GETTING IT RIGHT!

Creating Customer Value for Market Leadership

PHILIP WEINZIMER

John Wiley & Sons, Inc.
New York • Chichester • Weinheim • Brisbane • Singapore • Toronto

ISBN 0-471-29188-9

Printed in the United States of America.

10 9 8 7 6 5 4 3 2 1

To my parents, Isidore and Frieda, who taught me the importance of respect, kindness, and love;

and my wife, Lynn, who has been with me on the roller coaster of life, and represents all the love that my parents wanted me to have;

and Danielle, our pride and joy, who in her own right respects others, imparts kindness to strangers, and will someday understand how much love parents have for their child.

CONTENTS

FOREWORD

During my forty-one years in the car rental business, 37 of them with industry leader Hertz, I have witnessed the increasing dominance of service businesses over manufacturing, and with that management's gradual but inescapable realization that an optimum level of service is a far more elusive bird than manufacturing excellence. It was this awareness that led me to spearhead the creation of the Hertz #1 Club Gold. I would never have predicted that this service would grow to over two million members, and account for 40 percent of our U.S. rentals as of this writing.

Most business professionals now recognize that quality control on the front line is harder than quality control on the assembly line. In fact, the very word "control" should never be associated with "quality," especially in the services sector. Control implies rigid boundaries and restraints, whereas service providers need flexibility and empowerment at every level to respond to their customers' constantly changing needs, wants, desires, and expectations.

At Hertz, we have empowered our employees with great success, so I read the "prepare your workforce" section of *Getting It Right!: Creating Customer Value for Market Leadership* with great interest. There Phil Weinzimer talks about how forward-thinking leaders are creating a new work environment where empowerment, cross-functional teams, and boundaryless behaviors are not just snappy buzzwords, but directly improve the quality of products and services.

I actually cringe when I hear executives speak of "motivating" their workforce. What managers really mean when they say this is that they are going to manipulate their employees to do things a certain way, namely, their way. In the right circumstances, most employees are motivated by themselves to accomplish personal and, by extension, business excellence. Motivation is not something a manager can do to employees, it is rather the end result of a supportive environment provided by an enlightened business enterprise.

Getting It Right! shows you how to create the right environment by preparing your workforce and organization to change from the internally focused organization of the past to the customer-focused model that works today. The workshops that follow each chapter are filled with interesting ideas and good tips that make the concepts work in the real world. I admire the author's courage in slaughtering some of Management 101's sacred cows. It is this down-to-earth, common-sense approach to preparing your organization that separates this book from so many others.

Even CFOs may gain insight when reading about the "discontinuous revenue stream." This brilliant analysis will show even the most unimaginative bean-counter that every time a customer is lost to a competitor, the revenue stream is lost until a new customer is gained. Seemingly obvious, it is amazing to me how such a simple truth is overlooked today when so many companies spend huge sums on advertising to attract new customers and very little on service enhancements to keep the customers they already have. Even when companies recognize the value of customer loyalty, how do they go about trying to achieve it? Usually by creating such short-sighted programs as the frequent-flyer awards dreamed up by the airlines. These are now so ubiquitous that they do not offer any competitive advantage, while the basic needs and wants of flyers, such as prompt arrivals, more leg room, decent meals, and friendly employees, go unsatisfied.

I am grateful to Phil Weinzimer for his use of examples that demonstrate how Hertz's focus on customer satisfaction is paying big dividends in keeping us the industry leader in a highly competitive and rapidly changing industry. But most of all I appreciate this book because it got me thinking. I know it will do the same for you.

Robert J. Bailey
Senior Vice President
Quality Assurance and Administration
The Hertz Corporation

Biographical Note: Robert J. Bailey, currently senior vice president, quality assurance and administration, joined The Hertz Corporation in 1956 and has held a variety of management positions, including vice president USA operations and vice president strategic planning. Besides spearheading the Hertz #1 Club Gold service, he also developed one of the company's most recent service enhancements, the GPS-based navigation system "Hertz Neverlost."

FOREWORD

In the natural cycle of business, even the most successful companies must either anticipate and adapt to changes in the marketplace, or fall by the wayside. Xerox ranks among the elite few who successfully make this difficult journey, with its transformation from copier company into The Document Company with the widest array of digital products and document solutions in the industry. The company's enduring and ever-strengthening focus on the customer is what made this impressive transformation possible. Customer focus unleashes the creative powers of a company, so its people can reconceive what its core products are, envision new markets, anticipate customer needs, and add the value that separates them from competitors. As I write this, Xerox has just won its second Malcolm Baldrige National Quality Award, more compelling evidence of the continuing success Xerox gains from customer focus.

Customer focus is built into the very framework we use to plan and improve our business, the Xerox Management Model, which states: "Current, past, and potential customers define our business." To me, customer focus means the ability to anticipate customer needs and create value for customers—not just meet their expectations. At Xerox, we call this obsession "Customer First," which is our brand name, if you will, for customer focus. And I am the corporate champion for Customer First. We define Customer First as the consistent, deliberate demonstration of reliability, responsiveness, relationship-building, and added value for the customer. Our mission is to make every Xerox employee a passionate customer champion whose top priority is doing what is right for the customer. Throughout the company, Xerox employees are going through training to learn in specific ways how they can demonstrate, whatever their job, the reliability and responsiveness needed to create value for the customer. We want Xerox people to look at the customer through the eyes of the customer. What would they do differently if customers conducted their annual performance reviews? We also want all employees to understand the "golden thread" that links them to the Xerox customer. And understand that customers evaluate us every day, in every encounter they have with a Xerox person, product, or process.

Philip Weinzimer gets it just right: It's not enough for senior management to talk about customer focus. For a company to maintain and expand its competitive edge, every employee must demonstrate such commitment every day, in real and tangible ways.

With its emphasis on specifics, on the practical over the abstract, *Getting It Right!* is recommended reading for anybody in the business world. Through a series of workshops that involve every employee in the organization, Weinzimer demonstrates, clearly and concisely, how to achieve the vital three: prepare the workforce, perceive customer needs, and provide customer value. It is very much a hands-on book that translates a customer-focused strategy into a series of learning exercises for all employees.

This is no dry textbook. *Getting It Right!* is also a great read, filled with compelling anecdotes and success stories from companies around the world. How the Australian postal service transformed itself into an all-purpose electronic customer service network Australians can use to do their banking and pay their bills, not just mail letters and packages. How the venerable Martin Guitar Company nearly priced itself out of business, then revitalized itself by focusing on a whole new segment, people who loved guitars but couldn't afford the expensive product Martin was offering.

One of my favorite vignettes describes the Xerox factory worker who asked himself what happens when a customer opens a crate and unpacks one of our machines. That simple question, asked from the customer's perspective, quickly led to a new process to make sure Xerox people understand the customer experience upon receiving one of our products. Machines awaiting shipment are now picked at random, moved around the factory on a forklift to simulate the activity at the customer's site upon delivery. We unpack the machine, load it with paper, and test it. As one Xerox person told Weinzimer, "Now when I work each day I don't just see metal. I see a group of people at a customer site unpacking the machine and testing it to make sure it functions the way it is supposed to."

Every Xerox employee must take to heart what Joseph C. Wilson, the first chief executive officer of Xerox, said many years ago: "It is the customer, and the customer alone, who will ultimately determine whether we succeed or fail as a company. Serving the customer is the responsibility of every Xerox employee." That is Phil Weinzimer's message too.

Customer focus goes to the heart of what we're all after: Profitable revenue growth, achieved by retaining the customers we have, growing the business we have with existing customers, and adding new customers. *Getting It Right!* can help. So read on!

A. Barry Rand
Executive Vice President
World Wide Customer Operations
Xerox Corporation

Biographical Note: Barry Rand, executive vice president in charge of Worldwide Customer Operations at Xerox Corporation, joined the company in 1968 and has won numerous awards for his accomplishments in sales and marketing during his career. He served as president of the U.S. Marketing Group before being named to his current position in 1992. He was inducted into the National Sales Hall of Fame in 1993.

PREFACE

Getting It Right! Creating Customer Value for Market Leadership is all about profitably growing your business and implementing a set of strategies that will lead to market success. It will help you prepare your workforce so they can better perceive market requirements and then deliver unmatched value to your customers with superior service. Customer value is not a difficult concept to understand but it can be difficult to implement successfully. We have all been inundated with the *what;* it's now time to understand the *how.*

After reading many books and working with clients on business strategy, organizational change, and operational improvements, I realized that no one book encompassed all the necessary concepts that an organization needs to achieve market success. It became obvious that any company that wants to succeed today must prepare its workforce. But what are the behavioral changes that employees have to make for the enterprise to succeed? A prepared organization should be better able to perceive customers needs, wants, and desires. A workforce that effectively listens to customers should be able to provide superior value. But how do you choose which opportunities to pursue? My goal was to include in one book concepts and ideas that have been tested in the field and share them with those who want simple yet detailed instructions for implementing successful change within an organization. The major objective is to create customer value and get it right the first time.

This book is designed for all levels of management. Senior executives can explore new concepts that lead to improved operational performance and market competitiveness through better methods of communicating strategies and leading their workforce. Middle management can learn how to apply a series of tools and techniques within a workshop setting that will lead to the reinvention of superior value in today's customer-driven organization.

I have divided the book into three parts. Part I helps prepare the workforce. Management will learn how to lead and motivate people to understand and articulate business strategies and translate them into profitable actions. This will help overcome the inevitable resistance to change, develop the new business behaviors the workforce needs in order to be successful, and also help identify the required changes in the corporate structure so the organization will be more customer focused. Since people are the most important element in a successful enterprise, I have devoted a majority of the material to this subject.

Part II of the book focuses on how to perceive the marketplace. It will help you to perceive value as customers see it, and develop listening and learning systems that help capture the needs, wants, and desires of customers and noncustomers. It will show you how to identify your markets and competitors by exploring the boundaryless marketplace and the advantages of strategic alliances. Part II will also help to benchmark your competitors—not to copy their processes—in order to spark new ideas and creativity in the workforce so it can provide new and innovative value to customers.

Part III of the book deals with providing superior value to customers. It explains the difference between core competencies and core capabilities and explores why process redesign efforts can fail. It gives you techniques to identify company and customer process components, potential constraints, and actions to create value. It provides a way to identify opportunities to create superior value by using a technique that aligns opportunities for business success, analyzes them for revenue, cost, and risk, and determines the degree of impact they will have on five customer focus capabilities.

Each chapter is filled with questionnaires, templates, techniques, and tips that will help the enterprise perceive, prepare, and provide value. The book is also filled with examples from leading companies around the globe, showing you how they have improved their ability to prepare, perceive, and provide value to their customers. Today, companies need to lead, not follow, and people in organizations need to work with, rather than for, each other. Management must create the inspiration and organizational structure that allows creativity to drive change. *Getting It Right!* will help you accomplish this. The goal, as always, is to improve profitability and competitive advantage.

One of the most important elements of this book is the workshops that appear at the end of each chapter. These are designed to help people in the organization understand the main concepts and to learn how to apply them through team exercises. I have used manufacturing examples because they are robust and easy to comprehend. However, these workshops are equally applicable in service companies and government agencies.

Each workshop has a similar look and feel. An agenda, along with facilitator notes, exercise instructions, and samples of completed exercises, walks you through each phase. Use the workshops as a guide, not a script; I encourage the use of a trained facilitator to help ensure their success.

For those who are looking for a quick summary of the book I have provided on the following pages a high-level overview that distills the key concepts of each chapter. At the end of Chapter 1 is a questionnaire that summarizes the main concepts of the book and enables you to determine the extent to which your company exhibits the Prepare, Perceive, and Provide capabilities.

I encourage you to communicate your comments and welcome your thoughts on how the concepts, techniques, and workshops in this book have helped you get it right. I can be contacted at pweinzimer@aol.com.

Phil Weinzimer
Allentown, PA

THREE P'S HIGH-LEVEL OVERVIEW

3 P's	Key Messages	Chapter	Company Examples
INTRODUCTION	• Prepare, Perceive, and Provide are the three keys to future success. • Position your company for market success (questionnaire). • People are the key to success.	1	Australia Post, Continental Airlines, Kaiser Permanente
PREPARE	• Dynamic leadership. • Communicate your vision. • Create enduring values, winning strategies, and a business focus for change. • Workshop—Strategy Awareness.	2	Higashimaru Shoyu, Hertz, Levi Strauss, British Airways, General Electric, Just Born, Unisys, Xerox
	• Prepare your workforce for change. • Value your people (questionnaire). • Identify creative leaders, middle-of-the-roaders, gradual followers. • Workshop—Assess Employee Readiness for Change.	3	AT&T, CWA, Super Automotive Parts, Xerox
	• Prepare for change with a business focus. • Develop new business behaviors. • Understand the difference between customer, organizational, and individual behaviors. • Workshop—Identify Business Behaviors for Your Organization.	4	Just Born, GE, Harding & Company, Hertz, Mercedes Benz
	• Develop a customer-focused organization. • Create an agile structure that effectively links the enterprise. • Utilize supporting subsystems to enable organizational success. • Workshop—Develop a Customer-Centered Framework.	5	LEGO, Wal-Mart, Hertz, Xerox
PERCEIVE	• Understand the business need to focus on customers. • Identify customer's needs, wants, and desires. • Develop effective listening and learning systems (questionnaire). • Workshop—Perceive Customer Value.	6	Xerox, Martin Guitar Company, British Airways, Raytheon, Hughes Missile Division

THREE P'S HIGH-LEVEL OVERVIEW

3 P's	Key Messages	Chapter	Company Examples
PERCEIVE	• Determine new opportunities. • Perceive your competitive environment. • Benchmark the best and analyze competitor strengths and weaknesses. • Workshop—Perceive the Competitive Landscape.	7	Northwest, Cinergy, Xerox, Ford, 3M
PROVIDE	• Understand the difference between core competencies and core capabilities. • Provide superior customer value with core capabilities. • Eliminate, automate, integrate, and simplify process constraints. • Workshop—Provide Robust Processes That Deliver Value.	8	Defense Automated Printing Office (DAPS), EDS, Computer Aid, Federal Express, Wal-Mart, Microsoft, Sony, Honda
	• Identify opportunities to pursue. • Align opportunities for business success. • Analyze revenue, cost, and risk and determine customer impact. • Workshop—Reinvent Superior Customer Value.	9	Hertz, ITT, Snap-on Tools
CONCLUSION	• Push the envelope to stay on top. • Prepare for your future, perceive change, provide for market success.	10	Microsoft, Olivetti, GE, Xerox, Otis, AT&T, Ritz Carlton, Home Depot, Hertz, Nike, Monsanto

ACKNOWLEDGMENTS

A few years ago, at an Agility Forum executive industry focus group I attended at Lehigh University's Iacocca Institute, Len Allgaier, one of my colleagues, used the words *prepare, perceive,* and *provide* during a presentation on strategy. During the next few days I thought of these three words numerous times, realizing how simple they are to say, yet how complex they are in relation to today's customer-driven marketplace. With those three simple words this book was born. Len, a former General Motors executive in advanced manufacturing, is founder of Leadership Manufacturing, an organization that helps companies create next generation enterprises and manufacturing systems. I thank Len for his friendship and inspirational words.

This book could not have been written without the help of many executives who shared their stories, frustrations, and accomplishments through interviews and telephone conversations. I want to thank Ross Born and David Schaffer of Just Born for their hospitality—as well as for the supply of jelly beans that helped keep me up many a night as I wrote. Thanks as well to James E. Rogers and Elizabeth Lanier of Cinergy for their vision and wealth of knowledge, and to George Lewis of PP&L for his historical perspective on the gas and electric industry. I want to thank Peter Ambeck-Madsen and David Lafrennie of LEGO for their insights; and Chris Martin of Martin Guitar for sharing his candid thoughts and challenges in rebuilding his company. I want to thank Peter Garcia, director of customer satisfaction at Xerox, for providing information on the Customer First program, as well as Noddie Gibson and Paul Lissy of Xerox Professional Document Services for sharing their insights on developing strategies for print-on-demand solutions. I owe a deep debt of gratitude to Robert Gray of the Australia Post and his colleagues Tony Widdows and Brian Cavagna for sharing their wonderful experiences; and to Dave Rapson of Unisys for providing background material for the Australia Post. I especially want to thank Michael Blunt of British Airways for his patience and help in providing information that helped bring the BA story to life, Chris Byron for his overview on how BA prepares its workforce, and Hilary Rickard for her perspective on customer service. I am very grateful to Thomas D. Hollman, president of Mainsail Associates, for providing his insights and experiences at General Electric.

Salomon Suwalsky of Olivetti Office USA was very gracious in allowing me to interview his management staff. I am grateful for his kindness and hospitality. I have respect for his insights and leadership in transforming Olivetti Office USA into a profitable twenty-first century competitor in just a few short years.

A warm thank-you goes to Robert J. Bailey of Hertz for writing a foreword to this book, to Dawn Bateman, his able assistant, to Joe Russo for the volumes of information he provided on Hertz, and to Jeremy Snook and Aidan O'Kelly for their help and information regarding Hertz activities in Europe. A special thank-you to John Morton of Hertz (who truly understands the meaning of customer service) for driving me from the Hertz lot in Heathrow to the main terminal to catch a flight so I could get home in time to share an important family event.

My thanks to Barry Rand of Xerox Corporation for taking the time from his busy schedule to write an insightful foreword; a very special thank you to Valerie Mason-Cunningham for her kindness, patience, professionalism and persistence in meeting an impossible deadline; and also to Brent Laymon for his editorial assistance with Barry Rand's foreword. A very special thank you to David Garnett of Xerox Corporation for his insight and guidance in recommending that Barry Rand write a foreword for this book.

I want to thank Chris Tung of Xerox Professional Document Services for his insight and guidance during the writing of this book as well as for helping me articulate some of its principles. Although Chris is young in years, his knowledge, insight, and dedication are refreshing for any who doubt that today's young minds are not capable of becoming tomorrow's leaders. I also want to thank Gerry

Pascale, Mike Spinelli, and Kirk Puterbaugh of XPDS for helping to clarify key points during the final stages of the book's development. I also want to thank my good friend Dr. David Hyman, an ophthalmologist, who reviewed the Three P's Overview with his keen eyes and identified some inconsistencies.

During the early stages of the book's development Richard Clark and I worked together at Unisys and spent many a night philosophizing over issues to include. Not only did these talks affect the final product but I also gained a good friend. Also, while at Unisys, Michael Collins and Iain Moss helped me to define some of the key issues that CEOs consider critical to achieve market success. I also am thankful to Ford Harding, a sales and marketing consultant who has written two books, and who guided me during the early writing. His coaching was invaluable.

I want to thank Mike Matza of Unisys and Ron Sims of CSC Consulting, whom I met while working at Unisys, for the countless hours we spent together solving the world's problems and developing strategies that we hoped one day would save corporate America from demise. Those times helped me envision many of the concepts included in this book. I thank my friend Larry Blenner for his counsel and guidance in shaping the book and for his continued support.

During my years at the Agility Forum I had the pleasure of meeting Steve Goldman, Roger Nagel, and Kenny Preiss. I thank each of them for the help, support, and friendship they gave as I began to crystallize the ideas and concepts for this book.

I want to thank Jeanne Glasser, the original editor on this project, who provided me with the opportunity to write the book, and Mike Murray for his illustration rendition of a company vision which appears in the workshop in Chapter 2. I want especially to thank John Boyd of Van Nostrand Reinhold for his continued support and for concise questions that helped make the workshops a more important part of this book; Noah Shactman for his persistence; Chris Boyd and Carl Germann who guided this project through its final days; and Angela Burt-Murray for her patience and understanding. Additional thanks go to Jo-Ann Campbell of mle design for working her magic in the design and composition of the book. I am forever grateful to the editor Rosemary Ford for her guidance, patience, and wisdom in knowing what to mold, improve, and rephrase; to her husband, Gene, for his understanding and patience as he fielded many of the late-night calls; and to their infant daughter, Cordelia, whose cries and laughter could be heard as Rosemary and I contemplated revisions and changes during telephone conversations.

There's an expression that goes, "You can count on the fingers of one hand the true friends you have in your lifetime." I have been fortunate to have three, whom I met in college. I want to thank Dan Bahr, Irwin Kirschenbaum, and Marty Kulberg for their understanding during the writing of this book as I canceled many events and gatherings that we need to reschedule.

Writing a book is both intellectually challenging and a rewarding experience. It is not achieved, however, without personal family sacrifices that are required when one works full-time by day and writes in one's spare time at night. My wife, Lynn, has always been by my side and was a driving force in helping me complete this book. It was not uncommon for her to come into my den at 11:30 pm and say, "How late will you be working tonight?" laugh, and then retire until she awakened the next morning saying, "How late did you work last night?" Nor was it uncommon for her to explore her passion, shopping, on weekends so I could spend some focused time on the book. When we met in high school I knew that we were meant to be together. The only problem was that it took her seven years to realize it. During those years I learned the true meaning of patience and persistence, traits which I often drew upon during the writing of this book. Lynn is the inspiration of my life and I will always love her for her patience, kindness, understanding, and love.

I want to thank my daughter, Danielle, who read through my earlier chapters and was strong enough to say, "Dad, you can do better than this." She makes me proud every day of her life. To my mother, Frieda, I owe special thanks. She offered me the encouragement, prodding, and inspiration I needed during the early stages of the book's development, when words were difficult to find and concepts hard to articulate. During the final months of writing it was not uncommon for her to call and say, "So! Is it done already?" During my childhood my father, Isidore, always urged me to pursue my goals and ambition. I thank him for his prodding and guidance and although he is no longer with us in body he is always at my side and in my heart.

To my family and friends I owe countless apologies for canceled social events. To our bridge group—Mike and Sue Stroock, Gene and Ann Ginsberg, and Seth and Kathi Katzman—I apologize for all the cancellations and beg your forgiveness as my book preempted our monthly event. I want to thank my good friends Mel and Sheila Lavin and Ed and Debbie Caplan for their continued support during the writing of this book. And, finally, thanks to my dog, Muffin, my faithful companion, who sat by me late into the night and on weekends while I struggled to find the right words.

Many other people, too numerous to mention, offered their input, comments, and support. You know who you are and I apologize for not including your names. I thank you.

CHAPTER 1

THE NEW
ENTERPRISE

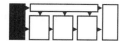

Major shifts are occurring in today's competitive environment and those organizations that don't adapt will not survive. These changes are unlike any we have faced before. We communicate and market our products globally. Information is available in nanoseconds with a simple keystroke on a computer. The pace is fast and the competition is fierce. A company can keep its eyes clearly focused on what it thought was the competition only to find that it has been outpaced by a newcomer it never even heard of. MCI, AT&T, and Sprint ignored Cable & Wireless Communications because they thought it was too small to be a threat. Cable & Wireless targets small- to medium-size businesses for telecommunications services and has grown at a rate of 20 percent annually. It is now a competitor to be reckoned with.

Even municipalities and state governments are competing to enrich their tax base. Companies, and citizens in turn, are demanding value for their tax dollars or else moving to areas that provide more value. State governments that focus on value, like those in the mid-Atlantic states, attract more businesses and taxpayers and can use increased revenues to provide more services.

As the business landscape changes, companies like Microsoft, Wal-Mart, and CNN represent the new breed of competitor. These companies recognize that to be successful you need to offer customers new and innovative products and services that constantly must be reinvented. Revitalized competitors like Compaq and Bell Atlantic have realized that the old models no longer apply and have adopted a new way of doing business in order to survive in the globalized market economy. The new model is centered on the customer. It focuses on anticipating customer needs and delivering products and services that delight customers and keep them coming back for more. This concept is represented in Figure 1–1.

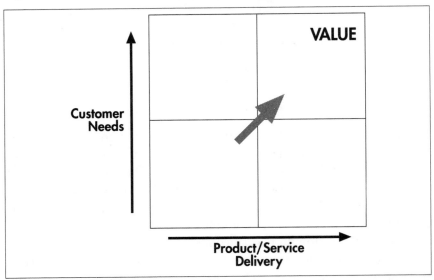

Figure 1–1. Customer-Centered Value Model

Global competition is similar to riding a roller coaster. Up one minute, down the next, with new market forces pulling you in different directions. In the past the ride was smooth; turns could be forecasted and stops along the way anticipated. Today, survival requires a new set of capabilities that focus on the customer and provide unmatched value. Companies like Honda and Benetton have adapted and prospered. Others have become secondary players or subjects of *remember when* anecdotes. American Motors and

Gimbel's are history while General Motors and Sears struggle to survive, finding periods of success but not really achieving market leadership.

The pace at which technology is advancing is so rapid that consumers are having difficulty keeping up with the latest products or services. Where customers had to write or telephone a company for information, they can now walk up to a kiosk at a local shopping center and get answers. Those customers too busy to go to the local shopping center can now access information through the Internet. While on the Internet, consumers can also purchase almost any product that they could buy in a store. You can even shop for an automobile online. And instead of having to wait in line to make a deposit or withdrawal at your bank, you can now conduct a variety of financial transactions on the Internet, including deposits, withdrawals, and even stock transactions.

Segmented markets are making it more difficult for companies to be successful, yet at the same time allowing companies to provide unique customer value. Sears became successful by providing a common set of products to American households. In those days, the market was *homogeneous,* and companies like Sears offered the consumer only a handful of product choices. As individuals prospered financially their tastes grew more sophisticated, and companies had to offer more variety and choices than before. Today, this phenomenon is captured in the phrase *one-to-one marketing,* where companies focus on individual customers rather than on groups of customers as before. Nike manufactures almost a hundred different types of sneakers. Toshiba manufacturers dozens of different laptops. Gateway and Dell will configure a personal computer to individual specifications. Cereal manufacturers provide hundreds of choices for consumers. Today you can walk into a store and be custom-fitted with a bicycle. Readers can customize their *Farm Journal* based on their individual needs.[1]

The new competitors realize that change is a normal part of the competitive landscape and should be embraced rather than feared. They focus on developing a set of strategic capabilities that enable a constant state of reinvention. They have succeeded in consolidating four dramatic shifts in the new world order—a globalized economy, new business models, segmented markets, and an explosive growth and redirection of innovative technologies—into a competitive weapon.

These companies shape the industry by getting to the future first and, as a result, lead instead of follow. They control their own destiny by redefining the rules. They recognize that global success requires a vision of the future that others don't have. They can identify opportunities and anticipate the needs of the marketplace, and develop robust competencies and capabilities that enrich the customer. They think globally but act locally. They recognize that succeeding in today's competitive marketplace requires a new style of leadership, new organizational structures, and new ways of harnessing the energy of empowered and knowledgeable employees. They develop an esprit de corps that drives the organization beyond what any individual thought possible.

THE THREE P'S: PREPARE, PERCEIVE, AND PROVIDE

In the past few years many companies repeatedly have latched onto the latest self-help acronym thinking that this one surely would solve their ailments. Business executives and managers have turned their companies inside out with reorganization after reorganization only to find, months later, that the competition is still beating them.

Many theories are out there, some of them excellent, but this book is not about theory; it is about making the theory work for your company. It is about how you can *prepare* your employees to become an effective, efficient, and focused workforce. How you can *perceive* your customers' needs so that they don't leave you for your competitor. How you can develop processes that *provide* your products and services to your customers quickly and with superior service. True strategic value lies in developing these three sustainable capabilities. *You must succeed at all three to achieve market leadership.* Preparing your workforce to become customer-focused is meaningless unless you can perceive each customer's needs. Both a prepared workforce and a perception of your customers' needs are necessary to provide new and innovative products that are delivered with the ultimate in customer service. These interactions are represented in Figure 1–2.

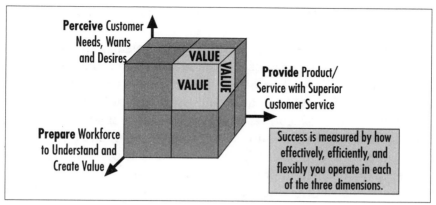

Figure 1–2. Customer Value Matrix

Dynamic leadership, an agile framework, and effective supporting subsystems are required if you want to properly prepare your workforce. Without the proper leadership employees are not motivated and have difficulty internalizing the company vision and strategies and linking them with the day-to-day actions required to achieve business success. An agile framework allows business partners to link their infrastructures in the pursuit of common business opportunities, employees to communicate with their business colleagues on a peer-to-peer level, and work teams to perform effectively. It also allows for the alternative organizational structures required to pursue a variety of business opportunities. Effective supporting subsystems reward individuals and teams, allow for information to be leveraged and shared across the enterprise, and prepare employees for a rewarding career by providing career development and education and training programs.

Every company needs to better understand how its external environment, the markets it competes in, and the existing and potential competitors within those markets affect its future. Today, unless you have an ongoing process to determine your competitive position in the marketplace you are headed for disaster. Competitors are springing up so quickly that time to market is now measured in months, not years. Northwest Airlines doubled its profits by analyzing its external environment. Your ability to manage the information that enables your perception of the environment, as well as to assess and strategically align these dimensions, is an important part of developing a profitable, competitive, and sustainable business.

Perceiving your business system environment requires a thorough understanding of your customers, company, and people and business network. Michael Feurer, president and CEO of Office Max, and Luciano Benetton, founder and president of Benetton, typify the new breed of executives who perceive their customers' wants, needs, and desires. Additionally, management must have a thorough understanding of the enterprise business processes to truly understand new and improved ways of creating value. AT&T would not have made a dramatic turnaround in recent years had it not invested in perceiving its existing business processes and how its employees perceive their customers. Only then did management realize what needed to be fixed.

The *provide* capability transforms customers' wants, needs, and desires into new and constantly evolving products and services. This is more than delivering a product successfully through the value chain; it involves adding services that are becoming more important than the product itself. Ritz-Carlton, Home Depot, United States Automobile Association (USAA), and a handful of other companies have all mastered the provide capability and continue to enrich it on a daily basis. To develop a provide capability you must assess your enterprise, select opportunities that are aligned for business success, and then reinvent the delivery channels to provide new and innovative products and services to your customers.

The ability to develop the three strategic capabilities, which I call the three P's, enables management to reshape an enterprise that is challenged by the market to one that leads the market. This concept, as depicted in Figure 1–3, is a road map for the book and appears in modified form at the beginning of each chapter. The shaded portion represents the subject of the chapter.

THE AUSTRALIA POST AND THE THREE P'S

A decade ago the Australia Post was riddled with inefficiency, poor service, and an industrial relations culture that defied remedy. Things got so bad that for several years new letter-sorting equipment sat in boxes as unions fought over manning levels. During the past eight years the Post has transformed itself from an inefficient bureaucratic government budget center into a service-oriented and profitable company with $2.9 billion in revenues, a 12-percent return on revenue, and a 15-percent return on assets. In 1996 it paid the Australian government more than A$500 million in taxes, loan repayments, and dividends. This transformation did not happen by accident; it was a well-planned strategic initiative that not only identified *what* needed changing, but also identified *how* to do it.

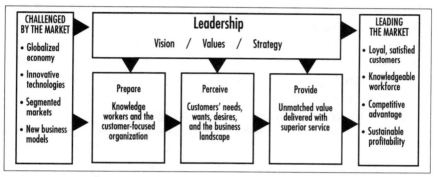

Figure 1–3. Prepare, Perceive, and Provide

In preparing its workforce the Post recognized that the traditional union/management adversarial relationship had to change. To help accomplish this, the company put together a joint settlement of understanding that outlined how the union and management would more effectively relate to each other. The settlement emphasized the need to change behaviors of both management and the workforce, to develop a new culture that focused on the customer, to find new ways to work more effectively in teams, and to increase investment in training.

Brian Cavagna, senior consultant for human resources, feels that two of the key ingredients for the success experienced were the industrial participation of the workforce in decisions affecting the workforce, and changing the behaviors of its workforce through their Quality Service Programs (QS1 and QS2). These programs concentrate on achieving high levels of customer service while also providing a platform for workplace flexibility and continuing improvements in day-to-day operations. The team-based programs have been so successful at instilling a set of business behaviors in the Post's workforce that Britain's Royal Mail is considering a similar approach.

To perceive customer needs the Post formed the Postal Services Consultative Council, which furnishes valuable knowledge about customers' expectations as well as feedback on the quality of services provided. Maurice Williams, chairman of the board, recognizes that the way to achieve long-term success is to understand customers' needs and to meet those demands with the highest level of service. The Post recognizes that every customer complaint and inquiry has to be handled to the customer's satisfaction or else he will move to a competitor. To monitor its customer service the Post tracks a set of key satisfaction areas: care for customers, staff knowledgeability, promptness of delivery, performance improvement, and value for money. In all but one of these areas, the Post has improved by over 10 percent in the last eight years.

In terms of providing value to customers, the Post is faced with a geographical challenge. Although its land mass is but slightly smaller than that of the United States, 85 percent of its population lives along the eastern coastline in an area less than 10 percent of the whole. The remaining 15 percent of the population lives in areas that are among the least densely populated on earth, with fewer than one person per square kilometer. In this difficult environment the Post delivers over 93 percent of the 3.8 billion pieces of mail that it handles per year within two business days. The cost of a first-class domestic stamp has stayed the same since January 1992 and remains one of the lowest in the world.

To provide new products and services the Post's 2,700 outlets utilize 8,000 computer terminals linked to a network that acts as a broad retail outlet for customers of Commonwealth Bank to conduct financial transactions. Customers of about 250 other organizations can pay their gas, electric, tax, and insurance bills at any Post outlet. A number of customers have monthly statements electronically sent to Australia Post Mail Centers that are closest to the delivery points. Here they are printed and delivered the next day. In July 1995 the Post started banking with its giroPost service. This provides online banking to the customers of nine banks. It allows customers to perform various financial transactions such as deposits, withdrawals, balance inquiries, credit card payments, account openings, and loan repayments. To provide a retail base of operations Australia Post has about 400 Postshops that offer customers a full range of postal stamps and post-related products, including stationery and greeting cards.

Australia Post realized early that the first step was to prepare its workforce to better understand the competitive realities of the business environment and the new set of business behaviors required for success. With this foundation in place, management and the workforce focused on how to perceive the true needs of customers and on providing value through development of a groundbreaking distribution system channeling for new products and services. As a result, Australia Post has positioned itself for the twenty-first century.

HOW WELL POSITIONED IS YOUR COMPANY?

In today's fast-paced environment many elements contribute to a company's success. If you could identify the few that form the core of a successful company you could well be on your way to achieving market success. The following are nine questions that will help you begin to think about your company in new ways. They won't provide answers, but they may generate a series of new questions you never thought of before.

Table 1–1. How Well Positioned is Your Company?

1. *How would your competitors describe your company?*

   Follower • • • • • Leader

2. *What drives the formulation of your strategy?*

   Catching up with the competition • • • • • Visualizing the future

3. *What word would best characterizes your ability to sense the surrounding environment (competitive markets, customer satisfaction, technological advances)?*

   Ignorance • • • • • Acuity

Table 1–1. How Well Positioned is Your Company? (continued)

4. How would your customers describe their experience in dealing with you?

    Part of a group   •   •   •   •   •   As an individual

5. How would you characterize your organization's structure and systems in pursuing business opportunities?

    Constricted and   •   •   •   •   •   Seamless and
    bureaucratic   virtual

6. How would your employees characterize their jobs?

    Indifferent,   Rewarding,
    boring, and   •   •   •   •   •   challenging, and
    uninvolving   linked to the customer

7. How would you characterize your company's use of information?

    Internally   •   •   •   •   •   Externally focused
    focused   toward the customer

8. How does your company utilize technology?

    Driver of change   •   •   •   •   •   Enabler of change

9. What type of effort do you apply in developing robust channels of distribution for products and services?

    Incremental   •   •   •   •   •   Reinvention
    improvement

Those of you whose pencil marks fell toward the left side of the page should take a step back and look long and hard at the direction your company is facing; you may be spending too much time looking behind you. If your scores fell toward the right of the paper you are becoming a market leader but need to work on how to maintain your leadership role. If your marks fell somewhere in the middle you need to focus on how to move toward the right. Developing a prepare, perceive, and provide capability will help you move toward the right of the paper and stay there. This test helps you to see how well your enterprise fares in implementing the three P's. Keep it close by and periodically take the pulse of your enterprise.

THE IMPORTANCE OF PEOPLE

In the past, corporate strategy managers used traditional command and control techniques to direct dedicated employees. In today's customer-focused marketplace, strategy that remains in the board-room will fail because it is *people* who implement strategy, with managers guiding and coaching them to success.

Companies that struggle with new processes and capabilities often fail to recognize that successful implementations of change are dependent on the business behaviors exhibited by the workforce. You can copy a process but you cannot imitate the culture that makes that process work in a successful company. Australia Post invests approximately 2 percent of its payroll—almost A$ 25 million in 1996—in training programs for its 30,000 employees. The programs focus on customer value, customer retention, and other customer metrics, as well as skills improvement programs that help personnel become better team players and make empowered decisions.[2]

In today's business environment a company that doesn't invest in its workforce will find its competitors passing it by. Companies like General Electric and British Airways realized this very early. They became market leaders because of their groundbreaking change programs for employees. Hertz invests heavily in training its 18,000 people working at 5,000 locations around the world on how to be sensitive to customer needs, how to react to unhappy customers, how to ameliorate customer complaints. By investing in people Hertz stands out among its competitors as the preeminent service provider.

Continental Airlines has transformed its reputation for the worst customer service in the airline industry to winning the J. D. Power and Associates Customer Satisfaction Award in both 1996 and 1997. Nobody has ever gone from worst to first in the history of the J. D. Power customer service surveys. To do this Continental invested heavily in its people, explaining company strategies, its vision, and how each employee could shape the future of the company. "We changed the way we measured success and rewarded employees in our company, so we got a very different behavior, one more closely attuned to what customers value," says Gordon M. Bethune, Continental chairman and CEO. He likens his workforce to a watch; every employee, like every part of a watch, is important. "Everybody has to work together or the whole thing stops. It's a team sport."[3]

People are vital today because service is such an important element of customer value. The success the carmaker Saturn has achieved is the direct result of understanding the importance of quality and customer service. Kaiser Permanente, headquartered in Oakland, California, is a health-care provider to seven million people in 16 states. It invested heavily in people when it realized that duplication of effort, a lack of customer focus, and varying cultures throughout the vast organization were affecting operating performance and, as a result, is better able to provide a service that meets customer and business requirements. The new metrics for employee effectiveness, customer satisfaction, cost and efficiency, quality of care measured by clinical outcomes, and member growth drive companies like Kaiser Permanente to make record profits year after year.

The most effective way to communicate change to employees, and possibly partners, suppliers, and even customers themselves, is to hold a workshop where people from different parts of the enterprise work together, under the guidance of a skilled facilitator, to understand how to be successful in today's competitive marketplace. What does the company vision really mean? What actions are necessary on a day-to-day basis to achieve company strategies? Where does the customer fit into the business equation? Workshops can help employees internalize the company's vision and strategy, translating it into an image that can be effectively articulated through role-plays and exercises in which business situations are acted out. This approach allows employees to demonstrate how well they understand the company strategy and helps them to work more effectively in teams. Workshops can also simulate real work environments, allowing employees to test new ideas in a safe environment.

Transforming your company into one that masters the prepare, perceive, and provide capabilities will take much care and patience. Change is not an easy process and must be managed delicately. It is also a never-ending process as practiced by those who truly understand the power and success that it can bring.

QUESTIONNAIRE: TEST YOUR PREPARE, PERCEIVE, AND PROVIDE CAPABILITY

Today's complex business environment requires you to constantly take the pulse of your prepare, perceive, and provide capability. The self-test below is designed for three applications. The first is to compare your company with other companies that have taken the self-test. Second, it can be used to compare how well each of the business units within your enterprise prepare, perceive, and provide for market success. The third use is to have groups of employees answer the questions as part of a workshop where each capability and associated questions are discussed; the goal is to understand how the company can more effectively prepare for, perceive, and provide customer value.

Each section represents an important element of the three P's strategy and begins with a visualizing statement that sets a general theme. Within each are statements reflecting successful characteristics.

For each characteristic, rate the extent to which the statement is true about your organization, using the following scale:

1=not at all 2=to a small degree 3=to a modest degree 4=to a large degree 5=to a great degree

PREPARE

People are the most important asset in your enterprise. Prepare them well and they will help your enterprise achieve market success.

1. Our executive management team exhibits a dynamic leadership style. _____

2. We have a vision that our employees can understand, articulate, and internalize. _____

3. People can translate the vision into clear actions that will achieve company strategies. _____

4. Our company is very people-focused. _____

5. Our management team recognizes that resistance to change is a natural emotion and helps the workforce understand the personal and business benefit required to implement change. _____

6. We work together to identify the customer, organizational, and individual business behaviors we need to exhibit if we are to succeed as a company.   _____

7. We have an agile structure that allows the enterprise organizations—our company, business partners, customers, and suppliers—to efficiently band and disband to pursue market opportunities.   _____

8. We have supporting subsystems that enable our people to flourish and work effectively within team environments.   _____

9. Our people are customer-focused.   _____

10. Our people want every customer interaction to be memorable and to provide a level of value unmatched by any other company.   _____

Total your score.   _____
Divide your total score by 50.   _____

PERCEIVE

To achieve market leadership we must perceive the needs, wants, and desires of our customers, competitors, and the marketplace.

1. We understand the importance of customer retention and its impact on revenues and cost.   _____

2. We differentiate among customer needs, wants, and desires.   _____

3. We understand the importance of interacting with customers in order to capture their needs, wants, and desires.   _____

4. We use listening and learning systems to capture, analyze, and identify new opportunities for creating customer value.   _____

5. We measure the effectiveness, efficiency, and adaptability of our listening and learning systems.   _____

6. We continuously look for ways to expand current markets.   _____

7. We exploit the marketplace to identify new and profitable opportunities.   _____

8. We use strategic alliances to expand market opportunities.   _____

9. We use benchmarking to gain insight to spark new ideas that help create superior customer value.   _____

10. We analyze our competitors' strengths and weaknesses.   _____

Total your score.   _____
Divide your total score by 50.   _____

PROVIDE

We must provide our customers with new and constantly evolving products and services if we are to achieve sustainable competitive advantage and market leadership.

1. We constantly identify and assess the core competencies and core capabilities we need to be successful in the marketplace. _____

2. We regularly assess the effectiveness of our core competencies and core capabilities. _____

3. We continually seek new levels of service for our customers. _____

4. We identify the company value and customer value for each major process in our company. _____

5. We constantly monitor and review our core processes to ensure that every activity adds value to the customer and to our company. _____

6. We are always looking for opportunities that can improve our revenues and competitive position in the marketplace. _____

7. We evaluate opportunities to ensure that they align with enterprise competencies, capabilities, customer value, and business strategies to ensure maximum enterprise value. _____

8. We evaluate opportunities for their impact on revenue, cost, and risk. _____

9. We compare each opportunity against the five customer-focused capabilities (speed, consistency, acuity, agility, and innovation) to ensure that customer value is optimized. _____

10. We constantly revisit our strategies and push the envelope to get it right and create customer value for market leadership. _____

Total your score. _____
Divide your total score by 50. _____

HOW TO SCORE YOUR RESULTS

After rating the statements in each section, add up your score and divide by the maximum possible score per section (50). The resultant percentage represents the degree to which your company is aligned with this segment of the business landscape. Figure 1–4 shows a scoring circle that is divided into three sections, each representing one of the three P's. Starting at the center of the circle for the appropriate segment, shade the percentage that corresponds to your score. For example, if you scored 50 percent on perceive, shade 50 percent of the segment starting at the center. When you have completed this for each of the three P's you can visually assess your effectiveness at a glance.

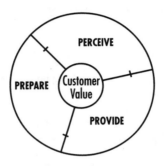

Figure 1–4. The Three P's: Scoring Your Results

ENDNOTES

1. Joe Pine has written extensively on this subject in the *Harvard Business Review* and his book *Mass Customization,* Boston: Harvard Business School Press, 1993.

2. Australia Post Annual Report, 1996.

3. "From Worst to First," *Leaders Magazine,* January/February 1997.

PART I

PREPARE YOUR WORKFORCE

CHAPTER 2

WE DID IT OURSELVES

---

*A leader is best when people barely know he exists. Not so good when peo-
ple obey and acclaim him. But of a good leader who talks little, when his
work is done and his aim fulfilled, they will say we did it ourselves.*

Lao-tzu

Higashimaru Shoyu Co., Ltd., is the third largest firm in the Japanese
soy sauce industry, with a 5-percent market share, revenues of
US$170 million, and 510 employees. In spite of a rapid new-product
development strategy, profits fell sharply in the mid-1980s as a result of growing competitive pressures. Plant manager Toshio
Okuna, a 23-year veteran of the company, realized that his workforce performed what they were told to do and no more. To turn
around the old ways of doing things Okuna developed a series of
programs that focused on long-lasting behavioral change.

In order to help workers gain a better understanding of the eco-
nomics of business, he devised a price control system (PCS) that
treated each of the plant's subunits as a profit center. To make the
PCS more real he created the fictitious Higashimaru Bank, operated
by the production control department. Play money was printed and
each of the six departments—preparation, fermentation, manage-

ment, pasteurization and filtration, bottling, and shipping—had to "sell" its work to the next department in the process. Okuna worked out a pricing scheme that allowed each department to make a "profit" on each unit of production it sold. At the end of the month department group leaders closed the books and prepared statements that were reviewed at a monthly plant meeting. "Bills" were presented to the other group leaders for services and goods rendered, raw materials consumed, and so on. After each group paid its bills and collected its revenue, it would determine its profitability. If a group ran out of money it had to borrow from the bank. Okuna routinely toured the plant; he would praise a particular work group at the next plant meeting when he found innovative changes being implemented. He rewarded profitable groups and counseled those that weren't profitable. It didn't take too long for each group leader and the department employees to understand the drivers of their success.

To improve group leaders' management skills and reduce team members' dependence on their leaders, Okuna instituted a program he called *tasumaki* (tornado). Leaders met to learn how to communicate with other group leaders as well as with their subordinates. To make them more sensitive to customer and market requirements, Okuna arranged for group leaders to visit local supermarkets and other stores to learn how their products were advertised and sold. Later they visited companies with similar concerns, such as Toshiba, where a conveyor system similar to that in Higashimaru's bottling area is used. The group leaders also met with sales, marketing, and accounting personnel to understand how departments interrelate.

Without warning, Okuna occasionally announced paid three-day periods during which team leaders were not allowed to work or to communicate with any of the team members. Subordinates had to learn how to manage the department without any direct guidance. This meant that group leaders spent more time training subordinates how to manage the department.

In the first year of the program production costs were reduced by 10 percent. Improvement in process flow eliminated duplication and bottlenecks, resulting in increased productivity. The ultimate result was that Okuna turned a business where profits were falling dramatically into one that not only maintained its market position but grew. What he accomplished was more than a temporary solution; he provided Higashimaru with the capability to accept, embrace, and exploit change. Okuna faced many of the same challenges as managers in other organizations. What made his approach successful was his recognition that leadership has changed dramatically over the last few years.[1]

LEADING THE WAY

The classic strategy-structure-systems model epitomized by Henry Ford placed the following three positions at the top of the organization:

1. chief strategist
2. architect of organizational structure
3. developer and manager of information and control systems

As leaders looked down from their thrones they saw an orderly and very structured organization. The view from the bottom was quite different. Managers were besieged by demanding controllers who required reports and analyses, more reports and more analyses, a vicious cycle that resulted in what General Electric's chairman and CEO Jack Welch calls "an organization with its face toward the CEO and its ass toward the customer."[2]

Under this model, management dictated the step-by-step process that employees had to follow. Employees constantly had to refer to their superiors. Today's management must provide a clear vision and goals that can be articulated by every employee. It must also define a set of values that inspires employees to perform their best. The decision as to *how* to perform each task is then left to the employee. Dr. Ronald Sims, a principal with CSC Consulting, says, "The old model hinged on control; the new model stresses trust in employees' instincts and capabilities."[3]

Leaders have to refocus their traditional roles. Influencing, measuring, decision making, and goal setting must be replaced by a new emphasis on people and teams who will design customer-focused products and processes. Dynamic leaders guide, coach, mentor, and listen instead of dictate, monitor, command, and control. Empowered employees need the freedom to pursue their creativity within appropriate boundaries. Management can provide the proper guidance to enforce these boundaries and help to build the skills of individuals by mentoring them. The leaders of tomorrow will be more like architects who provide the framework for innovation. In the past, rules and organizational level dictated control. Tomorrow a shared vision will allow employees to harness their energies and determine the necessary actions that will result in organizational success.

A shared vision has helped the computer chip leader Intel achieve phenomenal productivity. Despite the soaring complexity of technology, Intel has launched development of a new microprocessor every four years starting with the 286 (130,000 transistors) in 1978, the 386 (275,000 transistors) in 1982, and the 486 (1.2 million transistors) in 1986. With the Pentium (3.1 million transistors), the generation gap shrank to three years and the design effort for the P6 (5.5 million transistors) was launched in 1990, only one year after the Pentium.[4] Andy Grove, CEO of Intel, ensures that everyone in the workforce understands the business environment and the changes required for success. The dramatic reduction in cycle time and improvement in capacity of the microchip would never have been possible without including the workforce as *part of the team*. It's not uncommon for Intel employees to attend, as part of an ongoing education and training program, workshops where they review the current business environment, the changes that the company has made, and what they plan to do in the future.

Real leaders and visionaries must encourage an entrepreneurial style that can be found in companies like Higashimaru and Intel. Good leaders do what they say and say what they mean. Saying what you will do without the appropriate follow-up actions is meaningless. Leading by example is the most powerful method of eliciting desired behaviors of others. Leadership that finds its way to the operating levels of the organization energizes employees to perform their best.

THE IMPORTANCE OF VISION

One of the most important tasks of leadership is to articulate a vision that can be understood by every employee and transformed by them into specific actions. A successfully communicated vision instills a sense of commitment in the workforce, driving individuals to actions leading to learning and change. As John Kotter, the Konosuke Matsushita Professor of Leadership at Harvard Business School, says, "Without a sensible vision, a transformation effort can easily dissolve into a list of confusing and incompatible projects that can take the organization in the wrong direction or nowhere at all."[5] The successful vision is a dream that inspires employees and gives them something to strive for.

In 1981, when Lord King became chairman of British Airways (BA), the airline was losing 200 U.S. dollars a minute. King was determined to turn the airline around. He initiated the process by creating a vision statement, "the world's best airline," that BA adopted. It quickly became part of the corporate culture that helped the company become successful. In 1996 BA carried 25.5 million passengers, leading all other international airlines as well as leading its competitors with an astonishing $7 billion dollars in net profits.

William L. McKnight led 3M from 1929 to 1966, and today 3M is an industrial giant despite its humble origins in abrasives and adhesives. McKnight's vision was simple: Innovation through creativity. With a philosophy that fosters creative thinking, thousands of breakthrough entrepreneurial initiatives have been undertaken. Today 30 percent of 3M's sales come from products fewer than four years old.

Komatsu, the Japanese manufacturer of construction equipment, adopted a two-word vision statement in the 1980s that targeted its foremost competitor: Surround Caterpillar. The leaders of Komatsu, at the time, felt that out of these two words employees could build an organization that would trounce the competition. The vision inspired Komatsu to grow rapidly and make gigantic strides in the marketplace.

The leaders of each of these companies have guided their organizations to prosperity with a vision that was articulated clearly and communicated on an ongoing basis to employees.

CREATING A VISION STATEMENT

It is profitable to have a vision. Studies have shown that companies with a vision of which employees feel a part outperform companies without a vision by a huge margin.[6] A vision statement should be simple. It should depict in the mind of the employees how the organization wants to see itself in the future. It must also possess the following three characteristics:

1. an image that people can visualize
2. a sense of purpose
3. the expectation of success

The British Airways vision has all three (see Figure 2–1). The image is one employees can immediately visualize, it communicates a sense of purpose that is worth committing to and achieving, and yet it is also a realistic aspiration.

Definition

An image of what the organization aspires to be in the future

Characteristics

1. Conceptual reality—*an image that people can visualize*
2. Sense of purpose—*creates value, worth achieving, requires commitment*
3. Expectation of success—*realistically achievable*

Example

British Airways

"To Be the Undisputed Leader in World Travel"

Figure 2–1. Vision Statement Framework

The computer reservation company of a U.S.-based airline has the following as its vision statement:

> To satisfy each external and internal customer by providing caring yet professional service that exceeds all our customers' expectations.

Although the ideas are clear and the goals are admirable, this generic statement is difficult to visualize because it does not conjure up an image. Its all-purpose message could apply to any sector and thus lacks a specific business connection that employees can identify with. It also does not convey a vision of how the company sees itself in the future.

Vision statements are generally formulated at the very top of the organization, sometimes with the help of outside consultants. For example, a group of senior executives, including a designated facilitator from within or outside the organization, meets for one or two days. During the first morning executives articulate where they see the company going during the next five years. The statements are recorded by the facilitator and can be of any length. An important part of this segment is that it is not too structured. People should not be constrained. The facilitator's role is to extract as much information as possible. In the afternoon a description of the future company is encapsulated in a series of bullet points that summarize the morning's thoughts.

On the morning of day two the executives identify key words that depict the future vision of the company. During the afternoon a series of three or four vision statements are formed using these key words. The vision statements are then tested with key employee groups via a questionnaire. It is important not to let too much time pass at this stage or else the momentum can be lost. See Figure 2–2 for a sample questionnaire.

The fourth question is deliberately open-ended and seeks to capture the employees' own words. Because vision statements have to motivate employees, management should pay attention to what they say. Employees' words can sometimes be more meaningful because it is they who represent the organization and its image on a grassroots level. They will also feel ownership if their comments on the vision are heeded. During final fine-tuning of the vision statement, the employees' words can be used if they are more appropriate.

---

1. Which statement of those listed below best depicts your vision of the company in the next five years? *[Provide a list of possible vision statements.]*

2. How easy is it to envision an image of each of the statements? *(very easy, easy, not at all)*

3. Which vision statement will best inspire you to action?

4. Describe the image that you see when you read each of the following statements. *[Provide space for comments.]*

Figure 2–2. Vision Statement Questionnaire

Getting the workforce involved in the process is what helped Gil Amelio transform National Semiconductor. In his 1996 book *Profit from Experience,* he tells how important it is to involve the workforce in developing a company vision. To lay the foundation, Amelio gathered a group of senior executives and brought in a graphics facilitator, David Sibbet. As the senior executives brainstormed a vision, Sibbet translated their words into a creative visual rendering on a sheet of paper stretching several feet that was taped to the wall. With this as a foundation more than 700 employees added on and continue to add to the artistic rendition of the vision that appears as a six-page foldout at the end of his book.[7]

COMMUNICATING YOUR VISION

As John Kotter states: "Executives who communicate well incorporate messages into their hour-by-hour activities." In every organization a communication channel exists, both formally and informally, that can be used to help communicate your vision. In most companies, communication methods evolved over the years to deliver both meaningful and unmeaningful messages. It is important to evaluate every channel of communication so that those wasted on nonessential information are replaced.[8]

The following are ways to communicate your vision:

DEVELOP STORIES THAT EPITOMIZE THE VISION

A company's culture is the culmination of experiences that can be articulated in short stories. For example, the senior manager of an East Coast candy manufacturer told the following story when he met with employees to share information on the progress of their transformation. The company was one year into its new vision of being a leading supplier of jelly beans and marshmallow products. The workforce seemed to be motivated but a plant manager couldn't help worrying when he was told that a union representative wanted to see him urgently. What the manager thought was going to be a major labor headache turned out to be a suggestion from the workforce to improve quality and reduce the cost of one of their major products.

Stories can be told at employee meetings, stockholder meetings, press conferences, and other venues where an example is worth a thousand words. To learn more about how real experiences can be used to epitomize vision, read *Get Better or Get Beaten! Leadership Secrets from GE's Jack Welch.*[9]

CREATE AN ENVIRONMENT THAT INTERNALIZES THE VISION FOR EACH INDIVIDUAL

Employees must be able to internalize the vision and develop one of their own. This is not the same as being able to memorize and repeat a corporate slogan. Success can only be achieved if individuals develop a vision of their own that supports the corporate vision. Workshops where individuals can share their thoughts, enrich the vision, and debate their point of view with others must be supported and encouraged. It worked at British Airways, where as a result of employee workshops the delivery of food service aboard the London–to–New York flights was improved. The team translated the vision into a specific event that improved service to the customer.

It also works at Disney World. There are no employees at Disney World, only cast members, regardless of function. This designation is a natural evolution of the vision at Disney: Everyone is there to entertain and make the customers happy. New cast members listen to a history of the company, its vision and goals from other cast members. The orientation sessions are interactive and aimed at soliciting ideas from the new members. This encourages an environment where new cast members can continue to contribute throughout their relationship with Disney.

DEVELOP THE LEADERSHIP, STRUCTURE, AND SYSTEMS THAT WILL ENABLE THE VISION

A vision is effective only if the mechanisms are in place to support it. If management provides too much structure, rigidity, policies, and procedures, then the old-style command-and-control structure stifles individual creativity. If you are envisioning the future and want individuals to contribute to its realization, you must develop the appropriate support structures and systems to ensure this.

For instance, at the Information Services Group of Unisys Corporation, executive management wanted its 7,000 worldwide consultants to become creative team players. Previously, the organization was very structured and rigid in its policies and procedures. To facilitate this open new environment, Unisys chose IBM's Lotus Notes software. Client histories, previous project histories, success stories, and a host of other information to help consultants be more effective became available at the stroke of a key.

A Unisys consultant working on a systems integration project in Europe can check to see if a similar project exists in the history database. The consultant can review problems that occurred, techniques used to mitigate risk, and even find the project team roster if she wants to speak to any of its members. Unisys management provided the structure and systems to ensure that the objective—to provide quality information management services to its clients—was more than just a slogan. As a result, consultant productivity improved by over 15 percent in one year and operating margin improved by 20 percent. In addition, regional consultant teams were transformed into an effective network of global teams working together to provide value to their clients.

BE PASSIONATE

Being passionate about a vision helps provide the impetus for others to share it. Successful leaders, organizations, and teams are not just committed to but passionate about their vision. Today's notable leaders, including GE's Jack Welch, IBM's Lou Gerstner, and Microsoft's Bill Gates, all exude passion when speaking about their company and their vision. Their passion can communicate more than words alone. What they say is memorable and exciting because of it.

CREATING ENDURING VALUES

Values are the beliefs and moral principles that exist within a company culture and underlie its behaviors. They are the deeply ingrained operating rules or guiding beliefs of an organization. Statements or slogans cannot instill values; they must be accomplished through management behavior. When management stands behind its values they resonate in behavior throughout the organization, and when there is life in corporate values, a strong and meaningful culture results. If management does not live its values, however, people within the organization go about their day-to-day activities with their own individual agenda.

To create an effective, value-based strategy you should:

1. Define and communicate a set of values for the organization.
2. Ensure that company policies and procedures embrace these values.
3. Demonstrate these values in management behavior.

DEFINE AND COMMUNICATE A SET OF VALUES FOR THE ORGANIZATION

Most companies define a set of values for their employees. They document them and then plaster posters all over the place. For employees to reflect values in their behaviors, however, they need to understand these values and why they are important to the company's success. This requires a two-way communication process that includes management and the workforce.

Robert J. Bailey, senior vice president, quality assurance and administration at Hertz Corporation, strongly believes in a two-way communication process. "If Hertz is to establish itself as the best value in car rentals by consistently providing high-quality service that meets customers' needs and expectations at competitive prices, our employees must understand the type of behavior we expect from them."

- We will conduct business ethically and honestly in dealing with our customers.

- We will treat our employees in the same fashion as we expect them to treat our customers—with dignity and respect.

- We will consistently provide the highest level of customer service and quality of vehicles, and differentiate ourselves from our principal competitors through innovation.

- Profits are the ultimate measure of how efficiently we provide customers with the highest level of customer service and quality of vehicles. Profits are required to survive and grow.

- The overall No. 1 position in airport revenue market share is a key measurement of industry leadership.

Figure 2–3. Hertz Values

Getting the message out was not an easy task. Hertz could have done what many others do: Send out a memo and declare victory. But Bailey and Hertz president Craig Koch thought that written communication would not connect with employees. Instead, they both crisscrossed the United States in 1992, meeting with employees in interactive workshops to discuss Hertz's values and their importance to company success. Bailey adds, "In addition to telling our employees about our plans, we also wanted to listen to what they had to say. If we didn't take the initiative and meet the employees then our credibility would be zero."[10]

Nordstrom Corporation is a highly respected Seattle-based retailer of upscale clothing. It uses a one-page employee handbook to communicate company values to new employees (see Figure 2–4).

WELCOME TO NORDSTROM

We're glad to have you with our company. Our number one goal is to provide outstanding *customer service. Set both your personal and professional goals high. We have great confidence in your ability to meet them.*

Nordstrom Rules

Rule #1: *Use your good judgment in all situations.*

There will be no additional rules. Please feel free to ask your department manager, store manager, or division manager any question at any time.

Figure 2–4. Nordstrom's Employee Handbook

ENSURE THAT COMPANY POLICIES AND PROCEDURES EMBRACE ITS VALUES

When you define a set of values, make sure that your company's policies and procedures support it. Paul A. Allaire, chairman and CEO at Xerox Corporation, thinks that employees should be encouraged to give to their communities. He believes that employees are not machines but human beings who want to work intelligently and find a balance between work life, home life, and social responsibility. This belief is reflected in company policy. At Xerox, any employee is paid his regular salary for up to one year if he volunteers to help his community. Bell South supported its community by developing an interactive weather system that allows students at public schools to learn and participate in weather forecasting. General Electric spends millions of dollars each year in support of environmental projects. In these ways, companies can ensure that their values are transformed from paper into tangible actions.

DEMONSTRATE VALUE IN MANAGEMENT BEHAVIOR

A $5 billion Fortune 500 computer manufacturer says it places a high value on the individual. The parking lot at its executive offices, however, is separated into two distinct areas. The first, marked *restricted,* is closer to the main entrance and is reserved for vice presidents and their secretaries. The second area is farther away and is an open area for all other employees. In the mornings the open area is filled with cars by 8:15 AM, the official starting time, while the restricted area isn't even half full. In this small but significant way, the workers get the message daily that they are less privileged than management, and management's credibility is undercut by its own actions.

Levi Strauss has demonstrated the success of a value-based strategy. Chairman and CEO Robert D. Hass, the great-great-grand-nephew of founder Levi Strauss, believes "in the interconnection between liberating the talents of our people and business success." Louis Kirtman, president of Levi's Britannia Sportswear division, cites walking the talk as a major reason for the company's success. "We started to improve at Levi's when we stopped talking about values and started behaving that way." Hass explains that "our values are really our conscience. The fact that people realize that the outside world and our own employees are watching forces them to be thoughtful about the consequences of their actions." When you look at Levi's values, Figure 2–5, you begin to see that they deal very much with behaviors that employees should exhibit.

NEW BEHAVIORS

Management must exemplify "directness, openness to influence, commitment to the success of others, and willingness to acknowledge our own contributions to problems."

DIVERSITY

Levi's "values a diverse workforce (age, sex, ethnic group, etc.) at all levels of the organization....Differing points of view will be sought; diversity will be valued and honestly rewarded, not suppressed."

RECOGNITION

Levi's will "provide greater recognition—both financial and psychic—for individuals and teams that contribute to our success ...those who create and innovate and those who continually support day-to-day business requirements."

Figure 2–5. Levi Strauss & Company's Values

ETHICAL MANAGEMENT PRACTICES

Management should epitomize "the stated standards of ethical behavior. We must provide clarity about our expectations and must enforce these standards throughout the corporation."

COMMUNICATIONS

Management must be "clear about company, unit, and individual goals and performance. People must know what is expected of them and receive timely, honest feedback...."

EMPOWERMENT

Management must "increase the authority and responsibility of those closest to our products and customers. By actively pushing the responsibility, trust, and recognition into the organization, we can harness and release the capabilities of our people."

Figure 2–5. (continued)

In order to implement these behaviors Levi Strauss had to change the way it does business. It defined a new set of behaviors for management that was more than just words. It held face-to-face meetings in which management and employees had a dialogue instead of a one-way lecture. In order to demonstrate empowerment, management began to shed its authority and transfer it to the lines. These values have been transformed into business success.

Hass feels so strongly about instilling a sense of value into his workforce that he backs it up with an investment in training. Almost half the company's employees and most of its managers have already completed three required courses: leadership, diversity, and ethical decision making. At the end of each course participants complete an analysis that captures their comments regarding the gap between the stated ideals of the company and the actual practice in the workplace. This is not just an exercise; Levi's management makes sure that these gaps are filled quickly.

Has this philosophy paid off? In 1994 Levi was a $6 billion company. Today it is a $7.1 billion company that is still growing. It is ranked fifteenth among *Fortune*'s most admired corporations.

DEVELOPING WINNING STRATEGIES

Vision describes *what* the desired future state of an organization looks like. Strategy identifies *how* the business will fulfill its vision. Vision is the destination and strategy is the road map. It's easy to confuse vision and strategy if you don't understand the difference between the *what* and the *how*. To be effective a strategy should be:

> *Actionable:* It conveys an idea of what is required to implement the strategy.
>
> *Succinct:* It makes its point with a simple phrase or expression that is easy to remember.
>
> *Customer-focused:* It defines customer value and how your company will deliver that value.

The following are five strategies employed by British Airways to achieve its vision:

1. Understand customers wants, needs, and desires.
2. Train the workforce to be more customer-focused.
3. Create customer-friendly processes that can be effectively delivered worldwide.
4. Develop the infrastructure to deliver superior customer service.
5. Develop an advertising campaign to communicate the new image to the marketplace.

If BA did not have an effective set of strategies, employees all over the company would be saying, "We know we want to be the best airline in the world, but how do we accomplish this?" If each and every employee's actions *link* to a corporate vision and strategies his actions will not conflict with those taken by others in the company. The challenge is to effectively define those strategies that will fulfill the vision. The level below strategy includes the operational goals and objectives of the organization. These define the day-to-day activities that will result in achieving the strategy, which in turn will achieve the vision.

Management needs to know that the workforce understands the enterprise strategy. Understanding does not mean *hearing* the strategy; it means hearing, absorbing, and articulating the strategy. This helps the workforce to implement it. Communication is effective only if there is a return mechanism for feedback, such as small discussion groups or workshops. The workshop approach provides an effective interactive mechanism that, if used properly, allows the workforce to buy in and contributes to effective strategies that will result in business success. The Strategy Awareness Workshop, at the end of the chapter, is an excellent way to communicate your vision and strategies to enterprise members. In a workshop setting employees not only get to hear the vision and strategy but also have the opportunity to demonstrate ways to link the vision and strategy to actions they can implement to achieve the strategy.

ENCOURAGING A BUSINESS FOCUS AND SENSE OF URGENCY FOR CHANGE

Change for change's sake doesn't accomplish anything. If people within an organization do not understand the reason for change, behaviors will never be altered. For instance, one morning the management of a Fortune 500 company herded a department of 150 people into a large auditorium, where they listened to a speech by an executive vice president. The message was simple: A large reengineering effort would begin shortly in the company. This meant that everyone would be performing their jobs differently in the future. The workplace would be more innovative and everyone would be working in teams. According to the executive vice president, it would be a more fun place to work. During the next few days, clusters of workers discussed the meeting. No one understood what the executive was talking about. Everyone felt that business was good and couldn't understand why there was a need for change. Furthermore, no one could understand or articulate how the change was going to affect them as a group or individually. Management had failed to communicate its vision and strategy for the future and, as a result, the following four months of reengineering activity produced no measurable improvements.

Only when employees truly understand the business objectives of the company and realize the urgency with which change is required can successful change really take place. Over time, the workforce must demonstrate a keen understanding of the business purpose of the enterprise as well as an awareness of customer expectations and the value delivered to the customer. If you are going to empower workers, they need to know the business so that the decisions they make are consistent with the business plans and objectives. This can be a hard lesson to learn in enterprises with a workforce that is hired for skills other than business acumen. As a senior manager at GE said, "Our technical people are so wrapped up in the engineering aspects of the business, they don't always see the business perspective."[11]

Every employee must learn to understand the competitive environment, the factors that differentiate the organization from its competitors, and the company's definition of the formula that will enable it to succeed and become a market leader. Otherwise, decisions, actions, behaviors, and judgments will be misguided.

PUTTING PEOPLE FIRST—THE BRITISH AIRWAYS CHANGE PROGRAM

British Airways prepared its workforce for a new strategy by establishing a sense of urgency and defining a business case for change that was communicated throughout the organization.

In 1983 Lord King hired former Avis executive Colin Marshall (later Sir Colin) as CEO of BA. King and Marshall agreed that their objective was to become a customer-focused airline. To achieve this goal they developed an interactive program for all corporate staff that mixed cross-functional employees in a series of two-day events; 120 people attended each event during 1983.

The program, called Putting People First, was part of an overall drive called Putting the Customer First. The major question addressed during the two days was: Why focus on the customer? King and Marshall wanted to ensure that all BA employees understood the importance of the customer. Historically, employees had been wedded to the operational aspects of the business, such as safety and getting the aircraft underway. Customer surveys indicated, however, that *"care"* and *"attention"* were what passengers wanted. Warmth, care, and friendliness were characteristics that BA employees needed not only to understand but actually to exhibit. Marshall personally attended over 95 percent of the two-day programs to convey the importance of the effort to BA's future success.

Once people within the organization realized that customer focus was at the center of the airline's business case for change, the second of a group of major change programs was put in place. Managing People First was a five-day training program attended by over 2,000 managers between 1983 and 1985. Again, Marshall attended over 95 percent of the meetings, which focused on people, trust, empowerment, coaching, and facilitating. The program provided a strong message for all employees: BA thought people were important and believed life would be better for all if everyone took a little more care with each other. It was as much a philosophy of life as it was a framework for improving the airline. Participants were asked how they greeted family members when arriving home as well as how they greeted and handled customers. In this way employees were asked to compare corporate values with their own private values in order to integrate a corporate mission that included caring and solicitude.

To speed up the change process, BA ran a number of initiatives concurrently. Chris Byron, senior general manager for manpower at British Airways, says:

> We had to change the image of the company. We changed our advertising agency and changed our image by introducing new uniforms. We symbolized the change with a different corporate identity. Also at the same time we were surveying our customers to find out more about their needs.[12]

The total change cycle encompassed ten years and was a very defined program that yielded remarkable results in an organization comprising almost 55,000 employees. The company also recognizes that the change process is ongoing and launches new people programs every few years. Two such programs focus on teaming and empowering the worker.

BA's transition started with a sense of urgency and a communication of the business case. People within any deliberately changing organization need both to understand the reasons for change and to be able to link them with the business case. Many change programs have employees experiencing the touchy-feely issues, but these programs tend to fall flat on their face *if they are not linked to business issues.*

THE WORK-OUT AT GENERAL ELECTRIC

In the mid-1980s General Electric (GE) was bulky, hierarchical, and bureaucratic. As a result it was slow to respond to changing market forces.

Meanwhile, technological innovations were occurring at a record pace and global competition was knocking on GE's doorstep. Something had to be done. The Hardware Phase, created by chairman and CEO Jack Welch, represented the first of a series of efforts that focused on the mechanics of improving revenues and earnings. It involved a massive reorganization. Many offices were closed and many people lost their jobs. Afterward, Welch faced a crisis in morale. When employees no longer had a job for life, how were they to be motivated? What was to be done to improve the inefficiencies created by the downsizing effort? Could employees feel more like owners of the business than cogs in a bureaucratic machine? Thomas D. Hollmann, now president of a Boston-based organizational effectiveness consulting firm, Mainsail Associates, Inc., was then manager of organizational effectiveness at the GE Aerospace Division in King of Prussia, Pennsylvania. With a Ph.D. in psychology as a base and a twenty-year career with GE, Hollmann remembers the ten-year period ending in 1990 as a tough time for all.

> Here we were downsizing a mammoth conglomerate. The workers left but the work was still left behind. Those that were left were working very hard but frustrated and in an organization that had shed one third its weight.

Empowerment was the core of the program following the Hardware Phase in 1989. It was called Work-Out. Tom Hollmann was responsible for its strategic direction within the GE Aerospace

Division. The idea behind the program was to assemble a cross-functional group of approximately 50–75 workers and managers and have a dialogue centered on changes that could be made to eliminate unnecessary work. Business leaders would ask the groups: What can we do to work smarter? What can we do more effectively and efficiently? The objective was to eliminate unnecessary tasks and reduce bureaucracy. The focus was on teamwork and more rapid decision making. As Hollmann explains, the idea during these sessions was to "get rid of the work that was no longer necessary and did not provide value to customers ..."—hence the name of the program, Work-Out.

The objective of the sessions was to get people focusing on three main areas that Jack Welch at GE called speed, simplicity, and self-confidence. *Speed* was meant to improve the work process and reduce cycle times. *Simplicity* meant clear messages to workers and customers—simple designs with fewer parts, and directness and honesty when dealing with one another. *Self-confidence* meant allowing individuals a broader scope of empowerment whereby they could learn to make decisions and function with greater autonomy, knowing they would get management backing, even in failure, when their intentions were correct. Work-Out changed the culture within GE and provided the foundation for a learning organization. Was it effective? Why did it work? Read Jack Welch's own words:

> Work-Out is many things...meetings...teams...training... but its central objective is growing a culture where everyone's ideas have value...everyone plays a part...where leaders lead rather than control...coach rather than kibitz.[13]

Under Welch's leadership GE reached unforeseen success. During the 12-year period ending in 1993, sales more than doubled, from $25 to $60 billion, profits more than tripled, from $1.5 billion to $5.2 billion, and GE downsized its workforce by almost half, from 400,000 to 230,000. With a new focus on the worker, revenue per employee rose from a meager $3,000 to almost $23,000, an increase of 225 percent.[14]

WORKSHOP: STRATEGY AWARENESS

The Strategy Awareness Workshop that follows is the first step in implementing a change program for your company. It provides the framework for all other change program activities by making sure employees understand the link between the change program and business success.

This is a very intense workshop because it deals with strategic issues most employees never get involved in. Therefore, the material that follows is very detailed. The workshop is also interactive and dynamic. It should ideally have a maximum of 15 attendees, excluding the facilitators. This allows enough interaction when the group breaks into teams composed of five participants, with one facilitator for each team. The best mix is nine employees and three managers for every workshop. With one manager on each team as well as the facilitator, the employees get enough help to ensure a successful workshop. It is vital to recognize that the mix of participants is important to the success of the workshop. I suggest that you read the workshop in Chapter 3, which deals specifically with identifying and categorizing types of employees. This will add greatly to the success of each workshop.

Table 2–1 represents the agenda for a one-day Strategy Awareness Workshop. The objective included for each agenda item is especially important because participants can capture the intent in a few words. You could add a slide that identifies the objective of each section of the workshop, but having a simple table that summarizes the entire workshop in the form of an agenda provides a clear overview for the attendees. Never leave the participants questioning what the objective of a segment is or what they will be doing.

1. SETTING THE STAGE—60 MINUTES

This is the opening session of the workshop; the lead facilitator provides an overview for the participants that includes the objectives, agenda, and administrative matters (location of restroom facilities, phone messages, and so on).

Table 2–1. Strategy Awareness Workshop

Agenda
8:30 AM – 9:00 PM

Time Frames	Time Allotted	Workshop Exercises	Facilitator	Objectives
1. 8:30–9:30	60 min	Set the Stage	Glen R.	To discuss the learning objectives and capture participants' expectations.
2. 9:30–11:00	90 min	The Business Realities of Our Vision and Strategies—*Warm-Up Exercise*	Sharon T.	Share our understanding of the company vision with our colleagues.
3. 10:15–10:30	15 min	Break		
4. 10:45–12:30	105 min	Linking Stategies To Business Results —*Team Exercise*	Bryan S.	Understand how the company strategies effect our business success.
5. 12:30–1:30	60 min	Lunch		
6. 1:30–3:00	90 min	Linking Strategies To Customer Value —*Team Exercise*	Sharon T.	Understand how the company strategies impact customer value.
7. 3:00–3:15	15 min	Break		
8. 3:15–4:00	45 min	Next Steps	Bryan S./ Sharon T.	Identify the actions necessary that will ensure our future success.
9. 4:00–4:45	45 min	Workshop Debrief	Sharon T./ Bryan S.	Capture and share the benefits of the workshop with our colleagues.
10. 6:00–9:00	180 min	Group Dinner	Group	

Lead Facilitator: Glen R.   Facilitators: Sharon T./Bryan S.

The workshop opens with the lead facilitator introducing himself to the group and welcoming them to the workshop as well as stating the objectives of the workshop using a slide such as that shown in Figure 2–6.

1. to understand the business implications of our new company vision and strategies

2. to understand how our new company vision and strategies impact customer value

3. to identify the actions we will need to take to ensure successful implementation of our business strategies

Figure 2–6. Sample Slide: Workshop Objectives

It is beneficial in this particular workshop to hang posters of the company vision and strategies on the walls of the meeting room.

This provides a constant reminder of the business issues that confront all the attendees and helps to clarify concerns that surround them. There is ample time during the Graffiti Warm-Up exercise and team exercises to explore the company vision and strategies in more detail.

At one workshop participants asked the facilitator to explain the use of the word *entertainment* in the vision statement (see Figure 2–7). Fortunately, a senior manager was in attendance and explained to the group that if "we begin to view ourselves as being in the entertainment business it helps broaden the types of products and services that we can offer our customers." He then spent a few minutes providing examples of products and services that were different than those they had produced before but would have value to customers in the marketplace. At the request of other participants in the workshop the senior manager spent another fifteen minutes reviewing the vision and strategies using the posters on the wall. He even went up to the posters with a marker to make notes and clarify certain points.[15] Combining visual displays with narrative helps participants comprehend the message. Techniques that use as many of the five senses as possible help people learn.

> To be the premier toy manufacturer that provides entertainment for our customers, a rewarding work environment for our employees, and profitability to our stockholders.

Figure 2–7. Sample Slide: Vision

For introductions you can show a slide (see Figure 2–8) that asks the attendees to respond to a short set of questions within two minutes. As each of the participants expresses her objectives for the workshop, one of the facilitators should write them on a flip chart and post it on one of the walls. As items are addressed during the workshop the facilitator should check them off. At the end of the workshop this list can be used to check if each item was addressed. If not, the facilitator needs to discuss each point. This helps personalize the workshop for each attendee.

In less than two minutes please introduce yourself to the rest of the group using the following framework:

1.   Name, position in the company, years with the company.

2.   Work and educational experience.

3.   Family members and hobbies.

4.   Personal objectives for the workshop.

Figure 2–8. Sample Slide: Introductions

2. THE BUSINESS REALITIES OF OUR VISION AND STRATEGIES—90 MINUTES

It is important to get the participants into the proper frame of mind at the beginning of the workshop. The Graffiti Warm-Up Exercise allows them to express their understanding of the vision in a drawing that they create with their team members. Figure 2–9 shows instructions for this exercise.

Each team is assigned a corner of the main meeting room and given a flip chart and a box of crayons. Facilitators are assigned to each team and along with the senior manager in each team they explain the vision and strategies to the group. The facilitator reminds the team when the 20-minute discussion period has elapsed so the team can start designing its drawing. When the teams have completed their drawings they explain them to the rest of the group in a five-minute presentation. When all the teams have presented the facilitator engages the group in a discussion to identify the drawing that best represents the company strategy. Remember that a vision that cannot be represented in a picture does not work.

When all the teams finish, the lead facilitator reviews each drawing with the other teams. This allows the teams to express their understanding of the vision and strategy verbally. The benefit of this exercise is that participants feel less constrained when expressing their understanding of the new company vision as a drawing. Following Figure 2–9 is a graphic illustration of a team's interpretation of their company's vision, to be the world's best toy company.

1. Break into assigned teams.

2. Discuss the vision and strategies with your team members for *20 minutes*.

3. In the following *30 minutes,* develop a drawing that represents your team's understanding of the new company vision using materials supplied.

4. When the drawing is complete notify the lead facilitator.

5. When all drawings are complete each team will explain its drawings to the other teams in a *5-minute* presentation.

Figure 2–9. Sample Slide: Graffiti Warm-Up Exercise

Illustration by Mike Murray.

3. BREAK—15 MINUTES

There should always be a scheduled break in the morning and afternoon of the workshop. This doesn't mean there shouldn't be other breaks if the facilitator feels that the group needs one. The tendency, however, is for breaks to last longer than the allotted time. To prevent this the facilitator should announce the time of the break, the current time, and the time at which the group is to reconvene. It is also beneficial to have the facilitators help the group return to the main meeting area as the break approaches its end.

4. LINKING STRATEGIES TO BUSINESS RESULTS—90 MINUTES

This exercise is designed to help each participant link strategies to specific business benefits that will be achieved. Because these subjects might be relatively new to the group it is best to provide an overview before launching into the exercise. The facilitator can review basic business principles with the group, namely that businesses exist only if they are profitable and that in today's marketplace the customer is a vital element in the business equation. The facilitator explains that this exercise focuses on the business side of the equation; the next exercise will focus on the customer side of the equation. This segment usually takes approximately 20 minutes. The facilitator should gauge the time based on the needs of the participants.

The facilitator then reviews the exercise instructions with the group. Figure 2–10 is the slide that was used for one company workshop.

It is very important for the facilitators to recognize that the participants may not have the business knowledge required to perform the exercise without some guidance. This is why they have a 10-minute session with the teams before discussion begins.

To see how a team from a toy company completed the worksheet, take a look at Table 2–2. This team had the advantage of having an excellent facilitator in the vice president of manufacturing, who had run similar workshops before and used the ten-minute discussion sessions very effectively.

Linking Strategies to Business Results and Customer Value

1. Break into assigned teams and work areas.

2. For no more than *10 minutes* your facilitator will lead you in a discussion about the business impacts to achieve success.

3. For the next *30 minutes,* identify the business results, in terms of sales, costs, and customer satisfaction, expected from each business strategy. Document your results on the worksheet provided.

4. When you are finished, return to the main meeting area, where each team will present its findings in a *5-minute* presentation.

5. When all teams have completed their presentations, a *10-minute* discussion will summarize the exercise results.

Figure 2–10. Sample Slide: Team Exercise Instructions

Table 2–2. Team Exercise Results—Linking Strategies to Business Results and Customer Value

Strategies	Business Results
1. Understand our customers and translate their needs into new and innovative products and services.	1. Increased sales, improved customer relationships, more employment, better wages, greater profit plan distribution.
2. Provide products that are safe and nonviolent, that encourage creativity, expand minds, and promote physical development.	2. Improved market image, more exposure in media, more productive variety for customers to choose from, increased sales, increased customer retention.
3. Provide prompt and accurate delivery of all products and services.	3. Increased customer satisfaction, improved manufacturing efficiencies, lower costs, reduced inventories.
4. Provide the marketplace with complete information about our products and services so existing and potential customers can make informed purchasing decisions.	4. Linking of customer to our company, improved decision time to purchase, improved customer satisfaction, improved market penetration of product and service offerings.
5. Build long-term relationships with our customers who will continue to purchase products and services from our company.	5. Improved customer retention, reduced selling costs, wider customer marketing base, future generation of customers established.

5. LUNCH—60 MINUTES

Lunch is an opportunity for the participants to relax and spend time with their colleagues. It is important that facilitators join in general conversation at lunch and not sit apart from the workshop participants. The ideal is to have three tables for lunch with one facilitator at each table. If table size prevents three separate tables than facilitators should spread themselves among the participants and not sit side by side. The facilitators can plan a question such as "What changes do you think will be necessary for the new company strategy to be successful?" This will stimulate dialogue and help prepare the teams for their next exercise.

6. LINKING STRATEGIES TO CUSTOMER VALUE— 90 MINUTES

In the previous exercise the teams identified the business results that derive from successfully implemented business strategies. In this exercise the teams begin to identify examples of value customers should receive from each business strategy. The facilitator starts off this workshop segment with the exercise instructions (Figure 2–11).

Linking Strategies to Customer Value

1. Break into assigned teams and work areas.

2. For no more than *10 minutes* your facilitator will lead you in a discussion about the various ways customers benefit in today's marketplace and how customer value can be linked to business strategies.

3. For the next *30 minutes* identify examples of value customers would expect to receive based on each business strategy.

4. When you are finished, return to the main meeting area, where each team will present their findings in a *5-minute* presentation.

5. When all teams have completed their presentations, a *10-minute* discussion will summarize the exercise results.

Figure 2–11. Sample Slide: Team Exercise Instructions

The facilitator explains to the group that they will follow the same process as in the previous exercise. The main difference is that in the previous exercise the focus was on business results, while this exercise focuses on customer results. The group then breaks into its teams; each meets with its facilitators to begin the exercise. Each team facilitator needs to help switch the focus from the business side to the customer side. To help the team make this transition, she can begin the 10-minute discussion by asking the members to start thinking like customers: "Look at each business strategy and tell me what you would want as a customer." This helps the team members start to articulate the customer issues. The facilitator records their responses on a flip chart. The goal is to try to capture three or four customer values for each strategy so that the team can discuss each and determine which they can agree on as their team answer. Table 2–3 is a completed worksheet from one of the teams.

Table 2–3. Team Exercise Results—Linking Strategies to Customer Value

Strategies	Customer Value
1. Understand our customers and translate their needs into new and innovative products and services.	1. Products and services are developed that meet customers' specific requirements.
2. Provide products that are safe and nonviolent, that encourage creativity, expand minds, and promote physical development.	2. Satisfies parents' desire to provide a safe and educational environment for their children.
3. Provide prompt and accurate delivery of all products and services.	3. Provides the product ordered in a time frame that meets customer expectations.
4. Provide the marketplace with complete information about our products and services so existing and potential customers can make informed purchasing decisions.	4. Provides customers with the opportunity to find out everything they need to know when making purchasing decisions and eliminates questions that would prevent purchase.
5. Build long-term relationships with our customers who will continue to purchase products and services from our company.	5. Provides customers with the knowledge that they will always be able to purchase a quality product that satisfies their needs.

7. BREAK—15 MINUTES

As noted above, this day can be very stressful for the participants, and breaks need not be limited to one in the morning and one in the afternoon. The facilitators should use their best judgment as to when to announce breaks. If the participants get fidgety and keep moving around in their seats, it is an indication that it might be time for a break. Also, participants sometimes ask for a break. Toward the end of the day the participants are tired and, therefore, more difficult to control. Facilitators should wander around and help the group to return to the meeting area. The current time and the time the participants are expected back in the meeting room should be announced before the break starts.

8. NEXT STEPS—45 MINUTES

This is the part of the workshop in which the participants get a chance to identify the next steps that ensure the business strategies are successfully implemented. With five exercises completed in one day, participants have had an excellent opportunity to identify the changes that are going to be necessary for the company to succeed.

The facilitator starts by asking the group to identify specific actions. He needs to draw out certain responses from the participants. These responses help tie the workshop together and reinforce the main learning points. As you can see from the following list, developed at one workshop, the facilitators did an excellent job of helping the group understand and articulate the three P's.

1. We have to develop measurable business results that will help us determine if our strategies are being implemented successfully.

2. We need to have a better understanding of how we can focus more of our energies on our customers.

3. We need to prepare our workforce to ensure that we successfully implement our business strategies

4. We need to identify specific ways in which we effectively perceive customer needs, wants, and desires.

5. We need to really understand the concepts around pro-
    viding superior customer value.

It is very helpful for the facilitator to make an overhead trans-
parency of the worksheet from each team (see Table 2–3) and show
them to the group. This provides the necessary spark to help the
group identify the necessary next steps.

9. WORKSHOP DEBRIEF—45 MINUTES

To conclude the workshop it is very effective to generate a one-page
summary of the benefits derived by the attendees. A technique to
use is represented in Figure 2–12. The facilitator asks the participants to describe in a few words the lessons learned from the workshop and writes their responses on a grid on the flip chart. It is important that everyone participate because this is a team effort. At
one workshop the facilitator used a computerized display that projected a blank grid on a screen. As each participant provided input,
another facilitator recorded the comments; these were immediately
projected onto the screen. At the end of the workshop each participant was provided with electronic copy of the lessons learned.

People implement strategy.	Customers can value services more than products.	Understanding our customers is a full-time job.	Customers need to be included in our business processes.	We will have to learn how to exhibit customer-focused skills.
Processes have to be constantly enriched to provide value.	Keeping customers reduces our selling costs.	Customers are both channels and consumers.	Our business partners must be part of the change process.	We need to better understand how children develop.
A vision must be clear and understandable.	We need to focus our energies toward the customer.	We will have to learn how to team more effectively.	We need to transform the way we conduct business.	Change is a never-ending process.

Figure 2–12. Lessons Learned

It is sometimes hard for participants to come up with a few words
to express a lesson learned. What works well is for the facilitator to

start working her way around the entire room, moving from one participant to the next. The participants should be told that it is okay to pass initially. Choosing a few words to express an idea is not easy and is a skill unto itself.

10. GROUP DINNER—180 MINUTES

Close the workshop by thanking everyone for a hard day's work. If there is a dinner the facilitators can remind the group of the time it starts. Dinner is a good opportunity for the group to be rewarded, relax, and have some fun. It can also provide an opportunity for an exercise. The Strategy Awareness Workshop requires hard work by each of the participants and each should be rewarded with an enjoyable evening. To help stimulate discussion and reinforce the learning process a facilitator should sit at every table, if possible. This can help to continue the discussion on change. At one of the toy company workshops the facilitator made acetate copies of the lessons learned slide and handed it out at dinner. People at each table were instructed to identify the two most important lessons learned and four reasons for their importance. The table facilitator helped promote discussion. A blank acetate was distributed, along with marking pens, that the teams could use. After dinner each team had an opportunity to review its new slide with the entire group. This helped to reinforce the workshop experiences.

To conclude dinner the facilitator needs to remind participants that this workshop is only the beginning of the change process but provides the foundation for a successful change program. At one dinner the facilitator concluded with the following comments:

> Today we have embarked on the first step of a journey that will result in each of you developing and enriching your skills and knowledge. Our company will take on a new focus that centers around the customer. We can't expect you to do this alone and you will participate in other workshops, similar to the one you attended today, that focus on helping you to prepare your workforce, perceive customer wants, needs, and desires, and provide superior customer value. In today's marketplace change is a

reality and we must learn to embrace it and make it part of our success. Thank you for your participation in the workshop today and I look forward to seeing you at future workshops.

ENDNOTES

1. Robin Cooper and M. Lynne Markus, "Human Reengineering," *Sloan Management Review,* Summer 1995.

2. Robert Slater, *Get Better or Get Beaten! Leadership Secrets from GE's Jack Welch,* New York: Richard D. Irwin, 1994.

3. "A New Frontier," *Solutions,* Unisys Corporation, Fall 1995.

4. "Intel: Far Beyond the Pentium," *BusinessWeek,* February 10, 1995, p. 88.

5. John P. Kotter, "Why Transformation Efforts Fail," *Harvard Business Review,* March/April 1995.

6. Gil Amelio and William Simon, *Profit From Experience,* New York: Van Nostrand Reinhold, 1996, pp. 14-15.

7. Ibid.

8. Kotter, 1995.

9. Slater, 1994.

10. Telephone interview with Robert J. Bailey, October 1994.

11. Interview with a senior manager at General Electric, February 1996.

12. Interview with Chris Byron, September 1994.

13. Slater, 1994.

14. Ibid.

15. Here, and throughout the remainder of the book, I have taken quotes and comments from attendees at workshops that I have facilitated over the course of my career.

CHAPTER 3

INTRODUCING CHANGE

Change is easy if you understand why. It is difficult if all you focus on is the outcome. It is almost impossible if you try to force it.

Anonymous

The president at Super Automotive Parts was concerned that his company was losing competitive position in the marketplace (the name has been changed at the request of the company). Customers had told him that product costs were not competitive and that the company was slow to respond to customer needs. The company manufactures brake systems and parts for the automotive after-market. It had experienced significant growth until 1995, when sales stagnated at $250 million while competitors were growing at about 10 percent per year. The senior management team discussed the subject for over four hours at a monthly meeting.

Founded in the mid-1920s, the company had grown using the traditional top-down management style: Management made all the decisions and the workforce faithfully carried out its commands. The president's father had started the company and on the day he announced his retirement he gave his son this advice: "Keep your distance from your employees. If you get too close they won't listen to you."

Three years later the son realized it was time for a change. He told his colleagues, "We need to get our people more involved in our problems. This way they may be able to help us with the solution." The group agreed. After discussion they decided on the three points they felt the workforce needed to understand:

1. We are not competitive in the marketplace.
2. We need to create a new work environment that will result in an organization more effective in responding to customer needs.
3. We need to cut costs.

For over two hours the team debated how to pass these messages on to the 1,500-member workforce. They concluded that the best approach was to meet with groups of 100 during a two-week period. The meetings would last about an hour and management members would rotate as speakers.

Unfortunately, the plan backfired. Instead of instilling a sense of purpose in the workforce, management instilled a sense of fear. Employees heard the one-hour speech and immediately began to worry if their jobs were in jeopardy and what new work rules would be instituted to improve productivity. No time had been allotted for questions after the senior managers had communicated their message, and rumors emerged all over the plant about a major layoff. Employee morale deteriorated. Instead of the hoped-for rise, productivity slid by over 20 percent in the following month.

This is an example of how to skewer a good idea by implementing it poorly. Many of the components of good leadership were in place. The management team recognized that times had changed, and it had a clear and communicable vision of the future. What it failed to account for was that when people are asked to change they build an emotional brick wall. Fear, anxiety, and concern come to the surface, blocking all other responses. Instead of hearing "We need your help to transform this company into one that is more responsive to customer needs," employees heard "the company has to cut costs so your jobs are in jeopardy."

The single most significant obstacle to changing people is their resistance to change. If management understands that any change in an organization is going to be met by initial resistance from the workforce followed by a forecastable cycle of behaviors, it can successfully plan the change process.

BECOMING PEOPLE-FOCUSED

Companies that don't focus on people can fall into the *Jaikumar Trap:* mistakenly focusing on machines rather than people as a means of increasing efficiency. In 1986 R. Jaikumar published the first study that really showed how focusing on people and not machines profitably impacts business.[1] The study documented how Japanese companies, using the same equipment as U.S.-based companies, were 1,000 percent more productive because of how they utilized *people* (see Figure 3–1).

Area Measured	United States	Japan
Number of systems studied	35	60
Average number of systems per company	7	6
Number of parts manufactured per system	**10**	**93**
Annual production per part	1,727	258
New parts introduced (ratio)	1	22

Figure 3–1. How People Make a Difference

Many companies now realize that their future success is dependent on a new focus that values the people in their organization. Companies in the early 1990s began to realize that people really do a make a difference and implemented one or more elements of the chart in Table 3–1. A "futuretecture" team at Xerox developed a new, three-level organization chart showing corporate staff at the bottom supporting business teams and districts at the top. The new chart focused on people rather than the corporate hierarchy because it is people who interact with the customer.

People-centered companies forge close, trusting relationships with their workers and organize them into empowered multifunc-

tional work teams that develop new products, processes, and services. You've heard about GE, 3M, Intuit, Microsoft, and other large
companies. Now, more and more small to mid-size companies and
unions are becoming people-focused.

The one-million-member Communication Workers of America
(CWA), led by its president, Morton Bahr, has worked with management to focus on people for the past fifteen years. The CWA believes
that improving the skills and knowledge of the worker will result in
improved processes, products, and services that will generate
more revenue and ultimately more jobs. At a Dallas AT&T facility in
the early 1990s a major remodeling project integrating four facilities
into one was accomplished by union members on time, on schedule, and without losing a single day of work despite the geographic
disparity of the four sites.

Table 3–1 describes a shoe manufacturer located in the mid-
Atlantic region of the United States that turned itself around after almost closing its doors. The son of the CEO had tried for many years
to convince his father that the competitive environment was changing and unless they did something at their plant they would continually lose business to their competitors. Finally the father began to
listen to his son's warnings and together they began to transform
the company from a command-and-control environment to one
where the people focus on providing value to customers. You can
see the change in how they valued their people. In 1990 they rated
their people value at 8. In 1995 they rated their people value 31. Today the company is thriving and profitable.

Table 3–1. Does Your Company Value People?

(Rate your company from 1 to 5;   1=Unimportant   5=Very Important)

Element	Non-People-Centered	5 Years Ago	Today	People-Centered
EDUCATION				
How important is it for your workforce to continue their education while employed by your company?	Suppress and stifle knowledge.	2	4	Aggressively foster and encourage people to increase their knowledge.

Table 3–1. (continued)
(Rate your company from 1 to 5; 1=Unimportant 5=Very Important)

Element	Non-People-Centered	5 Years Ago	Today	People-Centered
SKILLS AND KNOWLEDGE				
How important is it for your employees to use their skills and knowledge in their work?	Functionally oriented departments perform repetitive tasks requiring minor training of personnel.	1	4	Workers translate their skills, knowledge, and experience into new and constantly evolving products, processes, and services.
ORGANIZATION OF PEOPLE				
How important is it for your workforce to be organized around customer-driven processes?	Workers are organized in functional silos where there is little communication between departments.	1	5	Workers from different department are organized around customer-driven processes and continuously try to improve customer value.
INNOVATION				
How important is it to foster an environment where employees can be creative and innovative?	Creativity is not a requirement in functionally driven work processes	1	4	People are encouraged and rewarded to create, develop, and implement new ideas.
EMPOWERMENT				
How important is it for your workforce to empower themselves in their work environment?	Decisions are made at senior levels of the organization and the workforce generally performs according to strict guidelines, policies, and procedures.	1	4	Senior levels set vision and strategy while operating levels define and implement goals, mission, and objectives, making all necessary decisions.
WORK TEAMS				
How important are work teams to the success of your enterprise?	Work teams are not required because work is organized around functions, with each employee performing specific jobs.	1	5	Empowered cross-functional teams form together to create new ideas with a high degree of accomplishment and involvement.
CHANGE				
How important does management consider change in the work environment?	Existing practices have been in place for a long time and any changes are directed from senior management.	1	5	Management recognizes that change is a reality and people are encouraged to promote change in the work environment with a focus on providing superior customer value.
	TOTALS	**8**	**31**	

Use Table 3–2 to evaluate how people-centered your company is. First rate the relative importance of each element to your company five years ago, with 1 being unimportant and 5 being very important. Then rate the importance of each element today. When you have completed rating your own company add the two sets of ratings. Although this is a subjective rating, the scores will give you an idea of trends between the two periods. One hopes for a positive change. Each company moves closer to valuing people at different rates. *The absolute value of the rating is not as important as the degree to which the scores have changed over the past five years.* If the difference between the totals of the two scores is less than 10, you need to rethink how your organization values people. If the difference between the two totals is between 10 and 20, you are on the right track and should look for more ways to focus on people. If the difference is greater than 20, you should be commended. Use this self-test periodically to determine whether your score is continuously improving. If it is, you are on the right course.

Table 3–2. Does Your Company Value People?

(Rate your company from 1 to 5; 1=Unimportant 5=Very Important)

Element	Non-People-Centered	5 Years Ago	Today	People-Centered
EDUCATION How important is it for your workforce to continue their education while employed by your company?	Suppress and stifle knowledge.			Aggressively foster and encourage people to increase their knowledge.
SKILLS AND KNOWLEDGE How important is it for your employees to use their skills and knowledge in their work?	Functionally oriented departments perform repetitive tasks requiring minor training of personnel.			Workers translate their skills, knowledge, and experience into new and constantly evolving products, processes, and services.
ORGANIZATION OF PEOPLE How important is it for your workforce to be organized around customer-driven processes?	Workers are organized in functional silos where there is little communication between departments.			Workers from different departments are organized around customer-driven processes and continuously try to improve customer value.

Table 3–2. (continued)

(Rate your company from 1 to 5; 1=Unimportant 5=Very Important)

Element	Non-People-Centered	5 Years Ago	Today	People-Centered
INNOVATION How important is it to foster an environment where employees can be creative and innovative?	Creativity is not a requirement in functionally driven work processes.			People are encouraged and rewarded to create, develop, and implement new ideas.
EMPOWERMENT How important is it for your workforce to empower themselves in their work environment?	Decisions are made at the senior levels of the organization and the workforce generally performs according to strict guidelines, policies, and procedures.			Senior levels set vision and strategy while operating levels define and implement goals, mission, and objectives, making all necessary decisions.
WORK TEAMS How important are work teams to the success of your enterprise?	Work teams are not required because work is organized around functions with each employee performing specific jobs.			Empowered cross-functional teams form together to create new ideas with a high degree of accomplishment and involvement.
CHANGE How important does management consider change in the work environment?	Existing practices have been in place for a long time and any changes are directed from senior management.			Management recognizes that change is a reality and people are encouraged to promote change in the work environment with a focus on providing superior customer value.
TOTALS				

HOW PEOPLE REACT

In the old days, change consisted of raising capital for a new plant and equipment, and focusing on producing high volumes of product at low per-unit costs. In today's business environment the biggest change for the workforce is learning new business behaviors. People naturally oppose change. Whether it is a move to a new neighborhood, finding a new job, entering a new relationship, or quitting smoking, we all remember the struggle and anxiety of the process. It is no different when change occurs in the work environment. Orga-

nizations, too, develop a behavioral culture over many years and
these behaviors become so ingrained that any effort to change
them is resisted, even when it is quite clear that the behaviors no
longer serve a good purpose. Adopting change follows three stages:
denial, awakening, and action, as shown in Figure 3–2.

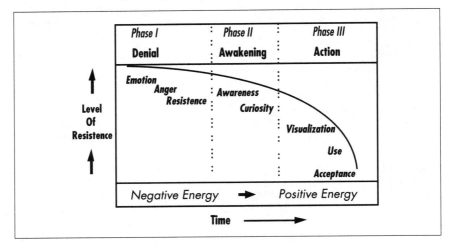

Figure 3–2. Adoption of Change Curve

Overcoming resistance in Phase I is the key to changing behaviors. It takes time to move from denial to action. How much time depends on how you approach the workforce with your change program. If you embrace them in the effort the timeline will be short. If
you communicate your change effort without soliciting their input
you will experience resistance and the timeline can extend to over
a year.

People accept change at different rates, as shown in Figure 3–3.
Those who are creative and innovative will accept change early in
the process; they are usually a small group. There will be another
small group at the end of the change timeline. These are the most
resistant to change, the gradual followers. The majority of people
are middle-of-the-roaders. At the vanguard of this middle group are
positive influencers, while negative influencers bring up the rear.

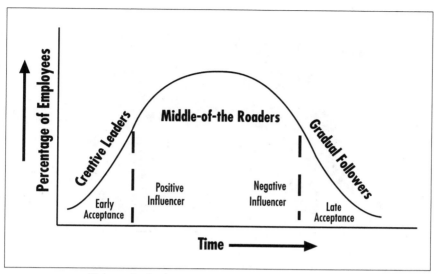

Figure 3–3. Acceptance of Change Curve[2]

CREATIVE LEADERS

Creative leaders go through a change cycle like everyone else. The difference is that their change cycle does not consist of obstacles but of positive enablers that help them accept the change. These enablers range from uninformed optimism—where people are confident the change is necessary but need more information to completely internalize the change—to completion, where the need for change has been completely internalized and understood. The timeline differs among creative leaders too. The important point is that all these individuals think positively about change. They do so even though they don't understand the reasons for it—*uninformed optimism*. As they receive information about the necessary change they get discouraged. They are overwhelmed with information and for a short time they doubt that change can happen—*informed pessimism*. When they begin to understand the reasons for the change individuals begin to internalize it—*hopeful realism* and *informed optimism*. Finally, they have a total understanding of the reasons for change and the necessary actions that are required to succeed at change—*completion* (see Figure 3–4).

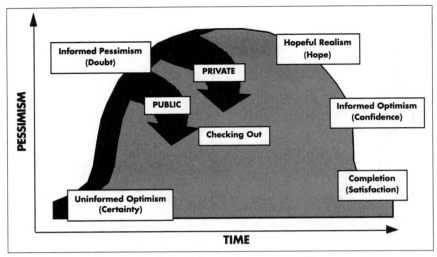

Figure 3–4. Positive Response to Change

Courtesy Kevin O'Sullivan, Unisys Corporation.

Creative leaders are always coming up with new ideas for doing things and seem to have an effective way of communicating their thoughts. Other employees look to them for leadership within the workforce. They have the vision and creative ability to see that change is necessary and accept it early. You can recognize these individuals because they always have a positive attitude about everything. They find ways to get things done instead of coming up with reasons why they can't get done. They also seem to take charge of a situation and volunteer to head a team or take on additional work because they know it is the right thing to do.

Creative leaders are found in the workforce as well as among management. For instance, at a welding supply distributor customers were complaining that orders were being shipped incorrectly. A number of superficial changes initiated by management didn't seem to work. A new shipping clerk heard about the customer complaints and asked his coworkers what they thought the problem was. No one could figure it out. One day he and a coworker were selecting products for shipment. The coworker had extreme difficulty reading the stock numbers and made a few mistakes. During the afternoon coffee break the new employee asked some of his coworkers to read stock numbers from shipping documents. They all had difficulty and interpreted the numbers incorrectly. Unlike his coworkers, who were in their late forties and early fifties, the new employee was young and had excellent eyesight. The printing on the documents was small, so the shipping clerk suggested to the supervisor that the font size be increased. After the suggestion was implemented shipping errors were dramatically reduced from 10 percent to less than 1 percent.

MIDDLE-OF-THE-ROADERS

The middle-of-the-roaders are the largest group. They are easily influenced by others and tend not to rock the boat. These people are the hard workers who make the business successful but they don't get involved in political disputes; they just want to do their jobs well and go home to their families at the end of the day. They usually follow certain individuals who influence them. This creates an opportunity for those instigating change. If a middle-of-the-roader is influenced by negative influencers and gradual followers, negative behaviors will be exhibited and any change effort will take a long time to succeed. If the middle-of-the-roaders follow the creative leaders and positive influencers, however, you can take advantage of forward momentum.

Influencers are usually part of the workforce. They take charge of situations. If there is an employee grievance they tend to stir up the troops. They have good communication skills and therefore people tend to listen to them. It is important to realize that influencers can be good and bad. An influencer who resists change can do damage to the organization by riling up the workforce with negative feelings.

At a small meat-packing plant in eastern Pennsylvania, management was trying to change some of the work rules to improve quality and customer service and ultimately to increase worker wages. One group thought the idea of changing the point at which quality checks were made would not only improve quality but also reduce operating costs. Many of the quality problems uncovered were created early in the manufacturing process, whereas quality checks were made toward the end of the process. By having the quality inspectors roam the floor instead of inspecting at the end, they could examine products at all points in the process. Management was willing to share the reduced rework costs with the employees on a 50/50 basis. Another group, composed mainly of quality control inspectors, resisted the change. They liked the easy life of inspecting at the end of the process. They could linger around, take frequent coffee breaks, and operate pretty much in an unsupervised part of the factory. In the proposed new process they would have to roam the floor and be scrutinized by other employees who would benefit from bonuses paid as a result of reduced rework costs. This meant that they had to work harder while in constant sight of other employees.

The first group had a positive influencer and the second group had a negative influencer. In the end the positive influencer was able to convince the second group that the new process would not only benefit the company but also benefit each employee with additional compensation. They accepted the new proposal.

Positive influencers exhibit leadership qualities. A positive influencer is one whom the workers look up to for advice and leadership. A negative influencer tries to organize a group to take an opposing view that is not in the best interest of the workforce.

GRADUAL FOLLOWERS

On the other end of the spectrum are the gradual followers. These are individuals who are set in their ways. Age is not necessarily a factor in this. People, both young and old, in an organization invest their time and energies in building skills. After a period of hard work, they can finally enjoy the comfort knowing that they can perform their tasks. Then one day someone comes along and says, "We are not doing the job this way anymore. You're going to have to learn new skills." They are crushed. After working so hard to learn their skills, they are being told that they have to learn new skills and processes all over again. You can't blame them for their feelings of anger and resentment. Management must recognize that there are many people like this in the organization. They are often hard workers, but they must be helped to accept change. On the positive side, gradual followers can make an important contribution to a discussion of change by adding the voice of reason. They check the validity of new ideas and question their value.

Gradual followers exhibit the responses to change described in Figure 3–5. For example, at a construction equipment manufacturer the order entry process was being shortened from a five-day turnaround to a targeted one-day response. The company manufactures compressors and other pneumatic equipment that construction crews use to build highways. Each of the ten order entry clerks had been with the company for at least fifteen years and was very comfortable with the cumbersome manual process that existed. This group represented the gradual followers. Initially they *denied* the need for change and then got *angry* when management told them that customers were complaining about delivery times. Over the next few weeks they became *depressed,* realizing that the change would happen but they did not feel part of it. They began to test the process, looking for information that would help them better understand the changes necessary. In the new process orders were checked as the process occurred instead of at the end. The workers questioned this until they realized how much longer it took to change errors uncovered at the end of the process than during the process.

To aid the change effort, a small group of managers who themselves had each been with the company at least fifteen years helped the order entry clerks with the new process for about four weeks. Management felt that the clerks would relate better to managers who were as senior in tenure as they than to some whippersnapper MBA. During the four-week period the order entry clerks began to see how much easier the new process was and realized that there were benefits to the changed process. Errors were corrected more quickly, team members worked with each other to process difficult orders, and covered for each other when a personal situation prevented someone from coming to work. The most important change was that as orders were being processed more quickly, customers began to comment on this to the order entry clerks. When the clerks saw the benefit they finally accepted the need to change their behaviors.

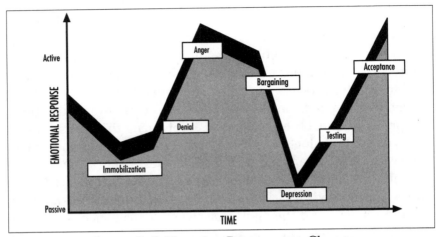

Figure 3–5. Negative Response to Change

Courtesy Kevin O'Sullivan, Unisys Corporation.

HOW TO SUCCESSFULLY ORCHESTRATE CHANGE

One of the primary reasons change efforts fail is that management does not take the time to understand people's emotional responses to change, both positive and negative, and the behaviors that ensue. The other reason change efforts often fail is that management does not know how to establish a dialogue with the workforce that will address negative responses and harness the positive energy the change is seeking to unleash. This is why the best way to begin any change effort is to perform an assessment of your workforce's readiness for change. Employees throughout the organization can participate in a simple one-day workshop in which management informs them of the planned change effort. Workshops capture feelings and measure the potential resistance to change while providing an opportunity to share and articulate the potential obstacles and benefits of the change program. Management can also assess the effort and priority of critical areas.

The key to organizing a successful change workshop lies in identifying five categories of people in your workplace. You can then select the people for each workshop group in a way that takes advantage of their strengths and what they have to give to each other. For instance, when a pharmaceutical plant wanted to shorten the time it took to process drug testing data it formed five process implementation teams of ten workers each. All the teams included at least two creative leaders and positive influencers. They delayed including gradual followers until the middle-of-the-roaders had accepted the new process. The strategy worked. Within two weeks the creative leaders had helped the middle-of-the-roaders buy into the new process. Subsequently, one to two gradual followers were included in the teams. With the majority of the team members already in favor of change it didn't take long for them to see the light.

If you put people together randomly, on the other hand, the different rates of acceptance can be puzzling. At a chemical processing plant about two dozen employee teams were looking at ways to improve operating processes. Three teams focused on marketing processes, three more on the order capture processes, four on manufacturing processes, and two on administrative processes. A number of the teams seemed to be moving at a quick pace while others moved much more slowly. On some teams there was one individual who resisted suggestions. Team members listened to the individual and then discussed the alternatives. Sometimes the team rethought its position; other times it had to have lengthier discussions to help the gradual follower understand the benefits of the process change. On other teams there were as many as four gradual followers who resisted the very idea of change. It took much longer to sway these gradual followers because of their sheer numbers.

The greatest benefit of change is the ability to harness the creative and intellectual energies of individuals and focus their efforts toward common business objectives. Unlike at any other time in history, the worker today has the opportunity to help the company succeed in becoming more competitive, more profitable, and more agile. As an employee at GE put it, "For twenty-five years you've paid for my hands when you could have had my brain for nothing."[3] The companies that will achieve the most success are those that anticipate changes in the marketplace and respond with new and constantly evolving products, services, and processes that provide superior value to customers. To do so management must make the necessary investments to help the workforce become more adaptable to change. It will also have to prepare the workforce to understand change and embrace it as an enabler of future success.

WORKSHOP: ASSESSING ORGANIZATIONAL READINESS FOR CHANGE

CATEGORIZE THE WORKFORCE

In improving the effectiveness of the workforce, managers are always faced with identifying the individual skills and work habits of their subordinates. The same is true when assessing people's readiness for change.

Several weeks before the workshop, management should divide the workforce into five categories: creative leaders, positive influencers, middle-of-the-roaders, negative influencers, and gradual followers. Although this is not easy, it is a necessary evil and will ensure success in the change process. At one company, to help them through this process, workshops were held for all managers and supervisors. Attendees were split into small working groups and asked to evaluate their direct reports, identify one individual for each of the five categories, and provide the reasons for the categorization. To protect each employee's identity, false names were used in the exercise. Managers then explained to the other members of their team how they categorized the individuals and the type of behaviors each exhibited.

This process helped the managers and supervisors become more familiar with assessing the behaviors exhibited by individuals in each of the categories. They were told to expect to shift people between categories several times before making a final determination and that at subsequent points in the process assignments could be reversed. Each manager was allowed three weeks to finalize his list. The managers were glad they had time to think. A senior manager at a paint manufacturing company commented:

> It was very uncomfortable at first when I had to place names in boxes. It felt strange. But during the three weeks before finalizing the lists I spent a lot of time analyzing people's behaviors. It was quite an eye-opener. Once I did that it was much easier for me to categorize my direct reports.

Table 3–3. Divide Your Workforce

Divide Your Workforce

Category	Employee	Behaviors Exhibited
Creative Thinkers	John	John always comes up with new ideas, follows them through, and is the consummate believer that change is necessary for success.
Positive Influencers	Sally	Peers look to Sally as a leader and constantly seek her advice. Sally listens well and communicates her ideas effectively.
Middle-of-the-Roaders	Bruce	Bruce is an excellent worker, has been with the company for 25 years, and never makes waves. He tends to follow the crowd.
Negative Influencers	Kathy	Kathy always looks for the negative reasons when there is a change. She is very articulate and her coworkers listen to her.
Gradual Followers	Gus	Gus has been with the company only one year and is fresh out of school. He is a hard worker but very set in his ways. Changes need to be explained to Gus in more detail than to others but once he understands the reasons for the change he performs his job well.

BRIEF THE CREATIVE LEADERS AND POSITIVE INFLUENCERS

Before the actual workshops, the lead facilitator—an employee with experience in these workshops or an outside consultant—should meet with a small group consisting of the senior management team, the management sponsor, and one or two creative leaders and positive influencers. This should be followed by a second meeting that includes all the creative leaders and positive influencers.

The purpose of the first meeting is to brief a small, influential group on the overall change program benefits, the change workshops, the attendees at each workshop, and their role in each of the workshops to ensure success. This will help to identify any potential obstacles to anticipate at the workshop as well as help the buy-in process of other participants. The second meeting with all of the creative leaders and positive influencers covers the same information plus an additional message: Creative leaders and positive influencers should be advised that their help is needed to ensure success in the change program. They should also be told that they will play an invaluable role in helping to facilitate the change workshops. Tell them that they will receive proper training in how to facilitate. As discussed earlier, creative leaders and positive influencers usually do very well at accepting change and by their sheer desire will help make the workshop a success.

By this point in the process the workforce should have been divided into the categories. Management and facilitators can now review the lists to see if there are concerns about mismatches. This is a good opportunity to get other opinions about the categorization; some changes usually occur at this point. At one such session creative leaders thought that two individuals on the list should be categorized as positive influencers instead of middle-of-the-roaders. A meeting was scheduled between the supervisors of the two employees and the creative leader who challenged the categorization. After an hour of discussion the two employees were recategorized. It seemed that the supervisor didn't know the employees as well as the creative leader, who was able to cite instances where the employees in question had influenced peers and were in fact sought out by peers for advice. In subsequent workshops these two employees made valuable contributions as facilitators.

No more than fifteen people should attend each workshop, and each workshop should be facilitated by two creative leaders and/or positive influencers as well as one lead facilitator who is either an experienced employee or an outside professional. Remember that having too many negative influencers in one workshop could sway the entire group the wrong way. Make sure you have a proper balance by pairing the negative influencers with the creative leaders and positive influencers who feel comfortable with them. At the same time you can also ask the group which middle-of-the-roaders each of the creative leaders and positive influencers would want in their workshops. Table 3–4 can be used as a guide to determining the proper mix of participants in a workshop.

Table 3–4. Ideal Workshop Participant Profile

Ideal Workshop Participant Profile	
Participant Category	**Number**
Creative Leaders	2
Positive Influencers	1
Middle-of-the-Roaders	9
Negative Influencers	1
Gradual Followers	2
Total	**15**

The process of managing change in the organization starts with planning for the workshops in a way that ensures success. Planning is the key to success and will improve your odds in implementing successful change.

ASSESSING ORGANIZATIONAL READINESS FOR CHANGE

The objective of this workshop is for participants to assess their company's readiness for change. It is not as intense as the Strategy Awareness Workshop presented in Chapter 2 but builds on the information it generated. Participants enjoy this workshop because they really have an opportunity to contribute to the change process and have fun at the same time. Table 3–5 represents the agenda for an Assessing Organizational Readiness for Change one-day workshop.

1. SET THE STAGE—60 MINUTES

The lead facilitator provides an overview of the workshop that includes the objectives, agenda, and administrative matters (location of restroom facilities, phone messages, and so on). The participants introduce themselves and voice their expectations for the workshop. To help participants with introductions the facilitator can show a slide similar to the one used in the Strategy Awareness Workshop (see Figure 2–8).

The major workshop objectives and the agenda can now be reviewed in a series of slides. It is beneficial in this particular workshop to hang posters of the company vision, strategy, and values on the left and right walls of the room. This provides a constant reminder of the business issues that confront all the attendees and helps to clarify concerns that surround them.

Table 3–5. Assessing Organizational Readiness for Change

Agenda
9:00 AM – 9:00 PM

Time Frames	Time Allotted	Workshop Exercises	Facilitator	Objectives
1. 9:00–10:00	60 min	Set the Stage	Joe S.	Discuss the learning objectives and capture participants' expectations.
2. 10:00–10:30	30 min	Warm-Up Exercise	Bill W./Sally F.	Understand different aspects of change and how it can effect the individual/organization.
3. 10:30–10:45	15 min	Break		
4. 10:45–11:30	45 min	Warm-Up Exercise II	Bill W./Sally F.	Understand different aspects of change and how it can effect the individual/organization.
5. 11:30–12:30	60 min	Lunch		
6. 12:30–2:30	120 min	Assess Obstacles and Benefits of Change —Team Exercise	Bill W.	Assess the obstacles and benefits of change in team exercise.
7. 2:30–2:45	15 min	Break		
8. 2:45–4:45	120 min	Assess Key Management Areas Required for Change—Team Exercise	Sally F.	Assess effort and priority of key management areas required for successful change program.
9. 4:45–5:15	30 min	Next Steps	Joe S./Bill W.	Identify necessary actions to ensure that the change program will be successful.
10. 5:15–6:00	45 min	Workshop Debrief	Joe S./Bill W./ Sally F.	Capture and share benefits of the workshop.
11. 7:00–9:00	120 min	Group Dinner		

Lead Facilitator: Joe S.   Facilitators: Bill W./Sally F.

- to inform individuals within the organization of the planned change effort
- to capture feelings and measure the potential resistance to change
- to share and articulate with others the potential obstacles and benefits of the change program
- to assess effort and priority of key management areas required for a successful change.

Figure 3–6. Sample Slide: Workshop Objectives

2 & 4. WARM-UP—75 MINUTES

This exercise is crucial in providing a sound foundation for the rest of the workshop. A change workshop requires attendees to be relaxed and to have a clear understanding of what change is about. A warm-up exercise that personalizes change is the best approach. Everyone has experienced change at some time in his life. Personalizing the change will make it easier for individuals to understand the phases of change that can be applied to the business environment.

The warm-up exercise has three stages. First, ask for volunteers to share a personal experience that involved change. Three to five examples taking no more than a total of fifteen minutes is sufficient. Second, break the group into teams of no more than five people for a thirty-minute exercise. Each team member is to share a personal change experience. As teams the participants then develop a list of phases that apply to the change process. Third, when all the teams return to the main room, a spokesperson from each shares the list of change phases developed, taking no more than about fifteen minutes for all the presentations. Figure 3–7 represents a team's identification of the phases experienced during the purchase of a house.

Buying a New House

Phase	Description
1. Fear	1. Fearful of the experience
2. Apprehension	2. Not sure the decision was correct
3. Concern	3. Wanted to make sure we make the right decision
4. Anxiety	4. Nervous about all the decisions we had to make
5. Information Gathering	5. Obtaining all the information needed to buy the house
6. Happiness	6. Satisfaction in the decision making process

Figure 3–7. Sample Slide: Warm-Up Exercise

To conclude the warm-up exercise, in the final fifteen minutes the facilitator helps the group reach consensus on what it believes are the phases that individuals go through when experiencing change. It is extremely helpful at this point to capture reasons why change efforts fail. The point of this exercise is to show that change is a process of phases that individuals must experience in order for the change to be successful.

3. BREAK—15 MINUTES

The tendency is for breaks to last longer than the allotted time. To prevent this the facilitator should announce the time of the break, the current time, and the time at which the group is to reconvene.

5. LUNCH—60 MINUTES

Use lunch as an opportunity for the group to learn and to provide the facilitators feedback on the morning workshop. Facilitators should spread themselves among the participants, ideally at three separate tables. To help the participants each table facilitator encourages them to express what they found interesting about the morning session. The facilitators should meet before the workshop resumes to share the discussions at the table. This is a reality check. Is the message getting through to the group? If there are any disconnects the facilitators can address these when the workshop resumes.

6. ASSESS OBSTACLES AND BENEFITS OF CHANGE— 120 MINUTES

This team exercise links the personal change experience with changes required in the business environment. Attendees rate the effect they experience from a defined set of obstacles and benefits and give reasons for their assessment. Facilitators should use the five change-related categories of people as a basis for assigning individuals to teams and use Figure 3–3 as a reference for determining the proper mix of participants. Breaking up the group into three teams of five makes this exercise much easier to complete. It is probably the first time any of the attendees have been asked these types of questions and process is more personal with a small group.

The two-hour segment can be divided into three effective mini-sessions. The first twenty minutes is used as an overview. The next hour is for the team exercise. The last forty minutes is for the teams to share their results with the rest of the group.

Figure 3–8 shows an instruction slide used during one workshop.

Assessing Obstacles and Benefits of Change

1. Use Worksheet A and rate the degree to which each obstacle and benefit impacts you as an individual.

2. For each obstacle and benefit provide the reason you chose the rating.

Figure 3–8. Sample Slide: Team Exercise Instructions

To help cross the bridge between personal change and business change the facilitators should review each element of the worksheet (see Table 3–6) before sending the teams off to perform the exercise. This helps accomplish two objectives. First, no one likes to admit they don't understand the meaning of words; by explaining the elements facilitators prevent individuals from embarrassing themselves. Second, the review provides common definitions that everyone can apply in the exercise.

At this stage in one workshop the facilitator recognized that the attendees didn't seem as motivated as she would have liked. To help stimulate interest she gave a pep talk to encourage participation in the exercise.

> Each of us will have to undergo some change as we transform this company to be more competitive in the marketplace. Change will not be easy and it is normal for us to feel uncomfortable about change. The purpose of this exercise is to think about how the change program will impact you as an individual. We need to make this change process succeed and we will need your help. This workshop is

designed to help each of us understand the reasons for change and to help us experience it in a positive way.

As a result of the talk the teams became more alive and responsive during the team meeting that followed.

A facilitator should be assigned to each team to help maintain focus on the exercise. Each facilitator should guide the participants through the process of completing the worksheet by repeating the instructions, providing examples, and answering questions.

Figure 3–6 is a completed worksheet. As you can see from the responses, this employee has been with the company for twenty years performing the same job. She is fearful of change but understands the benefits it brings. This individual was concerned that the company would not be patient with her because she is so set in her ways. Under additional benefits to change this employee noted that the company would be more profitable and more fun. (Only two other workshop participants added "more profitable company" as a benefit. This indicates that the workforce still doesn't understand the business issues surrounding change. The facilitator spent some time discussing the business issues with the group. After about a ten-minute discussion others agreed that a benefit of change would be a more profitable company.) It is evident from this employee's comments that she wants the company to succeed but is afraid that she may not have the patience or capability to change without a fair amount of help.

Table 3–6. Assessing Obstacles to and Benefits of Change Worksheet

ELEMENT	IMPACT RATING (1 = High; 2 = Med; 3 = Low)	REASON FOR RATING
Obstacles to Change		
1. Loss of job	2	I am afraid that management will look at reducing employees as a way of cutting cost.
2. Loss of power	2	I won't have the power that I had before if we form teams and everyone has a say.

Table 3–6. (continued)

ELEMENT	IMPACT RATING (1 = High; 2 = Med; 3 = Low)	REASON FOR RATING
Obstacles to Change (continued)		
3. Need to learn new skills	1	I have been doing the same job for 20 years. How will I learn a new skill quickly?
4. Need to learn new behaviors	1	This is all new to me and I don't know if I will be able to change.
5. Difficulty dealing with change	2	I think I understand the concepts of change but I am not sure if I will handle it well.
6. Difficulty understanding the need for/benefits of change	3	I understand the need for and benefits of change but being able to change is an entirely different process.
Other Obstacles You Wish to Identify		
7. Finding help to deal with changes	1	I want to do what is good for the company but feel that I may need more help than others to change my behaviors.
Benefits		
1. Learn new skills	3	I want to learn new skills but have been performing the same job for 20 years.
2. Help the company achieve its objectives	3	I do want the company to succeed and will do whatever I can do to make that happen.
3. Easier to communicate throughout company	3	If we work in a more teaming environment then it certainly would be easier to communicate with one another.
4. Become more valuable to company	3	As we learn new skills we will become more valuable to the company and to the marketplace.

Table 3–6 (continued)

ELEMENT	IMPACT RATING (1 = High; 2 = Med; 3 = Low)	REASON FOR RATING
Other Benefits You Wish to Identify (continued)		
5. Greater ability to use creative skills	3	As I learn new creative skills the job may not be as boring as it is now.
6. Work with fellow employees in a team environment	3	I always enjoy talking with people and working with them.
7. More profitable company	3	More profits will mean a better work environment for us.
8. More fun	3	Enjoying work and having fun is important.

When the teams return to the main meeting room each shares its results with the entire group in a brief 5–10-minute presentation. After this, the facilitator should ask, "What did you learn from this exercise?" During one such workshop for a steel manufacturer an assembly worker raised his hand and said, "Analyzing change like this helped me better understand the obstacles and benefits of change." Others in the room felt the same way. It is important for individuals to share their learning experiences with the rest of the group. This helps reach consensus and builds camaraderie among group members.

7. BREAK—15 MINUTES

Toward the end of the day a group is apt to be more difficult to control so facilitators should wander around and help participants to return to the meeting area.

8. ASSESS KEY MANAGEMENT AREAS REQUIRED FOR CHANGE—120 MINUTES

Understanding the obstacles and benefits of change for individuals is one of the workshop objectives. The second major objective is to capture from the attendees the areas that management needs to focus on in order for the change effort to be successful. Timing is just as important in this exercise as in the first and the same time schedule can be used. Be prepared for comments. At one workshop an attendee was sarcastic: "It's about time we had our say about management. Now it's our turn to get even." Others laughed. The facilitator smiled, and responded, "Although you might look at this as an opportunity to criticize management, we should view this as an opportunity to help management effect a successful change process."

As with the first exercise, a slide that describes the instructions is helpful (see Figure 3–9).

Assessing Effort and Priority of Key Management Areas for Successful Change

1. Use Worksheet B and identify the effort and priority you feel are required to ensure a successful change program using the following rating scale:

    1 = High   2 = Medium   3 = Low

2. For each element provide the reason for your score.

Figure 3–9. Sample Slide: Team Exercise Instructions

This exercise is harder than the first because the concepts are more difficult to comprehend. In this exercise attendees deal with ideas such as leadership, vision, teaming, and communication, and the facilitators will have to spend more time explaining each and providing *explicit* examples. In one workshop, the lead facilitator reviewed each element of the worksheet and used a flip chart to capture an example. He had each of the two cofacilitators copy the same information on separate flip charts so each team could have its own poster as a guide. The more visual aids are used, the more successful the workshop. Again, a facilitator should be with each team to help it through the exercise.

When the teams return to the main meeting room they should present a summary of their findings. Table 3–7 shows a completed worksheet.

*Table 3–7. Assessing Effort and Priority of Key Management
Areas for Successful Change Worksheet*

Element	Effort	Priority	Reason
	Impact Rating (1=High; 2=Med; 3=Low)		
1. **Lead the charge.** Developing and practicing leadership skills at all levels to obtain support, commitment, and respect from workforce.	1	1	The current management style is very much dictatorial. If we are going to succeed at change we need to respect, not fear, management.
2. **Develop a vision.** Developing and articulating a clear and concise vision that motivates the workforce.	1	1	If we are going to change our company and be more competitive than in the past we need to understand what the vision of the management team is.
3. **Communicate the message.** Encouraging regular and open exchanges of information throughout the enterprise.	2	2	It will be very important to have an environment of open communication.
4. **Provide required infrastructure.** Ensuring the required infrastructure to support the new changes.	3	1	I don't really understand the infrastructure issue that well so I rated the effort as a 3 but feel it is very important if we are to be more responsive to our customers.
5. **Encourage participation.** Encouraging and supporting open and active participation throughout the entire company.	2	2	I think this goes hand in hand with the question on open communication. We have to remember that we have never been asked to participate or provide an opinion before so it may be difficult but yet very important.
6. **Train the workforce.** Providing the required training in new skills and capabilities for the workforce to pursue and succeed at existing and new strategies.	1	1	If we are to work together in teams we will have to learn new skills that aren't learned overnight.

Table 3–7. (continued)

Element	Effort	Priority	Reason
	Impact Rating (1=High; 2=Med; 3=Low)		
7. Assess opportunities. Developing the capability to assess and exploit opportunities to achieve success.	2	3	I believe that this is the result of all the actions we will take and therefore has a low priority.
8. Provide a learning environment. Providing an environment that encourages, supports, and rewards learning.	2	2	We will need to learn new skills to develop new products for our customers.
9. Create new rules. Developing rules that constantly challenge existing structures, systems, and policies.	1	1	I like this one but it could be dangerous if all of us think we can challenge everything.
10. Empower the workforce. Creating an environment where authority, responsibility, information, knowledge, and rewards are distributed throughout the enterprise.	1	1	It sounds like a great idea and is very important but somehow I think it isn't as easy as it sounds.

The facilitator should now ask participants for their reaction to the exercise. Another facilitator can capture their comments on the flip chart. At one workshop Angela, who had been with the company for ten years and worked in a variety of departments, raised her hand. She told the group:

> This was really difficult for me. At first I wanted to say that management didn't do anything right. This was more of an emotional reaction. But as Bill [the facilitator] described each of the key management elements and provided us with an example of each, I started to realize that this is important stuff and although I really didn't understand it well enough yet, I need to spend more time in the future learning what each of the elements mean and their impact to a successful company.

A coworker added, "We have been so sheltered on the work floor just doing our jobs that we don't really understand the business issues that would make this company successful."

The lead facilitator observed everyone's reaction. He asked the group if anyone else shared the same feelings. Almost every hand was raised. The facilitator then asked the group if it would be helpful for them to receive training in general business issues and the new dynamics in the marketplace. Everyone's hand was raised at this point. The cofacilitator walked over to the flip chart and titled the page "Parking Lot." This is a term for important thoughts that need to be addressed but are not the subject of the workshop. The participants agreed that they needed to have a better understanding about the business issues and market dynamics that make the business environment so complex today. Additionally, the group felt it needed more training in change and how it would affect each of them in their jobs. These points were summarized on the flip chart and the facilitators told the group that there would be more interactive sessions where they would have the opportunity to learn about change and to experience different aspects of change. To close the issue the facilitator said, "Management wants each of us to be part of the change process as well as be part of the success. They realize there is an investment that is going to have to be made and they are prepared to do this." Everyone applauded.

9. NEXT STEPS—30 MINUTES

This is the point in the workshop at which the attendees can really buy into the change process. It is their opportunity to identify the next steps that need to be accomplished for the change program to work. The facilitator can refer to the Parking Lot at this time for subjects to include. Figure 3–10 is a slide prepared during a workshop that described not only management's next steps but the benefits that would be realized from them. Everyone always has a suggestion as to what to do next, but to ensure that it has value the business benefits associated with the action must be identified. The employees really enjoy this workshop. As one said, "It's nice to know that management finally wants to include us in the process."

Next Steps	Benefits
1. Training in business issues and terms	1. Understanding how to link our actions achieving business success
2. Better understanding of implications of change	2. Greater success at implementing change
3. More workshops so people can network	3. Help us learn how to work more effectively in teams
4. Mixing management with workers at subsequent workshops	4. Better understanding by each level of the other's key issues and concerns.

Figure 3–10. Sample Slide: Next Steps and Benefits

10. WORKSHOP DEBRIEF—45 MINUTES

To conclude the workshop it is very effective to generate a one-page summary of the benefits derived by the attendees—for example, a grid capturing participants' responses to the question "What lessons have you learned?" Following is a sample lessons learned chart from an actual Assessing Organizational Readiness for Change Workshop.

Change is difficult.	It includes management and the workforce.	It requires hard work.	It means learning new skills.	It means growing personally.
Can cause fear and anxiety.	Not easy to accomplish.	Change is part of today's business environment.	Change is part of our lives.	Change is exciting.
Resistance to change is normal.	Not everyone can change.	It can be fun.	It can help us achieve business success.	Change should not be feared.

Figure 3–11. Lessons Learned

This exercise also provides an opportunity for attendees to explain what they mean by their lessons learned. In the workshop where Figure 3–11 was completed one participant who suggested that change is learning new skills explained that "change is good and that for progress to be made there needs to be change." This employee had been with the company for 18 years performing the same job and couldn't wait "to become more versatile and be trained to contribute in other ways."

11. GROUP DINNER—180 MINUTES

Close the workshop by thanking everyone for a hard day's work. If there is a dinner the facilitators can remind the group of the time it starts. Dinner is a good opportunity for the group to be rewarded, relax, and have some fun. It can also provide an opportunity for an exercise. At one workshop the facilitator said to the group before dinner:

> Don't forget. During dinner we want you to discuss the subject of change in more detail and write down the four main actions that the company should take as a first step in the change program. Each table is supplied with some blank overhead foils and marking pen. The group at each table should select a spokesperson who would then show the slide to the entire group and summarize the table discussion.

ENDNOTES

1. R. Jaikumar, "Postindustrial Manufacturing," *Harvard Business Review,* November/December 1986.

2. Adapted from *Handbook of Human Performance Technology,* Harold D. Stolovitch and Erica J. Keeps, San Francisco: Jossey-Bass, 1992, p. 181.

3. Interview with a former General Electric manager.

CHAPTER 4

EIGHT NEW BUSINESS BEHAVIORS

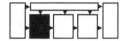

We believe that people are the greatest asset of a company. At Just Born, we encourage people to communicate openly. This invites curiosity and questions which give birth to imaginative ideas and new concepts. The end result, of course, is successful people and successful businesses.

Ross Born
Co-president, Just Born, Inc.

During my first 10 years in business I was trained to be a functional manager. The functional mind-set carried over into every action, including the hiring of employees. For a number of years I hired people based upon their functional skills. When I managed an accounting department I looked for individuals who knew accounting. When I managed a manufacturing organization I looked for people who could run a machine, read a blueprint, and so on. Some employees I hired needed guidance to perform better and others just didn't work out at all. I shared my thoughts with colleagues and discovered that they too were having the same experience. Hiring employees was like a crapshoot; I never knew in advance how well the employee would perform. One day I started thinking about the

most recent examples of employees who just didn't work out. In
each case performance was not the issue; it was their behavior. One
employee was a clock-watcher who took advantage of every break
to relax on the job. Another employee had difficulty working with
her peers. She was always testy and difficult to speak with. She
would never listen and always had her own agenda. A third employee was lazy and never took initiative in managing her department. I then decided that I would make a list of problems and put
down beside them the associated actions that would have fixed the
situation. Table 4–1 represents this list. I filed this list away under
the category of Employee Hiring.

Table 4–1. Historical Problem Log

Problem	What I Would Want Employees to Do
1. Customer complaints were not being reported to management.	1. Report complaints weekly in a report that is distributed to all department heads so we can satisfy customer requirements.
2. When speaking with an employee about his job he did not understand what business we are in and who our competitors are.	2. Know our company and our competitors so they know what we need to do to be successful in the marketplace.
3. Employee delayed changing trucking companies when she knew that the service was consistently poor, leading to lost shipments and, ultimately, customer complaints.	3. Understand that employees should make those decisions necessary to resolve problems.
4. Employee would not offer to accept or receive help from coworkers, making him difficult to work with.	4. Work with other employees and seek advice from coworkers to help and solve problems that individuals cannot solve alone.
5. Shipping personnel, in uncovering errors in shipment, tried to solve vendor problem without using purchasing personnel who were more qualified.	5. Try to solve business problems with whatever assets and resources are necessary from anywhere in the company.
6. Supervisor procrastinated in trying to solve a quality problem that resulted in a $150,000 customer return.	6. Don't wait to fix a problem or exploit an opportunity.

Table 4–1. (continued)

Problem	What I Would Want Employees to Do
7. Lost a million-dollar-a-year account because salesperson didn't think a customer's problem she was aware of was her problem to fix.	7. Take responsibility for solving a problem and don't try to hide it, hoping it will go away.
8. Obvious bottlenecks in manufacturing were overlooked resulting in shipment delays of 30 days and cancellation of $450,000 of customer orders.	8. Look for ways to perform tasks or processes more quickly.

A few months later I had to hire an employee in the purchasing department. When I met with the director of human resources I pulled out my list, which I had decided to use as a guide when interviewing prospective candidates for the position. As the interviews progressed I found that every candidate had the functional skills to do the job. However, it was obvious that only a very few had the behaviors that would prevent the problems on my list from occurring. I finally chose the candidate who I felt best exhibited the effective behaviors I had identified. As the weeks went by I noticed that the new procurement manager was very effective. From that moment on I used my list to hire employees. I kept track of the employees I hired and after a few years I found that almost everyone I hired had turned out be successful. My list became more valuable, and I shared it with my colleagues.

In the late 1980s I started reading about how Jack Welch, CEO of GE, was transforming his company by focusing on employee behaviors and not functional expertise using a program called Work-Out. The more I read the more I realized that my list was right on the money. I took out my list of behavioral attributes and some materials about GE's Work-Out program and compiled a list of eight behaviors critical to an organization's success (see Table 4–2).

Table 4–2. The Eight New Business Behaviors

Behavior	New Behaviors	Old Behaviors
CUSTOMER BEHAVIORS		
Process Focus	Improve customer processes by eliminating bottlenecks and unnecessary steps.	Focus on one single function without regard to the customer of the process or the final objective; do it the way it has always been done because that is the process.
Market Focus	Provide value to your customer by knowing your marketplace and your competitors; monitor, listen, and respond to the needs of customers; partner with other businesses.	Think that you don't need to understand the outside world; you know best what is good for your customer.
ORGANIZATIONAL BEHAVIORS		
Empowerment	Take the necessary steps to get a job done.	Wait for instructions and not be confident that you can solve the problem or exploit the opportunity.
Teamwork	Be willing both to give help and receive help from coworkers.	Act as a loner and be unable to help others.
Boundarylessness	Share resources, assets, and knowledge across organization and enterprise boundaries to solve business problems.	Define or defend your turf and refuse help from outsiders.
INDIVIDUAL BEHAVIORS		
Initiative	Take positive actions when something looks wrong or events don't match expectations.	Assume you are powerless and someone else will do it; fear rejection or failure.
Ownership	Take responsibility for a task and hold yourself accountable for how and when the task is done.	Be controlled by events and others' schedules; let impediments go unchallenged; exhibit not-my-job syndrome.
Speed	Look for ways to do things faster, reduce cycle times, and eliminate wasted efforts.	Overanalyze and endlessly discuss problems, contingencies, and what-ifs.

IDENTIFYING NEW CUSTOMER BEHAVIORS

Every manager I have ever met has difficulty getting employees to understand the business environment. This is understandable, because most employees have never been exposed to this element. Production control personnel analyze inventory levels and schedule production, accounting personnel manipulate numbers, shipping and receiving personnel know how to receive materials and package outbound freight. When you speak to them about customer requirements, competitive strategy, and market forces, they look at you in puzzlement. Yet every day we expect these same employees to perform tasks that impact customer satisfaction, competitive position, and market leadership. If employees better understood the dynamics that affect customers and the marketplace they would bring a business focus to their tasks.

PROCESS FOCUS

Process focus starts by never losing sight of the *customer.* Customer value is created through the series of business processes that together provide a product or service. For instance, a mail-order company in the Northeast was receiving complaints from its customers about how long it took to ship orders. At a weekly staff meeting management discovered that the current cycle time of nine days had, in fact, increased from five days the year before. The director of transportation volunteered to head a task force that included employees from all departments as well as a representative from each of the ten major vendors. During the next thirty days new processes were developed that reduced the order-to-delivery cycle time to two and a half days. This is an example of a process focus.

Process focus goals are to manage existing customer processes to ensure smooth handoffs, level loading, and timely output. Reviewing them is not a one-time event. The fast pace of the marketplace requires companies to constantly reinvent processes to obtain new or enhanced products and services. The process is the delivery mechanism. It is more important today than ever before because of the prevalence of change. When companies are developing new products every six months and new services at the same pace it is the business process that delivers the new product or service. It is necessary, therefore, periodically to reevaluate processes to eliminate bottlenecks and unnecessary steps or reinvent them to ensure that you are providing value. Also, never lose sight of the customer. If you do, failure is guaranteed.

Use the questionnaire presented in Table 4–3 to measure *process focus* behaviors within your enterprise.

Table 4–3. Process Focus Behavior Questionnaire

Element	Not Process-Focused	←1 2 3 4 5→	Extremely Process-Focused
Integrate	Employees work independently from other departments in functional silos.		Employees, customers, suppliers, and strategic business partners are integrated into peer-to-peer work teams.
Create Value	Individuals don't understand the meaning of market value—they just do what they are told.		Cross-functional enterprisewide teams focus on creating market value. No value—no effort.
Challenge	Individuals perform their assigned tasks, never challenging their value even when they know there is a better way.		Individuals/teams continuously challenge the existence of every policy, practice, and process.

To implement process focus behaviors you need to form cross-functional teams comprising your employees, customers, suppliers, and strategic partners for every major process in your value chain. For example, when Ford first designed the Taurus the team included designers, engineers, purchasing, and manufacturing personnel and was supplemented by representatives from strategic subcontractors as well as customers. These individuals were trained in effective teamwork techniques and empowered with challenging goals and objectives. Cross-functional teams need to constantly monitor their actions and enrich their work.

To create value you must first define the value of all the major business units/teams in your enterprise. Then you must train them to understand how to create value. This can be accomplished through workshops that help members be creative in developing new value for your customer. For instance, a process improvement team at a medical products company was formed to improve the manufacturing process for its incubators, a major product line for the company. Creative thinking workshops were held to help individuals and teams to think outside the box and to be more innovative and creative. With this type of training employee teams can evaluate processes with a new perspective and determine which enterprisewide activities contain value and which do not.

Creating value is not a one-time event. Value must be continuously assessed because what has value today may not tomorrow. Up to a few years ago companies that focused on telephone and mail for their orders were doing the right thing. Today, however, they can't ignore electronic commerce as an avenue for communicating with customers. Companies must challenge their processes to determine if there are better ways to create customer value. (Providing superior value is covered in greater depth in Chapters 8 and 9.)

MARKET FOCUS

In today's customer-driven marketplace it's imperative to understand how your business fits in with the competitive environment. Gone are the days when companies like General Motors and Sears had captive markets. Today management has to constantly be aware of the surrounding environment. To do so requires understanding that customers, competitors, and other market factors affect business success. A few years ago an individual with many years of industry experience started a one-person consulting company that helped small companies improve their marketing skills. He was really excited about this new venture. He talked to some of his contacts and placed an advertisement in the local Sunday paper.

He did not receive a single response.

Market focus is not sitting back and waiting for the phone to ring; it is a proactive process. It is obtaining and using knowledge from your business environment to achieve success. The marketplace is composed of your customers, competitors, business partners, and your company. The more knowledge people within the enterprise have of the market the better they will be able to execute their responsibilities. Ford Harding, an experienced consultant, started a business called Harding & Company to help companies improve their marketing and selling skills. He prepared extensively before venturing out on his own. He identified companies he would market to and analyzed competitors who already provided this service. He used his contacts to identify gaps that competitors were not able to fill with services desperately needed by companies. He then developed a marketing campaign around those gaps.

Figure 4–1. Market Focus Is Not Sitting Back and Waiting for the Phone to Ring

One area that companies were struggling with was how to motivate salespeople to provide excellent service rather than to sell a particular product. Many companies provided sales training but few were really able to produce measurable results for their clients. Harding developed an excellent training program around this area and has been successful ever since.

Figure 4–2 depicts this market focus in a graphic. Understanding *your customers'* needs, wants, and desires helps you create profitable value. Understanding *your competitors* enables you to minimize competitive risks. Understanding *your business partners* provides you the opportunity to work together developing new ideas, penetrating new markets, and developing opportunities. Finally, knowing more about *your own business* and where it fits into the marketplace helps you to understand your own strengths and weaknesses.

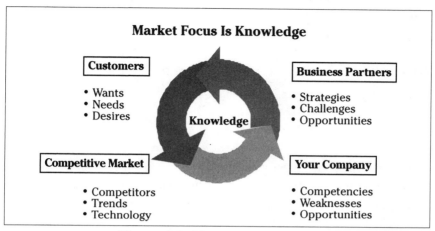

Figure 4–2. Market Focus Areas

Use Table 4–4 to measure market focus in your organization.

Table 4–4. Market Focus Questionnaire

Element	Weak Market Focus	←1 2 3 4 5→	Strong Market Focus
Customers	People perform jobs without regard to customer needs, wants, and desires.		Entire workforce understands customer needs, wants, and desires and how enterprise can provide profitable value.
Competitors	People are ignorant of competitive environment and have no understanding of why it is important.		People completely understand competitors and take the opportunities in the competitive environment to create value for customers.
Business Partners	People are unaware of who they are, what they do, and what value they provide.		People enjoy peer-to-peer communication with individuals/teams who are actively involved in major business strategies and the implementation of customer-driven business processes.

Table 4–4. (continued)

Element	Weak Market Focus	←1 2 3 4 5→	Strong Market Focus
Your Company	Information is limited to functional working environment.		People understand the breadth and depth of the business—strengths, weaknesses, and areas of opportunity.

If you want your employees to become market-focused they have to begin with an understanding of your customer needs, your business partners, your competitors, and market trends. (This is covered in more detail in Chapters 6 and 7.)

In today's business environment your business partners can be a great advantage. They have competencies that can complement your own to provide greater customer value. Understanding how you can work together effectively is an important element of the market focus. The more knowledge you have about your competitors, the better prepared you are to meet any threat. In fact, the more you know, the more you can anticipate and respond before your competitors can act. When Kodak was developing the disposable camera it realized that its competition, Fuji, was developing its own version of the disposable camera. Stores have only so much shelf space and first to market is critical in this industry. Kodak did away with traditional serial product development that was based on trial and error and reduced the traditional cycle time from two years to less than one. It formed product teams that included customers, business partners, and suppliers. By focusing very carefully on a product that customers wanted and by understanding the competitor's product and development cycle, Kodak was able to beat Fuji to the marketplace and achieve business success.

DEVELOPING ORGANIZATIONAL BEHAVIORS

The most powerful behaviors that a workforce can exhibit are those that improve the effectiveness of the organization. These behaviors enable teams to work efficiently, solve operational problems quickly, and make appropriate decisions.

Just Born, a thriving 75-year-old company with headquarters in Bethlehem, Pennsylvania, manufactures approximately 75 million pounds of jelly beans and marshmallow products each year for sale in the United States. For the past seven years it has experienced a 20 percent annual growth rate against a 5–7 percent average in the candy industry. The company achieves success by sustaining organizational behaviors that empower employees, provide a positive team environment, and allow individuals to cross over organizational boundaries to find resources to solve business problems

Ross Born and David Schaffer, co-presidents, "...respect people's ability to think. We strive to have each member of our organization feel that they can contribute as much as possible to making their company the best it can be." It is evident that the employees truly feel that Just Born is *their* company. "We are empowered to make decisions that help solve business problems," said one employee. "We have confidence in each other's decision making ability," said another. "We communicate with each other very well," said a third.

When asked to identify the most important element making the workforce so effective, an employee said, "We know we can depend on each other for help."[1] The employees are customer-focused, empowered, creative, and work effectively in teams. In short, they exhibit organizational behaviors that, when harnessed with dynamic leadership and an agile organizational structure, result in employees who focus on business issues and get results.

EMPOWERMENT

Empowerment has been a buzzword of the nineties. Once employees have been anointed with the magic of empowerment, however, the euphoria quickly dissipates. Words don't empower people; actions do.

Being empowered does not accomplish anything unless management provides an environment in which it can be effective. At one door manufacturing company the management team met with the employees and told them that they wanted to empower them to make decisions at the level that the work was performed. Realizing that empowerment was more than a word, management set up training workshops that helped employees understand how to use

Figure 4–3. Empowerment Is More Than Just Words

empowerment to become more productive and efficient in performing their job. The most difficult concept for employees to understand about empowerment is the circumstances in which they have
the authority to make necessary decisions without having to go up
the management chain for advice.

Sometimes management is more comfortable when empowerment is given limits. By not providing boundaries management
could feel it is giving away the store. For example, Hertz customer
service representatives are empowered to address customer complaints with a prescribed set of actions. They are not empowered to
go beyond the guidelines. For empowerment to be effective management needs to provide knowledge, information, authority, responsibility, rewards, and boundaries, as depicted in Figure 4–4.

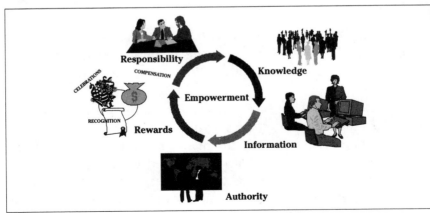

Figure 4–4. Empowerment Is an Environment

Use Table 4–5 to assess your organization's empowerment status.

Table 4–5. Empowerment Questionnaire

Element	Unempowered	←1 2 3 4 5→ Empowered
Knowledge	People have the skills required for internally focused, function-driven jobs.	People develop skills required to think strategically and execute horizontally oriented customer-driven processes.
Responsibility	People are limited to functional responsibility with no insight into other enterprise areas.	People are accountable for the successful execution of horizontally oriented customer-driven processes.
Authority	People's authority is limited and applied under strict guidelines.	People enjoy more individual control in execution of responsibilities and authorization to resolve problems without higher-level approval.
Information	Available data are limited to functional area or responsibility.	Enterprisewide information is available to all people.
Rewards	Rewards are tied to individual performance and awarded at the discretion of senior management.	Recognition for achievement, celebration of successes, and compensation rewards are tied to individual and team performance.

If you want to implement empowerment, first you should provide your employees with the information they need to think strategically and create horizontally oriented customer-driven processes. This means your workforce needs to understand your vision, values, and strategies as well as what customer focus means and how to create profitable value the customer will pay for. Management must also provide authority along with the responsibility for getting the job done. If customer service representatives have no authority to satisfy customer complaints, they are not empowered. Wherever you assign responsibility you must also provide the authority to fully implement it.

Management must reward for successes. Nothing is more satisfying than individual or team rewards for a job well done or an effort, although not successful, performed with vitality. Rewards do not have to be large. Even the smallest recognition goes a long way toward providing the impetus to continue and to exceed the current level of performance.

TEAMWORK

A team is more than just a group of people working together; it is a group of people who have a common objective and purpose. Team members are accessible, open, and communicate effectively. Sometimes teams form just because someone capitalizes on an opportunity. For instance, an employee at a communications company was complaining to his coworker about the inefficiencies in the accounting department during the month-end closing cycle. The coworker gathered a number of peers and formed a team to focus on reducing the month-end closing cycle from ten business days to three.

Figure 4–5. Teamwork Is Not Just People Working Together

Teamwork succeeds when performance goals and approach are shared by all. Effective teams agree on the objective and the approach to be used, and then determine goals and responsibilities. Each member of the team has to accomplish some portion of the objective, acting both alone and in concert with other team members as well as with other teams. Team members have skills that complement one another and all share mutual accountability. Figure 4–6 is my summary of effective teaming skills. It is important that teams really understand each of these skills and use them effectively.

The effective team:

- works toward common goals
- develops its members' skills
- accepts praise and criticism
- cooperates rather than competes
- welcomes challenges
- uses resources efficiently
- performs effectively and produces results
- teaches and learns from others
- resolves conflicts effectively
- embraces the diversity of its members
- shares pride in its accomplishments
- celebrates successes

Figure 4–6. Teaming Skills

Use Table 4–6 to assess the effectiveness of teamwork in your organization.

Table 4–6. Teamwork Effectiveness Questionnaire

Element	Using Teamwork Ineffectively	←1 2 3 4 5→	Using Teamwork Effectively
Commitment	Team members work to accomplish individual objectives/agendas that may not necessarily mean business success.		Team members are focused on achieving business success for the enterprise.

Table 4–6. (continued)

Element	Using Teamwork Ineffectively ←1 2 3 4 5→	Using Teamwork Effectively
Skills	Team members are not selected for their skills but for their availability and politics.	Team members develop/obtain requisite skills to achieve team objectives.
Accountability	Team members have individual goals and are accountable to their superiors.	Team members share mutual accountability for achieving team objectives.

To implement effective teamwork behaviors in your organization you will need to focus on commitment, skills, and accountability. To develop commitment, team members need to work as a group to identify the team mission, their objectives, and specific definitions of success. Everyone on the team has to participate and agree on these issues or the team cannot be effective.

Don't assume that everyone on the team has the skills necessary to be effective in a team environment. Members should identify the skills they feel are necessary for the team to be successful. Everyone needs to honestly appraise his own skill level and determine how to bridge the skill gap. Many techniques are available to help build effective teaming skills. The important point is to identify those skills that need improvement.

The third element of successful teams is accountability. Teamwork requires two levels of accountability. The first level is organizational; management must set the parameters for an acceptable outcome. The second level of accountability is individual; each member of the team is accountable to the others for honesty, trust, and open communication. These individual accountability skills are vital to team success.

BOUNDARYLESSNESS

Organizations that are internally focused have boundaries. They create walls between their customers, employees, and business partners, as depicted in Figure 4–7. Customers are treated as a necessary evil, employees as servants, and business partners as adversaries. Internally focused companies isolate themselves from the very elements that are needed to succeed in today's market-driven economy.

At first glance you might think that boundaryless behavior allows you to traverse the entire enterprise with unquestioned authority. On the contrary, management should always provide boundaries for individuals and teams to operate in. For example, asking a team to develop a new project without setting limits on time and budget can have disastrous effects. At an electronics manufacturing plant a project team was asked to look into improving the new product development process. Departments thought the team was acting with management's approval and had the authority to proceed and reengineer the process. Department heads started arguing with one another over the changes, and production levels fell. In fact, the team had started changing the product development process without management's concurrence. It took three months to undo the misdirected changes that the team had implemented. The senior manager who authorized the team had not set the boundaries and as a result the team failed in its effort.

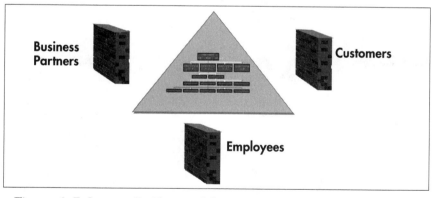

Figure 4–7. Internally Focused Organizations Create Boundaries

Boundarylessness is about sharing resources, assets, and knowledge across the organization and outside it to solve business problems.

A fast-growing manufacturer of newspaper inserting equipment was constantly running out of parts that affected customer deliveries. The company manufactures equipment used by newspapers to insert the comics, magazine, and other advertisements in the regular newspaper. The materials manager decided that numerous short-term process patches were not working because they didn't include the suppliers that manufactured 80 percent of the component parts. He had mentioned this to management before but nothing had changed. He decided to solve the problem himself. He realized that the problem affected all the departments and therefore decided that the other department managers should be involved. He called a meeting with the department managers, who all agreed that they, as a group, needed to solve the problem. They developed an integrated inventory control system that resulted in on-time shipments, reduced inventories, and timely customer deliveries of inserting equipment.

Use Table 4–7 to assess the boundary status of your organization.

Table 4–7. Boundary Behavior Questionnaire

Element	Bounded	←1 2 3 4 5→	Boundaryless
Decisions	Made at the senior levels of the organization, in days/weeks, by those furthest from the work.		Made on the spot, in minutes, by those closest to the work.
Communications	Intermittent, incomplete, and irrelevant.		Quick, easy, and seamless throughout all levels of the organization.
Layers	Ubiquitous, suffocating, creating unnecessary tension.		Few, penetrable, and integrating all levels of the organization.
Information	Requires lengthy approval cycles, never provides the answer to the question asked.		Easily accessible, seamlessly distributed, helps to create knowledge.
Skills	Developed in functional silos and hidden from others.		Developed and shared across the enterprise.
Leadership	Nonexistent; "followship" is encouraged through command-and-control tactics.		Leaders rotate through the company, gaining respect from their subordinates by motivating, mentoring, guiding and coaching.

Table 4–7. (continued)

Element	Bounded	←1 2 3 4 5→	Boundaryless
Focus	People work on different projects with conflicting strategies, objectives, goals, and metrics.		People work individually or in teams toward common goals and objectives using linking strategies, metrics, and rewards.
Creativity	New ideas are not recognized; they are discouraged and avoided.		New ideas are embraced, encouraged, and implemented.

If you want your organization to be boundaryless, first you must encourage and support initiative and leadership. In addition, you need to empower the workforce to make decisions at the appropriate level in the organization, which is where the work takes place. People cannot practice boundaryless behavior if they do not have the power to back up their actions. For instance, a team trying to improve customer service at an appliance manufacturer looked at ways to connect customer service representatives with technical personnel in order to help customers having problems using a product. The team identified individuals from various departments who could help such customers. The department managers were not happy that their employees would occasionally be taken away from their day-to-day responsibilities. The sponsoring executive stepped in and pulled the plug. Although he had told the team to practice boundaryless behavior, he wouldn't back up the team's recommendations.

Fostering a creative environment is important for boundaryless behavior. It is also important to make information available throughout the enterprise. For example, a team assigned the task of improving a manufacturing process required certain technical skills to help understand the current process. Members used a database that listed everyone in the company, their skills, experience, and location. This enabled them to identify those specific employees who could help the team better understand the problem. They formed a team and went out into various parts of the organization to reengineer manufacturing processes.

INTERNALIZING INDIVIDUAL BEHAVIORS

The expression goes, it's not how *hard* you work but how *smart* you work that counts. Employees who care about doing a good job exhibit individual behaviors focused on achieving business results quickly. For instance, an electronics company had just purchased a small firm that had been doing work for the government. In a routine audit it was discovered that for some time bookkeeping irregularities resulted in the government spending monies that were not authorized. The CFO contacted government officials and assigned one of his top accountants to resolve the situation. The accountant was very skilled but he never took real initiative or ownership of the problem. He always delayed and looked for help. This created many problems for the CFO as the government became impatient at the pace the investigation was going. Finally, the CFO had to put someone else in charge who had the behaviors to manage the project; the accountant was used as the technician. Individual behaviors that matter to the organization are initiative, ownership, and speed.

INITIATIVE

Initiative is like a built-in radar system. It is the ability to look for and take advantage of opportunities. An employee who takes initiative does something when events look wrong or don't match expectations. People with initiative are often risk takers who experiment with new ideas and new ways of doing work. They are willing to stick up for what they believe in, voice minority opinions, deliver bad news, and raise issues that must be dealt with even if there is risk of incurring anger.

A recently promoted shipping and receiving manager for an electronics company thought that transportation charges were too high. He brought this to the attention of management, who was not interested. Still concerned, the manager evaluated transportation charges for the prior year, then developed new business relationships with carriers, implementing a new transportation process that reduced costs by 30 percent and reduced delivery times by 20 percent. Management rewarded him with a generous one-time bonus and an apology for not listening to him when he first brought the problem to its attention.

Initiative must be linked to business needs to be successful. An employee who riles up his coworkers because he wants to extend the morning break from ten minutes to fifteen minutes is using initiative in the wrong way. If the requirement is legitimate, more subtle actions can be used. Using initiative to create hostility among employees is not effective.

Employees with initiative are action-oriented, creative, and willing to take a risk. In this context, *action* means movement within a loosely defined channel so that energy is always moving toward an objective. Individuals and teams need to commit to actions that achieve business objectives. Action not linked to business objectives is like a cat chasing its tail: There's much movement but no progress. A way to get this message across to the workforce is to conduct workshops where the attendees identify three recent actions and determine whether or not a business objective was achieved.

Thinking differently can take initiative. Old ways, although successful, may not work in today's marketplace. Thinking out of the box allows you to put aside past practices, habits, and biases and allows you to develop creative new solutions to challenges never faced before. Having initiative in this context means taking the first step toward solving a problem. Here, again, workshops can help employees understand initiative that achieves business results.

Last and most importantly, initiative requires you to take risks. Risk taking requires you to follow a path that has a very low probability of success. This means you have thought through the possible outcomes and feel comfortable proceeding. You will never have 100 percent of the information required to solve a problem. Some feel 40 to 60 percent of the information is enough to proceed because there will are always be factors that cannot be predicted. Most risk takers have a gut feel for when an action seems right and will proceed with limited information. These individuals have learned from their previous experiences.

The key to taking risks is the ability to recognize that problems will occur and that they have to be managed. Of course, risk has its failures. But in each failure there should be a lesson learned. Management at 3M rewards its product development teams even if their ideas do not result in a new product or process success because it

wants to create an environment where employees do not fear risk
but rather embrace it.

Use Table 4–8 to assess the initiative of your organization.

Table 4–8. Initiative Behavior Questionnaire

Element	No Initiative ←1 2 3 4 5→	High Initiative
Action Orientation	Individuals/teams procrastinate and assume someone else will get the job done.	Individuals/teams take appropriate actions when events don't match to expectations.
Creativity	Individuals/teams sit back and wait until the time is right to take appropriate action.	Individual/teams take necessary first steps to achieve results and do it quickly.
Risk Taking	Individuals/teams are conservative in their approach and cross every t and dot every i.	Individuals/teams take action without waiting for possible contingencies to be addressed and questions answered.

OWNERSHIP

In corporations all over the world individuals practice some elements of ownership as they carry out their job responsibilities. Ownership implies control. An individual or team that allows events to
control its actions does not have ownership. Hoping that someone
else will get the job done is not practicing ownership. Assuming that
a problem or issue will just disappear on its own is not practicing
ownership. Take a look at Figure 4–8. Here a product development
team has been asked by the area vice president to think about how to
solve a problem during a product improvement meeting.

Ownership is more than a word: It is a process. It includes accountability, commitment, and authority. Just like white blood cells
that rally when an infection invades the body, individuals who exhibit
ownership move quickly to solve problems. They have a business focus and understand that each problem gets in the way of achieving
business success. Accountability, commitment, and authority form
the basis for superior ownership behaviors. *Accountability* is being

responsible for a specific process, activity, or task. *Commitment* provides the drive and sense of urgency that ensures success. *Authority* provides the necessary resources to ensure that activities and tasks are carried out effectively, efficiently, and flexibly.

Figure 4–8. Ownership Issues

At British Airways there is always one individual or team who has ownership of an aircraft. The pilot has ownership from the time the engineering team turns over the craft for flight. After landing he turns over the ownership of the aircraft to the maintenance team. At no point is there doubt as to who has ownership of the aircraft; furthermore, the individual/team that has ownership has the accountability, authority, and commitment to perform job functions.

At a local school district in eastern Pennsylvania parents had been pressing the school board to build a new high school for over two years. Finally, the high school principal convinced the school board that the project needed an owner and that he would volunteer for the job. During the following two years he personally managed the design and building of the new high school, which was accomplished on time and within budget, while an interim principal was named to carry out his day-to-day functions.

Use Table 4–9 to assess the status of ownership in your organization.

Table 4–9. Ownership Behavior Questionnaire

Element	Non-ownership ←1 2 3 4 5→	Ownership
Accountability	Individuals are responsible only for functional activities. Success of the function does not ensure success of the process, activity, or task.	Individuals/teams are jointly responsible for the successful execution of a process, activity, or task.
Commitment	Individuals have a laissez-faire attitude.	Individuals/teams are keen to ensure the successful execution of the process, activity, or task.
Authority	Individuals are not empowered to make on-the-spot decisions or harness resources to achieve success.	Individuals/teams are given the resources required to achieve success.

SPEED

Being focused on time is not easy. Individuals who exhibit this behavior are planners. They learn from the past, fix problems quickly, and want to be prepared for and respond to others in a timely manner because they respect other people's time. Speed is not necessarily good unless it has a business focus. Figure 4–9 is a perfect example. People sometimes do their jobs quickly but don't achieve any business success. They are sloppy, they forget things, and they don't try to get all the facts before they take action.

For instance, a major insurance company reorganized its claim process around customer-focused teams in order to improve claims processing time and customer service. When selecting employees to be team members, management looked for teamwork skills, customer focus, initiative, and speed—the behaviors it felt would improve claims processing and customer service. An individual who had been with the company for ten years and had one of the highest rates of claims processing was not selected to be part of the team. A number of times he had rejected claims that were in fact correctly completed. When the error was pointed out, instead of apologizing he got angry at the customers and blamed bad handwriting or choice of words. This didn't promote the best of customer relations but the company tolerated the employee because of his high rate of claims processing. The employee exhibited speed but did not always succeed in the twin business objectives of processing claims quickly *and* providing superior customer service.

Figure 4–9. Misconceptions about Speed

Speed, although a matter of pace, should rather be looked at as the interaction of effectiveness, efficiency, and flexibility. *Effectiveness* involves making sure you accomplish your business purpose. *Efficiency* involves ensuring that you perform activities and tasks with a minimum of waste. *Flexibility* means being prepared to adapt to changing conditions. All three measures, performed well, combine to form speed. We all remember the race between the tortoise and the hare. In case you forgot who won, take a look at Figure 4–10.

Figure 4–10. The Tortoise and the Hare

Use Table 4–10 to assess speed in your organization.

Table 4–10. Speed Questionnaire

Element	Using Speed Unintelligently ←1 2 3 4 5→	Using Speed Intelligently
Effectiveness	We think we accomplish our objectives but don't understand how they link to business success.	We always focus on accomplishing business objectives that link to enterprisewide vision, mission, and strategy.
Efficiency	We work as hard as we can. The harder we work, the better it is.	We focus on value-added activities and eliminate non-value-added work.
Flexibility	We fear change and are not prepared to deviate from prescribed tasks.	Change is a reality and we prepare for unforeseen challenges.

If you want to implement speed in your organization make sure that all activities and tasks link to enterprisewide vision and strategy and that all actions achieve a business objective. Second, make sure that all employees understand that haste makes waste and that all actions should be accomplished as efficiently as possible. Finally, always be prepared to replan. Flexibility is a major component of the success formula for speed. In today's business environment one thing is certain: Change is a reality and we always need to plan for it.

IDENTIFYING BUSINESS BEHAVIORS FOR YOUR ORGANIZATION

In every organization some or all of these eight behaviors exist. Sometimes they are exhibited in pockets of the organization by teams and/or by individuals. Each organization prioritizes the types of behaviors it requires. Changing behaviors in an organization does not move from the top down. It moves from the bottom up, which means that all individuals in the organization need to be involved. Don't stop here. Most companies think only about their own employees. *Don't forget that today's enterprise model includes your company, other companies that partner with you to pursue market opportunities, your suppliers, and, of course, your customers.*

Methods for identifying behaviors include observation, surveys, interviews, focus groups, and workshops. Each builds on the others, culminating in the workshop, which is the most effective.

OBSERVATION

Observing people can help you determine what behaviors are and are not being exhibited in the workplace. This is an excellent first step in seeing what is actually going on. For instance, employees working in a mail-order company asked for more staff to answer the telephones. They complained that they were always busy and didn't have enough time to properly respond to customer requirements. Management used discreet observation techniques to find out that employees were taking excessive breaks and spent more time talking to fellow employees than answering the phone. Subsequent meetings with employees brought these behaviors to light, and within a few months the work environment had improved.

Overt observation doesn't work very well. When people know they are being observed they are on their best behavior. The observation method provides data that can be built upon with the other techniques.

SURVEYS

Surveys are an excellent way to gather information from large groups of people. The key to an effective survey is the construction of the document. Clear, concise questions result in useful information. If one of the objectives of your survey is to determine whether or not individuals can understand and identify with the company vision, you might ask a main and a follow-up question: "Do you understand the vision statement of the company?" followed by "Which of the following four choices [different perceptions of the vision] do you believe conveys the vision of the company?" This links the overall response to a quantifiable answer. Unless you ask the second question there is no significance when a *yes* answer is given to the first question. Try to test the survey with a small pilot group before you administer it to large groups of people. This can dramatically improve the effectiveness of the results by improving the quality and clarity of the questions asked.

INTERVIEWS

The interview is probably the technique most often used for obtaining information. Interviews provide the opportunity to establish rapport and gain insights that are not possible when using workshops or surveys. (Remember to interview your business partners and customers as well as your employees!) Use follow-up questions to gain insight. When an individual says, "I don't think that Paul is a good leader," you can ask for specific examples or probe with information from other interviews.

Questioning skills are very important to the interview process. Closed, open-ended, and confirming questions are the three types used. *A closed question* usually asks for specific facts. "What type of product does your company sell?" "Is it true that all employees are treated the same with respect to vacation policy?" *Open-ended questions* ask for insights and feelings. "Why do you think your customers buy your products?" "How do your employees feel about the vacation policy?" *Confirming questions* are closed-loop questions that allow you to feed back what you hear and ensure that you interpret the respondent's answer correctly. "Did I understand you to say that most of your customers are generally pleased with the level of customer service provided?" "Interviews with others in your organization indicate that the vacation policy is fair and earlier you said that all people are treated equally with respect to the policy. I would assume then that vacation policy is not an issue with your employees?"

FOLLOW-UP INTERVIEWS

The follow-up interview is a good method to determine if employees confirm the behaviors identified using the observation technique. For instance, one company videotaped employees with their permission and observed excellent business behaviors. Yet when the employees were interviewed they felt that they didn't have the required behaviors. When the interviewer showed them an observation video the employees were amazed at how effective they really were.

When German automaker Mercedes-Benz built a brand-new $300 million plant for sport utility vehicles on the outskirts of

Tuscaloosa, Alabama, management was more concerned about hiring employees with effective business behaviors than with specific business experience. More than 40,000 people applied for the 650 jobs available, and company executives subjected candidates to as many as 80 hours of intensive assessment in which they explored behavioral attributes. Mercedes was looking for candidates who were strong on team skills, concerned with continuous improvement, and knew that what makes Mercedes successful is a quality product delivered with superior service.

Companies like Mercedes and Higashimaru Shoyu, discussed in Chapter 2, know that employee behaviors influence customer and process focus, impact the effectiveness of the organization, and improve individual efficiency, productivity and profitability. Whether you own a corner grocery store or manage a 15,000-member workforce, understanding how to elicit these eight business behaviors in your company is critical to success in today's competitive environment.

WORKSHOP: IDENTIFYING BUSINESS BEHAVIORS FOR YOUR ORGANIZATION

The objective of the workshop is to help participants understand and demonstrate the specific business behaviors required for your company to be successful. The true measure of success is not how well you understand the concepts behind business behaviors but how well you can exhibit them in your daily work environment.

As Table 4–11 shows, the workshop is divided into three main segments. The first helps participants understand the behaviors by drawing on personal life experiences. The second helps them understand the behaviors in the business context. The third phase helps them demonstrate successful business behaviors. Each segment builds on the other, resulting in a dynamic and interactive workshop.

It is again important to have the right mix as well as the right number of participants in each of these workshops. Please refer to the workshop in Chapter 3 that identifies the process you should follow to get a good balance of participants.

As in the previous workshop, to provide the right business environment for the workshop post the company vision, values, and strategy on the walls of the main meeting room and also in the break rooms. This is to emphasize that behaviors are tied to business objectives.

Table 4–11. Defining Business Behaviors for Success

Agenda
9:00 AM – 9:00 PM

Time Frames	Time Allotted	Workshop Exercises	Facilitator	Objectives
1. 9:00–10:00	60 min	Set the Stage	Janet B.	Discuss the learning objectives and capture participants' expectations.
2. 10:00–10:30	30 min	Warm-Up Exercise	Joan L.	Get to know your colleagues.
3. 10:30–10:45	15 min	Break		
4. 10:45–12:00	75 min	Exhibiting Behaviors in Our Personal Lives—*Team Exercise*	Robert A.	Identify and understand how we exhibit behaviors in our personal lives.
5. 12:00–1:00	60 min	Lunch		
6. 1:00–2:00	60 min	Exhibiting Behaviors in the Business Environment—*Team Exercise*	Joan L.	Identify and understand how we exhibit behaviors in the business environment.
7. 2:00–5:00	180 min	Exhibiting Behaviors in Our Company—*Team Exercise* (including 15-min break)	Robert A.	Envision how we would exhibit business behaviors in our enterprise to achieve business success.
8. 5:00–5:30	30 min	Next Steps	Robert A./ Joan L.	Identify necessary actions to ensure we exhibit the correct set of business behaviors to achieve success.
9. 5:30–6:15	45 min	Workshop Debrief	Joan L./ Robert A.	Capture and share the benefits of the workshop with our colleagues.
10. 7:00–9:00	120 min	Group Dinner		

Lead Facilitator: Janet B.   Facilitators: Joan L./Robert A.

1. SET THE STAGE—60 MINUTES

The lead facilitator provides an overview of the workshop and a brief description of the agenda and the objectives. The participants introduce themselves and explain why they believe business behaviors are important. This makes participants aware of each other's various point of view and allows the facilitators to gauge the various degrees of understanding of behaviors. A group that has a fairly good grasp of the importance of business behaviors can spend more time in the demonstration phase of the workshop. If the level of understanding is not as great, the facilitators should balance the agenda accordingly.

2. WARM-UP—30 MINUTES

In an interactive and dynamic workshop it is important for participants to loosen up and get to know one another early in the process. A good way to do this is to use a Scavenger Hunt Icebreaker Exercise. This is designed to get everyone in the workshop moving around and finding out about each other in an unusual but nonthreatening manner. Figure 4–11 represents a scavenger sheet that everyone is given. The objective of the exercise is for participants to get to know one another. Everyone is instructed to spend 20 minutes speaking with others in the group, starting with any person, and finding out who matches a description on the scavenger sheet. When a participant finds a match, he writes the name of the person in the box. To ensure that people really move around, one cannot use the same person for more than one box. This is a fun exercise but requires facilitators to roam the room and make sure people move from person to person. By the end of the exercise, everyone has met.

A person who has more than three children.	A person you know who you've learned something new about.	A person who speaks more than one language.	A person who was born in another country.	A person who has earned a postgraduate degree.
A person who has a spouse who also works.	A person who enjoys the arts.	A person who has owned her own business.	A person who has published a paper or written articles.	A person who has held more than 4 positions within this company.
A person who has served in the military.	A person who is 50 years or older.	A person who you have never met before.	A single parent.	A person who has been with the company for more than 20 years.
A person who is younger than 45.	A person who is a different religion than you.	A parent of twins.	A person who is older than 45.	A person who participates in a regular fitness program.
A person who has traveled to an interesting country.	A person who is divorced.	A person who has five or more brothers and sisters.	A person who is married with no children.	A person who has been with the company for less than one year.

Figure 4–11. Scavenger Hunt Sheet

3. BREAK—15 MINUTES

This break is similar to the breaks detailed in the previous work-shops. Don't forget to announce the current time and the time you expect the participants to return to the main meeting room. The facilitators might also have to help the group return to the meeting room as the break comes to an end.

4. EXHIBITING BEHAVIORS IN OUR PERSONAL LIVES— 75 MINUTES

To help participants understand the concept of behaviors, the first phase of the workshop focuses on behaviors in personal life. This allows attendees to use something familiar—their personal life—as the framework for the learning process.

The facilitator starts this phase of the workshop by defining the word *behavior.* Figure 4–12 presents a simple definition that has worked well in a number of workshops. At some workshops the facilitator starts by asking the group to help define *behavior* with another facilitator acting as the scribe and recording the various definitions on either a clear acetate projected onto a screen or a flip chart. The important point is that everyone has a common definition of *behavior.*

> The manner in which one conducts himself or herself in a specific situation or environment.

Figure 4–12. Behavior: A Definition

The facilitator helps to reinforce the definition by asking the participants to provide examples of behaviors that they have seen. At one workshop a participant reflected on "a bank teller who was very friendly, courteous, and always very attentive. A number of times she corrected mistakes on my deposit slip." The facilitator should get participants to relate experiences and identify the types of behaviors that were exhibited.

Once the facilitator feels that the group understands the concept, a list of the behaviors is shown to the group along with an explanation of each. You can use some of the material from this chapter. To help the participants visualize the behaviors they are asked to provide an example of a personal experience where these behaviors were exhibited. At one workshop a participant described an airline flight where every seat was taken and the flight attendants had to work hard as a team to serve meals and attend to passengers. Another told of a sales clerk who was understanding when she was explaining a complicated return. While the lead facilitator solicited input from the group a second facilitator wrote the responses on a flip chart (see Figure 4–13).

BEHAVIORS	EXAMPLES
• Teamwork	• Flight attendants working together on a crowed flight
• Boundarylessness	• Friend helping our family move
• Empowerment	• Sales clerk helping others customers in another department
• Ownership	• A sales clerk who noticed a flaw in a purchased garment
• Initiative	• Technician who drove 150 miles to get part for heat pump
• Market Focus	• Looking at homes in other neighborhoods
• Process Focus	• Local supermarket always ensuring quick checkout service
• Speed	• Bank teller completing transactions accurately and quickly

Figure 4–13. Exhibiting Behaviors in Our Personal Lives

The key is getting one or two people to start talking. At one workshop the group was obviously nervous and not responding. In this situation the facilitator helped the group by listing a number of events on a flip chart: going shopping, doing yard work, and so on. When that didn't evoke a response he asked the group, "Did anyone ever have an interesting experience at a gas station?" Finally, one person responded, and after that the flood gates opened.

The objective of this phase of the workshop is for the participants to visualize a personal experience for each of the behaviors. This now sets the stage for relating these behaviors to business.

5. LUNCH—60 MINUTES

Lunch is an opportunity for the group to relax and get to know their colleagues better. To help stimulate the discussion about behaviors it is a good idea to have each table discuss a subject surrounding behaviors. For example, the participants can be seated at two tables. Two facilitators sit at one table (not next to each other) and one facilitator at the other. They help stimulate a conversation about behaviors by asking a simple question: What are some other experiences each of you have had that you can relate to one of the behaviors? The facilitator hands out a list of the eight behaviors to everyone at the table. This can generate an interesting conversation and reinforce the visualization of the behaviors for each participant.

6. EXHIBITING BEHAVIORS IN THE BUSINESS ENVIRONMENT—60 MINUTES

The next phase of the workshop helps the participants understand how the same behaviors explored in the previous exercise are exhibited in a business environment. Up to this point the learning process has been as a group. This is important because large groups share information in the way they respond to questions, ask questions, and engage in general discussion. For a new topic, such as behaviors, this is necessary. Also, groups need to *warm up* before being placed in small work teams. With this group work behind them participants are ready to be placed in teams.

The facilitator assigns participants to work in teams to: (a) identify examples of business behaviors within a general business environment; and (b) identify specific examples of behaviors that have positively impacted operating performance within the company. To help the process each team is given two templates that list the behaviors on the left and provide space for an example of each. Figures 4–14 and 4–15 are examples of completed templates from a workshop team.

The facilitators play an important role in this exercise. It is important that the teams understand how these behaviors are exhibited in the business environment because in the next exercise they will develop examples of business behavior. The transition from behaviors in one's personal life to those in a business environment should not be difficult. To help teams envision the behaviors facilitators should explore each of the examples in more detail. So, for example, in one workshop, when a team member used the example of employees working on process teams, the facilitator asked the individual to provide a specific example.

BEHAVIORS	EXAMPLES
• Teamwork	• Employees working on a process improvement team
• Boundarylessness	• Supervisor listening to suggestions from subordinates
• Empowerment	• Seeing and acting to resolve a problem
• Ownership	• Taking responsibility for the job you are performing
• Initiative	• Trying to determine why rejection rates are so high
• Market Focus	• Understanding the competitive environment
• Process Focus	• Always focusing on customer value and doing things right
• Speed	• Working quickly to improve customer response times

Figure 4–14. Exhibiting Behaviors in a Business Environment

When the teams return to the main meeting room they share their results with the rest of the group. To further help the learning process the facilitator should ask for other business examples for each of the behaviors. At this point the facilitator needs to make a judgment as to whether the group has grasped the concept. Again, if the group is struggling, the facilitator needs to step back and bring the group up to a level where it can perform the next exercise, where all the previous work is applied.

7. EXHIBITING BEHAVIORS IN OUR COMPANY— 180 MINUTES

This phase of the workshop is the most critical. It is here that the participants identify an event within the company where business behaviors negatively impact company operating performance. Then, through a 10-minute role-play, they have an opportunity to

BEHAVIORS	EXAMPLES
• Teamwork	• When John in accounts payable helped the receiving department resolve numerous errors on inbound shipments
• Boundarylessness	• When Jonathan offered to provide personnel to help Joe in final assembly
• Empowerment	• When Glenda and John in accounting developed a method of explaining monthly P&L statements to shop floor workers
• Ownership	• When Samantha in customer service analyzed numerous customer complaints to find common category areas
• Initiative	• When Lisa, Jan, and Bill decided that they would spend the time to uncover the reasons for customer complaints
• Market Focus	• When Larry suggested that the company identify the key areas that customers care about and what competitors offer
• Process Focus	• When Gabe and his team developed a Website that allowed customers to electronically communicate with the company
• Speed	• When Cynthia suggested a way to improve the time it took to process a customer complaint

Figure 4–15. How We Exhibit Behaviors Within Our Company

show how behaviors should be exhibited so that there can be a positive impact on operating performance.

To start the role-play exercise the facilitator needs to ascertain if any of the group has had experience with role-plays. At one workshop the facilitator asked, "How many of you have been involved in role-plays?" Only a few hands were raised. "Did the role-play help you, and if so, how?" The first participant who raised her hand said:

> Initially, I was scared, but the facilitators really helped me. It was also a lot of fun. Most importantly it helped to reinforce the verbal messages in the workshop. I thought I understood what was being discussed but until I played the role it didn't really hit home.

This kind of response is an excellent way for others to hear about the benefits of role-plays. However, if no one has been involved in a role-play the facilitator needs to spend some time explaining to the group the objectives of role-plays and how they help to reinforce learning. At one workshop where no one had ever been in role-plays the facilitator said to the group:

> Role-plays are fun. They are a way for you to experience real-life experiences, make mistakes, and learn, all without any of the real-life penalties. Acting out a situation is harder than the real-life experience. Therefore, we will have facilitators to help guide you through the process.

The role-play exercise is composed of three parts. The first part is identifying events within the company where behaviors negatively impacted operating performance. This should take no longer than 15 minutes. The second part is to identify a single event and use the worksheet (Figure 4–17) to help capture key information; this should take no longer than five minutes. The third part is to demonstrate in a 15-minute role-play business behaviors that would have positively impacted business operations. This should take approximately one hour to prepare for. While one team is role-playing, the other team will assess the situation using a template (Figure 4–19) to capture behaviors exhibited, how they were exhibited, and any general information they want to record regarding the role-play. This will be shared with the entire group after the role-play. The other team will then perform the role-play and be assessed accordingly.

To help the teams the facilitator needs to spend enough time on the instruction slide (Figure 4–16), and exercise worksheet (Figure 4–17), so that the teams clearly understand what is expected of them.

The objective of this part of the exercise is for team members to link behaviors to business results. If they can cross the chasm and grasp the impact behaviors have on operational performance, the workshop will be successful and the company change program will more likely be as well. Facilitators should be prepared to help the teams manage their time. This is a dynamic exercise and it is easy for people to lose focus and get distracted. Be prepared for teams to have some difficulty when they break into their meeting rooms. This is where the facilitators can provide guidance for the group and help lead them to completing the exercise successfully.

Identifying Negative Business Behaviors

1. Break into your assigned teams.

2. Spend 10 minutes identifying a number of events within the company where business behaviors negatively impacted the business environment.

3. As a team, choose the single event that had the most negative impact on business operations.

4. Using the worksheet provided, identify the circumstances surrounding the event, the behaviors exhibited, and how they negatively impacted the business environment.

5. As a team, discuss how the event could have resulted in a positive impact on operational performance if different behaviors were exhibited.

Figure 4–16. Sample Slide: Exercise Instructions

Worksheet

Event: _____

Background: _____
_____
_____
_____
_____

BEHAVIORS	HOW EXHIBITED	NEGATIVE IMPACT ON PERFORMANCE
Teamwork		
Boundarylessness		
Empowerment		
Ownership		
Initiative		
Market Focus		
Process Focus		
Speed		

How would operational performance have been positively impacted by the exhibition of different behaviors? _____
_____
_____
_____

Figure 4–17. Identifying Business Behaviors for
Achieving Business Success

The facilitator should ask the group if they have any questions. There is always someone who wants to ask a question but is afraid to be the one to look ignorant. Tom Connellan uses a catchy example in *Inside the Magic Kingdom* when he asks the group, "I know nobody ever likes to ask the first question. So, who would like to ask the second question?"[2] At one workshop when the facilitator used this technique, someone finally raised his hand—after about 30 seconds—and asked a question about the exercise worksheet they would be using during the first part of the role-play exercise. This helped the facilitator spend some time on the worksheet and explain its value to the group. If no one asks a question about the worksheet, the facilitator should spend time reviewing it anyway and inform the group that the facilitator assigned to each team will be able to provide guidance during the actual exercise.

The exercise worksheet is designed to help participants relate business behaviors with operating performance. It is designed so that the team members, working together, provide examples of business behaviors and examples of how these behaviors negatively impacted operating performance. The reason the worksheet focuses on the negative impacts is that people learn better from mistakes than by doing things right. At the bottom of the worksheet the team has an opportunity to record how behaviors could have been used to positively impact operating performance. Here team members can use what they have learned during the workshop and apply it to a real business experience.

Figure 4–18 is a completed worksheet. This rapidly growing mail-order company for novelty items was experiencing a downturn. New employees not properly trained in customer services, coupled with manufacturing and shipping problems, created many unhappy customers who stopped ordering. Over a three-month period sales dropped by $400,000. The president of the company asked the senior management team to meet, identify the problem, and recommend a solution. As you can see from the worksheet, the meeting was a mess and many negative business behaviors were exhibited. Fortunately for the workshop, one of the attendees was part of that meeting and helped the group really understand how business behaviors can negatively impact operating performance.

Worksheet

EVENT: Meeting with managers of customer service, manufacturing, and quality control to uncover why repeat sales are falling

IMPACT: Repeat sales dropped by 25 percent over a three-month period accounting for $400,000 in lost business

BACKGROUND: Repeat orders were falling and customer complaints were increasing. Customer service was blaming manufacturing, which was blaming quality control. A meeting of department managers to discuss the problem ended with no resolution. Everyone left the meeting angry. Two months went by with no improvement. The president of the company chaired a committee of the department managers and company personnel to look into the problem. A number of problems existed. The company was growing rapidly and new personnel were hired. New employees and turnover of key people in the customer service department resulted in untrained personnel who weren't customer oriented. Shipping errors resulted in increased complaints, and manufacturing problems resulted in back orders that customers were not happy about.

BEHAVIORS	HOW EXHIBITED	NEGATIVE IMPACT ON PERFORMANCE
Teamwork	Everyone argued with each other.	People who won't work together can't solve problems.
Boundarylessness	Everyone was protecting himself.	No one was concerned about the business impact.
Empowerment	Let someone else solve the problems.	The problem continued without anyone taking action.
Ownership	No one thought it was his problem to correct.	Status quo is acceptable.
Initiative	Everyone exhibited initiative in blaming others.	Being defensive instead of proactive prolongs problem.
Market Focus	Everyone ignored customers going to competitors.	Company sales were being lost to competitors.
Process Focus	Everyone thought about his own department.	Functional managers lost sight of customer.
Speed	Everyone thought the problem would go away by itself.	Problems that don't get resolved quickly impact revenue and cost.

How would operational performance have been positively impacted by the exhibition of different behaviors? If department managers focused on the business problems—lost sales—and worked together as a team they could have identified the cause more quickly and resolved the problem. Even when the problem was corrected very few of the customers reordered from the company. A subsequent survey showed that they went to the competition. No one felt empowered to do anything or thought of the business implications of the problem. No one single manager thought he had ownership of the problem. The president of the company runs a command-and-control environment. If management exhibited positive business behaviors we would still be growing instead of questioning where our old customers went.

Figure 4–18. Identifying Business Behaviors for Achieving Business Success

The next step is for the team to role-play the event using behaviors to positively impact operational performance. This is a fun part of the workshop where the team members can begin to demonstrate the behaviors they have been hearing about for the entire day. Sometimes the facilitators are lucky and get a real ham as part of the group who takes charge and gets the team going. Other times the facilitator has to take a proactive role because team members are shy and afraid of performing. The facilitator instructs the other teams that they will have to assess the role-play. To help them a template is provided to each team member and subsequently reviewed (see Figure 4–19).

Event Role-Played:			
Behaviors Observed	How were behaviors demonstrated? Physical	Verbal	Examples of How Behaviors Were Exhibited
Teamwork	☐	☐	
Boundarylessness	☐	☐	
Empowerment	☐	☐	
Ownership	☐	☐	
Initiative	☐	☐	
Market Focus	☐	☐	
Process Focus	☐	☐	
Speed	☐	☐	
General Observations			

Figure 4–19. Team Exercises: Observer Template

Physical	Verbal
Using our bodies to convey a thought, idea, or emotion.	The words we use or don't use to convey a thought, or idea, or emotion.

Figure 4–20. Exhibiting Our Behaviors

To help team members prepare for their role-plays and perform the assessment on the other team, the facilitators reviews a slide that defines the two ways behaviors are exhibited. At one workshop the facilitator helped the team as follows.

Behaviors are exhibited in a verbal as well as a physical manner. What you say and how you say it, or what you don't say, are examples of how behaviors are transmitted. When you ask your supervisor for permission to take a day off and he or she says, "I'll really have to think hard about it and determine if you deserve it," a hidden message is being sent to you. If the supervisor has his or her hands crossed and has a very grim expression on his or her face, a hidden message is being physically transmitted. You need to remember that you can use both physical and verbal methods of exhibiting behaviors.

Event Role-Played: Meeting to discuss falling customer reorder shipments with managers of customer service, manufacturing, quality control, and shipping and receiving.

Behaviors Observed	How were behaviors demonstrated?		Examples of How Behaviors Were Exhibited
	Physical	Verbal	
Teamwork	☑	☑	Everyone focused on solving problem.
Boundarylessness	☐	☑	Boundaries were ignored with focus on problem.
Empowerment	☐	☑	Group felt they had the power to correct problem.
Ownership	☑	☑	They felt that the problem was theirs to solve.
Initiative	☑	☑	Everyone had ideas on how to solve problem.
Market Focus	☐	☑	Everyone agreed the marketplace demanded quality.
Process Focus	☐	☑	Focus was on customer and how to recoup value.
Speed	☑	☑	Group felt the problem had to be corrected quickly.

General Observations

1. Manufacturing manager set the tone, asking everyone to leave their egos at the door and focus on the business problem at hand.

2. Calling lost customers to see how they would react to recommended improvements was quite a novel idea.

3. Everyone contributed to improving suggestions, such as when Joe suggested that we need the voice of the customer. Shelly suggested how.

4. Department managers more eager to hear solutions to problems in their own department from those outside their department.

5. Manufacturing manager helped prompt shipping manager to contribute after she was silent for first fifteen minutes.

6. Quality control manager helped stimulate discussion with thought-provoking questions when meeting stagnated.

7. When a roadblock to a suggestion was encountered, department personnel were called into the meeting to help.

8. Having the vision and strategies displayed on wall helped keep the focus on the business issues.

9. It was interesting how the group wanted the president to join the meeting to fill him in on the progress.

10. When the meeting adjourned, everyone was eager to implement the recommended solutions.

Figure 4–21. Team Exercises: Completed Observer Template

When the teams return to the main meeting room the facilitator needs to remind everyone that this is serious business and request that the observing team be quiet and courteous. The facilitator should also remind participants that they will be performing very shortly. Each team presents its role-play, which should last approximately fifteen minutes. When the first team is finished the second team huddles for about ten minutes to compare notes and complete a single observer template, which is then reviewed with the entire group. Then the teams change sides and repeat the process. Figure 4–21 is an example of a completed observer template.

The afternoon break takes the same form as the breaks in previous workshops. Remember that participants are more tired in the afternoon and it may be more difficult for them to return in just fifteen minutes. Therefore, it is often best for the facilitator to announce the break, admit to the group that the afternoon is a difficult time in any workshop, and that she would appreciate participants returning to the main meeting room in fifteen minutes. The break announcement should be concluded with the current time and the time participants are expected to return.

8. NEXT STEPS—30 MINUTES

This part of the workshop is to capture from the participants what they feel needs to be done in the immediate future to ensure that business behaviors are positively exhibited in the company. With the role-plays just completed the group usually has many suggestions. The area that participants usually struggle with is how to integrate these business behaviors with the normal working environment. At one workshop one of the participants said, "This workshop is really great but how will we be able to transfer what we learned here into our day-to-day working environment?" This is where the working experience of the facilitator can help. The facilitator responded to this question as follows:

> Don't think that you will be able to change your behaviors very quickly. This workshop was very focused and you were not in your normal business environment. This will take time. What I suggest you do is to have a depart-

mental meeting every few weeks and talk about business events and the behaviors people exhibited. What you will find is that your colleagues will become more sensitive to business behaviors and start exhibiting them or reminding their colleagues to exhibit them more positively. The most important message I can leave you with is that when you see positive business behaviors exhibited you should commend and reinforce this type of behavior. Reinforcement is an important element when trying to change behaviors.

It is important to have the group agree that behavioral change is necessary and that everyone needs to understand how to exhibit business behaviors that can positively impact operating performance.

9. WORKSHOP DEBRIEF—45 MINUTES

Providing a summary of the workshop benefits for all the attendees is an excellent way to reinforce learning. See the previous workshops for more details on facilitating this section, especially the Strategy Awareness Workshop in Chapter 2. Figure 4–22 is a completed grid from a behavior workshop.

Behaviors are important to business success.	Negative behaviors can impact business results.	Reinforce positive business behaviors.	I will think twice before I criticize a coworker.	Positive business behaviors impact P&L.
Focusing on behaviors can make you a better person.	Help others to see their negative business behaviors.	Changing behaviors is not easy.	Behaviors help others know who you are.	Display business behaviors for colleagues to see.
Understanding behaviors will help our personal lives.	I will be easier to work with.	I can now see negative behaviors more easily than before.	There is a link between behaviors and business results.	Positive behaviors will make me a better team player.

Figure 4–22. Lessons Learned

During one workshop, after all the participants provided input to the grid, a participant said, "I really learned a lot about how individuals can impact the bottom line of our company by the way we behave. I am going to laminate the grid and display it my work area along with other materials from this workshop to constantly remind me how I can impact the company's performance by the way I behave."

To provide a baseline for understanding business behaviors the facilitator finishes the workshop with a questionnaire that helps the group assess at a high level their comprehension of the subject. Figure 4–23 is a completed questionnaire from a workshop participant. This questionnaire helps the group begin to think about the different situations in which behaviors are exhibited and to assess how they exhibit these behaviors differently in their personal and business environments.

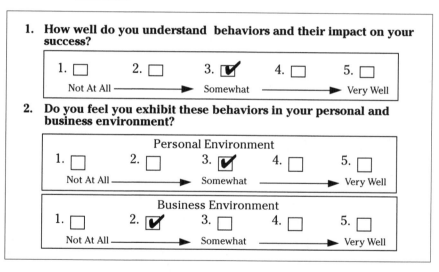

Figure 4–23. Assessing Your Behaviors

10. GROUP DINNER—120 MINUTES

The facilitators should try to integrate the subject of behaviors in the conversation. Sitting at different tables, they should ask participants an open-ended question that helps provoke discussion. At one workshop the facilitator at one table asked, "In the workshop today you had a chance to role-play an event where you could change the outcome of an event using positive business behaviors. What other events have occurred where business behaviors would have positively impacted business performance?" This question evoked plenty of discussion and was a good way to get the participants to start internalizing the change process.

ENDNOTES

1. Interview with Ross Born, September 1995.

2. Tom Connellan, *Inside the Magic Kingdom,* Austin, TX: Bard Press, 1997.

CHAPTER 5

THE CUSTOMER-FOCUSED ORGANIZATION

We are building a simplified, flexible and process-oriented organization that will enable us to react quickly to signals from the market, all over the world.

The LEGO Group
Special supplement to 1997 annual report.

Lots of kids grew up using LEGO plastic toy building bricks and until 1995 the 65-year-old U.S. subsidiary of the Danish company had a stronghold on the American construction toy market. Then feisty new competitors, including K'Nex Industries and Ritvik's Megablocks came on strong, while LEGO Group's customers, like Toys 'R' Us and Wal-Mart, demanded more variety and faster delivery.

Up to this point the LEGO Group had used a traditional market-driven structure, but as competition encroached on its market and customers demanded improved service and delivery, it was clear the organization was too cluttered with processes and procedures. A senior LEGO manager said, "With 50 companies and 9,500 employees working in 30 countries on six continents, it was very difficult to get anything done in a short period of time."[1]

In May of 1995 LEGO Group management initiated a revitalizing program called Compass Management. The first task was to create an enterprise structure more responsive to changing market conditions. Each of the 50 LEGO Group business units in Europe, North America, South America, and Asia would be more independent. Each business unit would adhere to a financial plan but be free to accomplish that plan based on its own strategies. "When our marketing department told us that our customers wanted some different product choices for the holiday season, we could respond to that quickly at the local level without having to go through the bureaucratic maze that existed at corporate headquarters in Billund, Denmark,"[2] said one senior U.S. LEGO Group executive.

Another problem was the supply chain. LEGO Group formed a supplier alliance so that all enterprises in the supply chain could talk to one another. This resulted in new efficiencies, leading to more rapid delivery of new products to market.

At the organizational level LEGO Group changed its policies and procedures to be more responsive to customers. Management at the North American business unit developed customer relationships and enterprise linkages so it could better understand customers and react quickly with new products and services. Key customers are invited to visit the LEGO plant in Enfield, Connecticut, on a regular basis. The purpose of these visits is to develop a closer relationship with customers and obtain input on how to be a more effective supplier. Teams of employees representing departments such as customer service, engineering, and new product development meet with the customers. These teams take suggestions back to their departments and work together to become more responsive to the customer. "This would have never happened in the old organization," said one LEGO group executive.

LEGO Group has enhanced its information systems. Employees at any location can obtain information needed to do their jobs quickly and share information effectively by accessing LEGO's *global village* on the Internet. LEGO Group has revamped the performance management systems. Instead of using internally focused measurements, LEGO's new metrics focus more on the customer. To help employees be more productive the company conducted training programs about business needs and areas for improvement. It established a communication organization at the corporate level to ensure a constant flow of information to all LEGO Group employees.

In 1996 LEGO Group introduced 182 new products to the marketplace, a 30-percent increase over the prior year. These products were on customers' shelves in less than 18 months, half the time it took previously. In the same year North American sales to retailers rose by 26 percent. Between 1995 and 1997, 60 percent of revenues were generated from products less than a year old, a jump of 25 percent. The company enjoys a two-thirds market share of the U.S. construction toy market and a young set of customers who keep coming back for more.[3]

ORGANIZING AROUND THE CUSTOMER

In meeting after meeting with executives and management I am shown the typical organization chart with its nice little square boxes. They bring out the chart and explain each and every box. After they explain the organization chart to me, I usually ask the following questions.

How dynamic is your marketplace? If it's a business that competes in the financial marketplace I usually hear about all the change from being a brick-and-mortar institution to one that operates in virtually every household via the Internet. This means new products and services that customers demand. It also means matching and exceeding new products and services that competitors supply. If it's an automotive manufacturer I hear about all the changes from being vertically organized to one that partners with suppliers to manufacture 50 percent or more of its parts. If it's a distribution company I hear about the new focus on the customer and how the supply chain is being optimized. In each of these cases the products and services being supplied to customers are going through such rapid changes that each month more and more new products and services are required.

The next question I usually ask is *How responsive are you to those demands?* The usual answer is "Not quite fast enough." My follow-up comment is *What I hear you saying is that if your organization could be more responsive to market demands you could be more competitive.* I then take out a sheet of paper, draw a square, and add some organizational boxes and a circle, as in Figure 5–1.

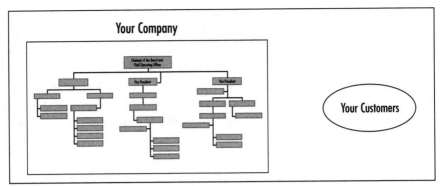

Figure 5–1. Your Company and Your Customers

I ask the executive to draw an arrow representing how the company is connected to the customer. She usually draws an arrow that points from the organization to the customer, as in Figure 5–2.

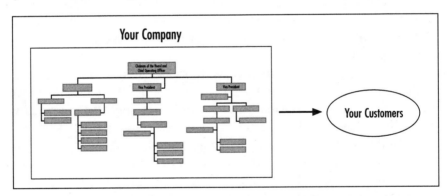

Figure 5–2. Your Customer in Relation to Your Company

I ask the executive to draw arrows indicating the activities that take place within the organization in the course of satisfying a customer requirement. I usually start with a customer order, then work my way through customer service, accounts receivable, product returns, etc. By the time I am finished the organization chart is full of arrows going in all different directions, like the one in Figure 5–3.

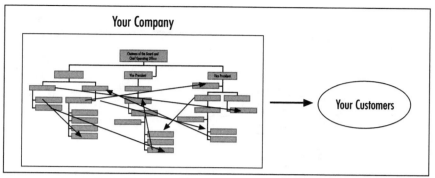

Figure 5–3. Typical Organizational Activity Diagram

I then take a fresh sheet of paper and draw two dots, as in Figure 5–4.

Figure 5–4. Creativity Exercise A

I ask the executive to look at the two dots and let A represent his organization and B the customer. I ask the executive to again draw the line that connects the company to the customer, as represented in Figure 5–5.

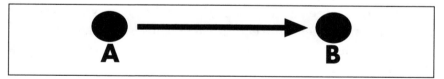

Figure 5–5. Creativity Exercise B

I then ask the executive to look at the organization chart with all the lines representing customer activities and replicate those lines underneath dot A. By the time the executive is finished the page looks something like Figure 5–6.

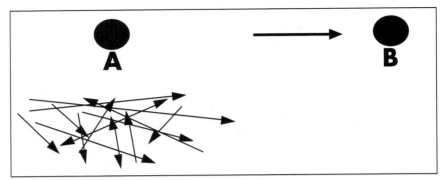

Figure 5–6. Creativity Exercise C

It's usually at this point that the executive sees that there is a lot of energy within the organization going everywhere except in the direction of the customer. The realization that an enterprise needs to be organized around customer processes is recognized by many but not really understood by all. The energy within an organization needs to be focused toward the customer. If not, a lot of activity occurs but no real benefit is achieved.

An agile structure allows your company, business partners, customers, and suppliers to join and separate as they pursue market opportunities. To ensure that employee actions are properly focused to create customer value, supporting subsystems move knowledge throughout the enterprise, provide compensation and other incentives to reward employees, and provide career development that helps retain talented individuals. This is the customer-focused organization model (see Figure 5–7). Without an agile structure and supporting subsystems the enterprise remains isolated from its customers, unable to respond to their changing needs with new products and services.

Management must try to understand which elements of an agile structure and which subsystems currently exist, which need development, and which need improvement. The best way to do this is to involve employees in a workshop like the one presented at the end of the chapter. This helps identify a customer-focused organization for your company. It will not only help your employees to prosper but your company to achieve its business success.

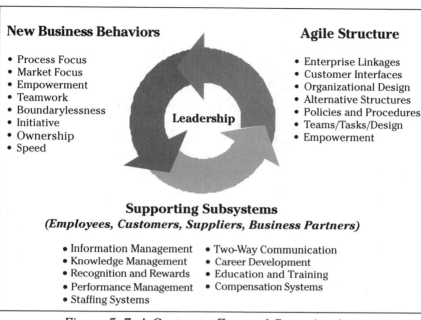

New Business Behaviors

- Process Focus
- Market Focus
- Empowerment
- Teamwork
- Boundarylessness
- Initiative
- Ownership
- Speed

Leadership

Agile Structure

- Enterprise Linkages
- Customer Interfaces
- Organizational Design
- Alternative Structures
- Policies and Procedures
- Teams/Tasks/Design
- Empowerment

Supporting Subsystems
(Employees, Customers, Suppliers, Business Partners)

- Information Management
- Knowledge Management
- Recognition and Rewards
- Performance Management
- Staffing Systems
- Two-Way Communication
- Career Development
- Education and Training
- Compensation Systems

Figure 5–7. A Customer-Focused Organization

THE AGILE STRUCTURE

The enterprise needs an agile structure to exploit profitable business opportunities. There are three levels to an agile structure. The *enterprise level* involves the ways suppliers and business partners within the enterprise link together and how the customer interfaces within the enterprise. The *organization level* deals with the structures, policies, and procedures that optimize the organization's productivity. The *individual level* enables both individuals and teams to operate efficiently and flexibly. Figure 5–8 summarizes these three levels.

CREATING AGILE LINKAGES AT THE ENTERPRISE LEVEL

To respond to changing market conditions quickly the enterprise has to form agile relationships with business partners and customers. These affect the pace at which products and services can be delivered. For instance, consulting firms contract with clients to perform a variety of services, some of which are subcontracted to other companies. If Andersen Consulting develops a customer service system for a client, it provides hardware and software services from Hewlett Packard, Novell, and other vendors in addition to its own services. If you often partner with the same companies it makes business sense to develop a master relationship agreement that sets out in detail how the two companies will work together with clients. These agreements cover purchase discounts for products and consulting services, invoice payments, handling of proprietary information, how employees will work together, electronic information sharing, investment sharing, and other important issues that would require months of discussions if negotiated separately for each project. With these master agreements in place, partners can quickly begin to work with clients to provide business solutions.

Enterprise Level **Enterprise Linkages**		Link the organizations of business partners into an integrated and effective enterprise to pursue profitable market opportunities.
Customer Interfaces		Exploit every customer interface to maximize customer value for the enterprise.
Organizational Level **Organizational Design**		Redesign organizational structures to allow individuals and team to create new customer-focused processes, products, and services.
Policies & Procedures		Reinvent enterprise policies and procedure to allow employees/teams to be more effective, efficient, and flexible in their work environment.
Alternative Structures		Provide for an environment where the organization can quickly reconfigure to effectively pursue appropriate market opportunities.
Individual Level **Teams/Tasks/Design**		Create an atmosphere and an underlying structure that foster the forming and effective interrelationships of enterprise teams.
Empowerment		Delegate authority and responsibility to the worker at the level in the organization where the work gets done in order to improve business performance and customer satisfaction.

Figure 5–8. The Agile Structure

In the manufacturing industry, companies like Wal-Mart have developed electronic interfaces with their suppliers to ensure that orders are communicated to the appropriate supplier so fast that they can be filled in as little as one day. In days past inventory cycle counting triggered a host of manual and time-consuming activities that not only lengthened the delivery process to months but required huge investments in inventories to cover the inventory replenishment period.

Every time an organization interfaces with a customer, maximum value must be achieved. Whether the customer places an order over the phone or via the Internet, mechanisms need to be in place to ensure that the customer is provided the best possible value. Additionally, every customer interface must allow for an exchange and capture of important information, even if it is a subtle complaint.

Hertz recognizes that unhappy customers will leave for the competition and that unhappy customers don't always communicate their feelings. "Every customer interaction is an opportunity for Hertz to capture a customer's feelings about their rental experience,"[4] says Robert J. Bailey, senior vice president for quality assurance and administration. Hertz has established an elaborate electronic mechanism to not only record customer feelings but provide an opportunity to maximize value. Hertz employees are trained to be sensitive to customer needs. For instance, a customer service representative may know that a family may not be comfortable with the specific vehicle they rented because it does not have enough trunk space. In this case the representative may recommend a car with a larger trunk.

Management must ensure that a customer interface strategy be developed for every phase of the business where there is customer contact. In the Hertz example, customers interface on a number of different fronts: when making reservations, when they are transported to the Hertz lot, when they pick up their vehicle, when they leave the lot, when they return the vehicle, and when they are transported to the airport terminal. One of Hertz's main strategies is to prevent customer complaints by recognizing these value points and training employees in recognizing potential problems and turning them into value-creating opportunities.

DEVELOPING AN ORGANIZATIONAL INFRASTRUCTURE

Employees must have a structure in which they can be productive. They need to be able to form teams quickly to achieve business objectives. Organization design now focuses on two main areas. First, it centers around business processes, away from a vertical functional structure and toward a horizontal cross-functional structure.

For instance, instead of assembly equipment being placed sequentially in the new Volkswagen plant built in Barcelona, the factory was designed so that teams of people can interact closely and help each other perform a variety of assembly tasks. The results were improved productivity and more satisfied employees.

Second, more and more organizations utilize what is known as a distributed work environment, where employees work out of their homes, other company offices, or the offices of business partners. In these situations an information infrastructure is required to hook up employees so they can communicate with each other and company business systems. AT&T had a sales office in northern New Jersey that housed over 250 people. It found that most of the time these employees were making sales calls and used the office less than 10 percent of their time. So the company formed distributed teams where employees worked out of home offices and developed an electronic network that allowed salespeople to communicate with one another and AT&T business systems. It was a win-win situation. Employees were happy because when they weren't traveling they could work out of their homes. Management was happy because it was less expensive to set up a home office than pay for office space in northern New Jersey.

Xerox Professional Document Services uses a similar approach. Most consulting organizations, up to a few years ago, had branch offices where consultants had desks, files, and work space to use when they weren't on client projects. As electronic communication enabled more information to flow efficiently from laptop to laptop, consulting companies started to deploy virtual teams. Consultants work out of their home offices or client sites. If they have to visit an office a small work area is made available. Again, it's a win-win situation for the employee and the company.

In a virtual environment, teams can form electronically wherever and whenever needed. Information systems should be created to supply and route information quickly to all team members. This is more than just purchasing computer hardware, connecting it, plugging it in, and declaring victory. Management must recognize that information within the enterprise not only must be captured but also managed and distributed. There is a distinct difference between information (data that can provide answers to questions), information management (how you manage information within and outside the enterprise), and information technology (the enabler that electronically captures, distributes, and represents information).

When people think of policies and procedures they think about rules and regulations that govern the work environment. In the old days these rules and regulations read very much like a military handbook. "All employees must phone their supervisors if they are sick or will be late. Any employee taking a sick day before a holiday will be charged with a vacation day." How about policies and procedures that foster creativity and innovation?

When an idea that could impact business performance is identified at 3M, management encourages teams to form and exploit the idea to its fullest. The company provides meeting rooms, electronic tools, and help in the form of outside facilitators to help teams get started. Even if the idea doesn't result in significant business impact and even if it fails to produce any impact at all, such teams are rewarded. 3M management strongly believes that it must foster creativity and an organizational structure that rewards teams. In this way policies and procedures are used not to govern but to nurture.

Construction companies use alternative structures in their business environment every day. Each project has its own identity, workplace, and objectives. Construction managers form teams around the project objective. A housing project might include one general foreman and a number of plumbers, electricians, and carpenters. A central place is established, usually a trailer, where they can meet. Otherwise they meet at the various housing construction sites. Building a manufacturing facility is more complex and requires a variety of environmental, electrical, and mechanical engineers as well as the traditional construction crew. Work crews don't meet only in trailers but in virtual team rooms all over the world. When Raytheon builds a power plant in the Far East, team members from the construction site, subcontractor offices, and Raytheon offices are hooked up by satellite so they can communicate instantly.

Companies all over the world are providing alternative structures for teams to function more effectively and efficiently. Ford Motor Company established a worldwide engineering team structure to design and develop a car, the Ford Contour, a feat that could not have been accomplished ten years ago. Such teams are necessary in today's complex business environment; they provide an agile sense-and-respond mechanism that yields superior customer value.

ENABLING INDIVIDUAL SUCCESS

We now understand that the individual in an enterprise can do more than ever before to create customer value. Individuals today need to excel in a team environment and use empowerment to produce business results quickly.

Management can foster teams with a structure that enables team members to be effective. For example, GE has an extensive training program that teaches individuals how to be more productive and efficient by improving individual and teaming skills. The company also provides an information infrastructure in the form of video-conferencing, facilitation guidance, mentoring, and other support.

When a group of employees at a bicycle manufacturing plant decided to pursue the cost-saving idea of one of its members, the team met once a week, discussed ideas, and made decisions as to which of them to pursue. As the team came up with more and more ideas, however, the plant manager decided that this traditional mode of operation was not effective. The manager then hired an outside consultant to help the team understand team process. During the early stages of brainstorming the team structure needs to enable creative thinking. Team members are encouraged to express their opinions, voice their concerns, and compare the benefits and pitfalls of each suggestion. The group breaks into subteams that work together to identify possible solutions. When the team meets to review the work products from the subteams, the focus is on deciding which solution is most cost-effective for the company. Within twelve weeks the bicycle manufacturer's team had decided on a solution, the approach to implement the solution, and had started to implement the solution.

Two factors make empowerment work. The first has to do with the empowerment behaviors discussed in Chapter 4; the second has to do with the structure that supports those behaviors. The two are different. For example, a Midwest manufacturer of welding equipment wanted to have an empowered workforce. The president of the company had a meeting with all 150 employees and told them to make decisions more quickly when it comes to improving customer service and to find better ways to cut manufacturing costs. He urged the employees to think from the perspective of the owner of the company and do what best serves the customer's interest. He hired a consultant to work with employees over the next two months to help them internalize empowerment behaviors. Unfortunately, he forgot about the second piece of the puzzle: the empowerment structure. The company continued to enforce the rule that any customer service adjustment greater than $25 required the president's signature. It required employee teams to obtain the president's approval before meeting on any cost-saving topic. What the president forgot to do was allow the employees the leeway to practice their empowerment behaviors.

Employees are not really empowered unless they have a structure within which to practice empowered behaviors. In this case the president could have increased the limit to $100 and arranged that employee teams meet whenever they want, simply providing him a report on their findings and future actions.

DEVELOPING EFFECTIVE SUPPORTING SUBSYSTEMS

Supporting subsystems, such as an agile structure at the enterprise, organization, and the individual level are shown in Figure 5–9.

Many companies look at the elements within supporting subsystems as individual initiatives. Human resources departments administer compensation systems, career development, education and training, and recognition and reward systems. Departmental managers look at staffing for their needs and develop performance measurement systems that help achieve departmental success. Information systems managers utilize the latest technology to move the same information around more efficiently but not necessarily more effectively. The problem is that executives do not understand the differences between information, information management, and information technology, while information systems managers do not understand business strategy. The result is that they stay away from each other. With companies spending about 3 percent of revenues on information technology investments senior management must focus more closely on where these millions are being spent. Each subsystem can affect business success if properly aligned. GE, Intel, and GM's Saturn plant achieve remarkable performance levels because management ensures that education and training, two-way communication, recognition and rewards, and other supporting subsystems are linked to business strategies and aligned to achieve specific business objectives.

Enterprise Level Recognition and Rewards	Develop appropriate incentives that enable individuals and teams to achieve sustainable customer focus and enterprisewide strategies.
Information Manager	Implement an information infrastructure that provides employees, business partners, suppliers, and customers the information they need when they need it.
Knowledge Management	Leverage the knowledge, skills, and experience across the enterprise that enables workers to be more productive, efficient, and flexible in the performance of their jobs.
Organizational Level Staffing Systems	Develop employee staffing systems that bring the most talented resources to the required project regardless of location.
Two-Way Communication	Create a process that ensures communication is a two-way process that includes listening, speaking, and articulating each other's messages.
Performance Measurement	Develop a process that links and aligns business objectives into performance objectives.
Individual Level Career Development	Provide employees the opportunity to improve their knowledge and skills while at the same time creating economic worth for the enterprise as they develop the necessary experience that enhances their business value.
Education and Training	Develop a program that enhances employees' knowledge, skills, and experience through a series of training programs that incorporate technology, mentoring, and outside resources.
Compensation Systems	Create a compensation system that incorporates year-round activities to monitor, measure, and, if necessary, realign employee performance metrics.

Figure 5–9. Supporting Subsystems

OPTIMIZING ENTERPRISE-LEVEL SUBSYSTEMS

The flow of information, the creation and distribution of individual and enterprise knowledge, and a reward and recognition system are the supporting subsystems at the enterprise level (see Figure 5–10). Together they allow individuals and teams to create superior customer value in an environment where learning is a core component of everyone's workday.

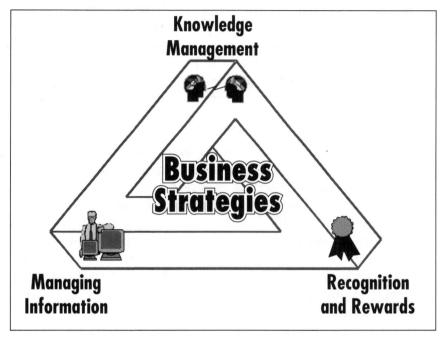

Figure 5–10. Enterprise Subsystems

Courtesy of Chris Tung, Xerox Professional Document Services.

Recognition and small rewards can help motivate individuals and teams beyond compensation systems. A small parts manufacturer in Pennsylvania rewards individuals/teams with sports tickets, team dinners, and even a dinner for the employee and his/her partner. When an employee goes beyond the normal effort this is recognized through a company newsletter, award certificate, or public recognition at an awards banquet.

You also want to reward those who exhibit the behaviors you want to instill in the rest of the workforce. When a mid-size manufacturer of health-care products rewarded employees for surpassing production quotas, management forgot to take into account quality and inventory targets. Rewards were given although business benefits were not achieved. Within six months of implementing this reward program, management changed its basis to the achievement of sales and inventory targets. Marketing and production personnel had to work together to benefit from the reward program, a behavior management wanted to instill in the workforce.

Among the biggest problems facing management today are lack of information, overflow of unnecessary information, and employees who do not know how to use the information available to them. With the demise of functional bureaucracies, employees work in a highly complex environment. People are asked to do much more than was required of them before. The bottom line is that they are more involved in gathering and analyzing information to do their jobs than ever before. In many companies, however, information systems are not holistic and, as a result, require employees to hunt for information in scattered business systems.[5]

A friend of mine once called his insurance company to ask about additional insurance. The first service representative he spoke to transferred the call to another department because the information required was not available to her. This happened three times and each time my friend had to repeat all his questions. Finally, after one hour on the phone and three service representatives, his question was at last answered.

This is not an isolated situation. Hundreds of thousands of times a day, all over the world, employees speak with customers and coworkers only to find out that someone else needs to be involved to obtain necessary information. Management should provide holistic information systems that allow all employees and business partners access to the information they need to do their jobs. Individuals would be more productive, customers better served, and the work environment more pleasant. For instance, at K-mart even suppliers have access to all the information they need to make business decisions about restocking.

Knowledge management systems are becoming more prevalent every day. It was not too long ago that you would call a major manufacturer when you had a problem with your washing machine, power drill, or telephone. You would find that the individual on the other end of the telephone was kind and courteous but could only direct you to the local service center. Today you can call a service representative who has access not only to an expert system that can help diagnose the problem over the phone but also places her in touch with an engineer who can join the call. Knowledge management systems provide a learning environment where individuals and teams can share information and apply it in a way they never thought possible. Employees are able to create new and innovative processes and products by sharing ideas that spark new ideas.

PREPARING EFFECTIVE SYSTEMS FOR ORGANIZATIONAL SUCCESS

Organizational subsystems allow the enterprise to match a skill requirement with the employee or enterprise team member who excels in that skill, wherever he or she is located. A performance measurement system provides a framework for individuals and teams to effectively perform in the creation, maintenance, and enrichment of customer value. Effective two-way communication across the entire company is essential to success.

Project teams all over the world are pursuing business opportunities that improve business performance. Although these teams comprise the best local talent, management is missing opportunities by not using the best *global* talent on projects. Teams of people distributed geographically can work together, via technology, as if they were working in the same room. One automotive company needed to improve certain manufacturing processes in its European manufacturing plants. Rather than use a European team, management matched the required skills and capabilities against a database that stores employee skills and project team accomplishments. The fifteen-member project team that redesigned the engineering processes was made up of seven employees from the European operations, five from U.S. operations, and three from South American operations. When the project was completed the team members assessed their accomplishments and updated the database so their peers around the world could take advantage of their skills in the future.

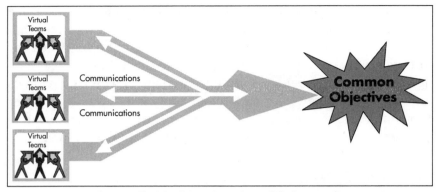

Figure 5–11. Organizational Subsystems

Courtesy of Chris Tung, Xerox Professional Document Services.

Managers at every company constantly communicate with people, supervisors always interact with their subordinates, and workers constantly advise each other on how to do their jobs better. In each of these interactions communication is *the* important element. However, communicating is not just speaking; it is also listening. Implementing these two components correctly will result in effective communications. There is a big difference between speaking and listening. When you speak you communicate an idea or thought. If the individual you are talking to isn't *listening,* then all your thoughts and ideas aren't being communicated. Listening is the ability to hear and interpret what the other person is saying.

Poor message reception isn't always the fault of the receiver. A manager at a steel manufacturing plant tried to convey to a shop floor supervisor that she needed to do a better job of motivating her subordinates. Two weeks passed and no change was evident. When the manager had a face-to-face meeting with the supervisor to find out why the message didn't get through, the supervisor said, "I didn't understand what you were trying to tell me." The manager said to the supervisor, "I thought I had made it perfectly clear when I said '*There needs to be more dynamic interactions interlaced with interpersonal communications effectively delivered and constantly monitored.*'" The supervisor said, "I had no idea what you were saying then and still have no idea what you are trying to say." The manager rephrased his comments. Within three days productivity and efficiencies improved. Effective two-way communication requires you to communicate *in a language that is understandable* to the person receiving the message.

The need for performance to achieve business objectives is an imperative that must never be forgotten. Yet all across the corporate landscape performance measurement systems reward employees for functional goals rather than enterprise goals. At a hand tool manufacturing plant, supervisors were rewarded for reducing downtime. At the other end of the plant, quality control supervisors were rewarded for catching errors in the manufacturing process. Management rewarded manufacturing for reducing downtime, ignoring the sacrifice of quality. Quality control supervisors were rewarded for catching production errors at the *end* of the process when in fact they should have been inspecting production *during* the process. Not only did costs increase because of bonuses but saleable production units decreased due to the extra manufacturing time it took to repair the defective products. Worst of all, customer shipments were affected and customer complaints increased. Such performance measurement systems are not tied to revenue or any other strategic objective.

It is clear that individual performance must be linked with business results. When developing compensation systems it is imperative to consider these two issues: the identification of goals and objectives that align with business strategies and the identification of goals and objectives common to individuals and teams who are not necessarily in the organization but who share a business process that provides value to the customer. For example, quality control personnel whose performance objectives include helping manufacturing reduce downtime and rework spend more time on the manufacturing floor working with production and engineering personnel than do quality control personnel who are rewarded based on the number of rejects they find at the end of the manufacturing process. People perform based on the measurement systems in place. Compensation systems that align with business strategies help employees focus on business issues and also help to ensure business success.

LINKING INDIVIDUAL SUCCESS WITH CUSTOMER VALUE

Individual subsystems provide a career path for workers to improve their skills and knowledge while at the same time creating business value for the enterprise. In contrast, compensation systems reward individuals and teams based on their contribution to customer value.

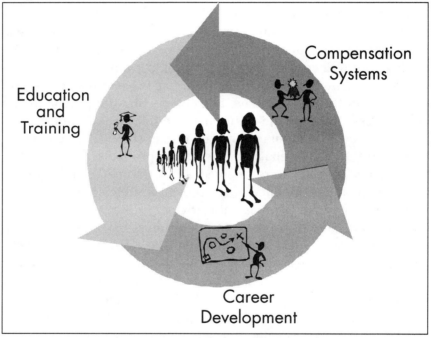

Figure 5–12. Individual Subsystems

Courtesy of Chris Tung, Xerox Professional Document Services.

Every company promises employees career opportunities. Their intentions are good but in many cases they don't have the systems necessary to implement a successful career development plan for employees. Many companies think career development is posting job opportunities for all employees to see. In almost every job interview the candidate articulates his career goals in response to a question from the interviewer. After the candidate is hired he is probably never asked about career goals again.

We've all heard how expensive it is for companies to obtain new customers. In fact, it costs ten times as much to get a new customer than it costs to keep existing customers. The same statistic holds true for employees. New employees need to be trained in their jobs and company policies and procedures, get to know other workers, and, most of all, absorb the company culture. Think about recent new employees and the time it took to get them *up to speed.* Career development is a five-step process that yields growth opportunities for employees and business success for the company.

1. Identify employee goals.
2. Determine skills and capabilities.
3. Develop a career plan.
4. Implement plan.
5. Continuously monitor for success.

Management should be aware of employees' ambitions. Therefore, employees have to be honest about them and not be constrained by their lack of skills and/or experience, which can be redressed over time. The next step is to assess each employee's skills and capabilities in order to identify the gaps that must be filled. Developing a career plan must also take into account whether or not the employee's ambitions can be satisfied within the enterprise. Remember, today's environment is awash in change, so don't assume that the company today will look the same in ten years—it probably won't. So develop a plan that helps the employee achieve the skills, capabilities, and experience needed to provide economic worth to your firm. If the employee can grow within your enterprise, then the investment will pay off handsomely. If the employee decides to move on to another company, she has still provided value to your enterprise.

Many corporations, including GE, AT&T, and Citicorp, have executive development programs that identify promising employees early in their career and rotate them through a well-defined track over many years. These assignments allow the employees to attain new skills and valuable experience that can be applied later.

Don't think career planning is limited to entry-level and junior executives. Succession planning is an area that is getting more attention than before. In the late 1960s almost 95 percent of all CEOs came from within the organization; in the late 1990s nearly 33 percent all CEOs come from the outside. This has led to new ways of grooming CEOs from within. Here are a number of best practices followed by companies that are known to succeed at succession planning:

- The board of directors is more involved than ever before in succession planning.

- Next-generation CEOs are encouraged to accept outside board assignments so they can get exposure to both the media and investors.

- Promising executives are given jobs intended to broaden their skills.

- CEO candidates are more involved and aware of business challenges, business plans, and strategies across the entire enterprise.

At Corning, Inc., the CEO and the board meet every February for a discussion devoted entirely to officer-level succession issues. "The more time you spend on succession planning and having the board involved, the better," insists chairman and CEO Roger G. Acherman.[6] At Air Products and Chemicals, Inc., the Pennsylvania-based global competitor in the gas and chemical markets, an executive succession plan targets vice presidents to obtain global experience as a prerequisite for career advancement. Three-year assignments in Europe, the Far East, and the United States are standard operating procedure for executives who want to get ahead.

Implementing career development plans is not easy. Often employees on a career track do well and their management does not want them to move on. Don't be swayed by short-term benefits. Think of the long-term benefits the company will achieve by having employees develop their career.

A successful career development plan does not end with implementation. Employees change their career plans. The needs of companies change as well. Continuously monitor career development plans by communicating with each employee on at least a quarterly basis. Get input from supervisors, peers, and subordinates, identify skill gaps that can be rectified, and let employees know about their success.

Whenever economic conditions begin to spiral downward, management looks at ways to reduce costs. Unfortunately, one of the first areas to hit is education and training. The mistake that management makes is that it considers education and training an expense when in fact it is an asset. Today's workplace relies more on mental than on physical power and thus must help workers enrich their skills and capabilities. Andersen Consulting realizes this and instead of cutting education and training budgets is finding new ways for people to expand their minds. Andersen is placing more emphasis on Computer-Based Training (CBT) than ever before. Where classroom training can cost hundreds of dollars a day per student, CBT training costs pennies. Traditional classroom training is expensive and limited to the time between the first and last days of class. CBT training relies on individuals to develop good analytical skills, progress at their own speed, and work with peers who use their education and training to solve business problems. Many companies are beginning to recognize that CBT training is not only less expensive but also more effective than traditional classroom training. GE has found that CBT training for its financial personnel is more effective than sending them to name schools like Wharton or Harvard.

Education and training go hand in hand with career planning, compensation systems, and reward and recognition systems. Giving employees the opportunity to expand their mind provides management with a workforce that is more creative and productive than ever before.

Every year there is a frenzy of activity in corporate America when it's time for employees to receive their salary increases. Most companies have annual review cycles where, in one-on-one meetings between supervisor and subordinate, they assess the individual's performance of the preceding year. Although these meetings don't last more than one to two hours, the preparation is cumbersome. Managers and employees spend countless hours documenting performance and reviewing the assessments that recommend compensation increases with upper management. Employees are not stupid. They know exactly what is going on and for a period of about two months before this performance review their focus on business is swayed by it. When the dreaded day of the meeting arrives, most are surprised at the results. An entire year has gone by and in this one hour events that took place months ago are mentioned for the first time.

Just like two-way communication, performance measurement systems usually result in a single, formal face-to-face meeting. Imagine if you, as a parent, let your child do whatever he wanted for an entire year, then had a one- to two-hour discussion about the previous year's behavior. I don't think any parent could responsibly raise a child under these circumstances. It's no different in the workplace. Most people want to do a good job and will do one if they are helped along the way. As a supervisor or manager it is incumbent on you to constantly communicate expected performance to subordinates and teams and reward them accordingly.

The annual review meeting should be a confirmation of performance review meetings that occur throughout the year. Supervisors should meet with their subordinates at least once a month to have open and honest *two-way* discussions about the previous month's performance. Better yet, if a supervisor sees an example of poor performance it should be addressed immediately. This goes for good performance too. Everyone is so busy these days that only the negatives get mentioned. Complimenting employees for a job well done goes a long way toward motivating them to perform even better.

In today's customer-focused marketplace, old rules don't work. Gone are the days when the main focus was to manufacture products at low per-unit costs. The new rules require companies to better understand who their customers are, what they need, and then transform those needs into new products and services that are delivered with superior service. However, it's not machines that accomplish this; it is people who work together in teams that include business partners, suppliers, and sometimes even customers, focusing on continually improving products and services to provide unmatched value to the marketplace. Unless you prepare your workforce with a clear vision that helps them articulate and internalize your business strategies, show them a set of business behaviors that translates those strategies into tangible customer value, you will never become a market leader. The customer-focused organization provides the dynamic leadership, agile structure, and supporting subsystems that enable the people within your organization to succeed.

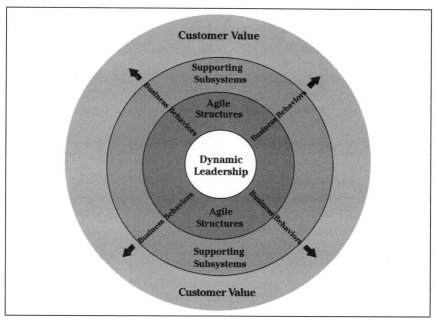

Figure 5–13. A Customer-Aligned Organization Model

WORKSHOP: CREATING A CUSTOMER-CENTERED FRAMEWORK

In this workshop participants get a chance to develop the enterprise infrastructure. It is here that employees can identify which elements of the structure and subsystems work well, need improvement, or don't even exist. It is important that participants have already attended the workshops detailed in earlier chapters, as they lay the foundation for this one.

Table 5–1 Developing a Customer-Centered Organization

Agenda

9:00 AM – 7:00 PM

Time Frames	Time Allotted	Workshop Exercises	Facilitator	Objectives
1. 9:00–10:00	60 min	Set the Stage	Howard O.	Discuss the learning objectives and capture participants' expectations.
2. 10:00–10:30	30 min	Warm-Up Exercise	Marcia B.	Get to know colleagues.
3. 10:30–10:45	15 min	Break		
4. 10:45–12:30	105 min	Developing an Agile Structure— Team Exercise	Larry T.	Understand and identify the agile structure elements required to achieve business success.
5. 12:30–1:30	60 min	Lunch		
6. 1:30–3:15	105 min	Developing Supporting Subsystems— Team Exercise	Marcia B.	Understand and identify the supporting subsystems required to achieve business success.
7. 3:15–3:30	15 min	Break		
8. 3:30–4:00	30 min	Next Steps	Larry T./Marcia B.	Identify necessary actions to ensure development of an effective customer-centered framework within our company.
9. 4:00–4:45	45 min	Workshop Debrief	Marcia B./Larry T.	Capture and share the benefits of the workshop with colleagues.
10. 5:00–7:00	120 min	Group Dinner		

Lead Facilitator: Howard O.   Facilitators: Marcia B./Larry T.

1. SET THE STAGE—60 MINUTES

The facilitator provides an overview of the workshop, its objective, and, using Figure 2–8 as a guide, has participants introduce themselves. To help attendees understand this workshop and the relevance of the previous workshops, the facilitator presents the following brief introduction.

> All of you have attended the previous workshops. In them you became more aware of our company strategy and how it links to customer value; assessed the organization's readiness to change; and defined the business behaviors necessary to achieve success. In this workshop we will identify the elements of the company infrastructure that make up a customer-centered organization, where the focus is on customer value linked to company strategies.

2. WARM-UP EXERCISE—30 MINUTES

The objective of the warm-up exercise is to get everyone relaxed and in the proper frame of mind. (Facilitators can refer to previous workshops for warm-up exercises.) At least 20 minutes should be spent helping participants to understand the value of a customer-focused organization. At one workshop each of the three facilitators prepared for it by reading up on agile structures and supporting subsystems. Using this material as background, they carefully facilitated a discussion, the objective of which was for the group to identify the elements of the agile structure and supporting subsystems without necessarily using these words. Facilitators used Figures 5–8 and 5–9 as background material to help guide the discussion. Figure 5–14 presents discussion questions used at a workshop.

Discussion Questions

What type of structure is necessary to achieve our company business strategy?

- At the enterprise level?
- At the organizational level?
- At the individual level?

What kinds of supporting sytems are required for individuals to excel in their jobs?

- At the enterprise level?
- At the organizational level?
- At the individual level?

Figure 5–14. Sample Slide: Team Discussion Guidelines

3. BREAK—15 MINUTES

As with all breaks, participants should be reminded of the time the break starts and the time they are expected back in the meeting room. Facilitators can guide them back to meeting room as the end of the break approaches.

4. DEVELOPING AN AGILE STRUCTURE—105 MINUTES

The objective of this team exercise is for participants to explore agile structure. Each of the three teams will focus on a different level. This technique is often used when an exercise would take too long to complete in its entirety and ensures good-quality responses.

The teams answer two questions designed to help them analyze the agility of the structure in their company and the effectiveness of a particular level. Figure 5–15 presents the exercise instructions that were used at one workshop.

Developing an Agile Structure

1. The facilitator will divide the group into three teams.

2. The facilitator assigned to your team will lead you in a *30-minute* discussion where you will explore the benefits and customer value of a specified level of the structure.

> Team A = Enterprise Level
> Team B = Organizational Level
> Team C = Individual Level

3. During the next *30 minutes* the teams will use the worksheet and answer the following questions.

   • What kinds of problems do you encounter with your coworkers, team members, suppliers, and customers that impact your performance and affect customer value?

   • What could be done to better the working environment that would also result in improved customer value?

4. The teams will present their findings to the rest of the group.

Figure 5–15. Sample Slide: Team Exercise Instructions

The facilitators work with each team, helping it to explore a specific area. They can use materials from this chapter to help the team understand the various elements. It's important for the facilitator to start at a high level and work into more detail. These concepts are not difficult to comprehend but for many it is an area they have never traveled before.

After the thirty-minute discussion the teams work at answering the two questions. Figures 5–16 and 5–17 are composites of the worksheets for the three teams from a paint factory. As you can see, they were able to come up with specific examples within the company for each level of the agile structure. This is where the facilitator can really help if a team is having difficulty relating the concepts to reality. A well-trained facilitator can adjust the break session to help the team members relate the concepts to their specific work environment.

When the teams return to the main meeting room, each takes five minutes to present its findings to the rest. When all the teams are finished the facilitator conducts a general discussion for the rest of the segment, which should be about fifteen minutes. The objective of this discussion is to solicit comments and have participants answer each other's questions. For example, at one workshop a participant said, "I am having trouble understanding how a customer-centered organization is developed. Should management do it alone or should we be part of the solution?" One of his colleagues responded, "During the team meeting we had a similar question. We decided that since a customer-centered organization structure really helps the workforce be more effective and efficient, then we should be involved in designing it. As a matter of fact, this exercise that we just went through helped answer a number of questions as to how we should do it."

5. LUNCH—60 MINUTES

Lunch can be used to reinforce learning points from the morning session. An excellent technique is to have each of the facilitators sit at a different table and pose a question to the group. At one workshop the question for each table was "How do you ensure that agile structures maintain their effectiveness? What process would you put in place to make sure that the structure in fact is agile and takes on new form based on business needs?" One participant told his colleagues;

My previous company's management invested hundreds of thousands of dollars in developing a process to handle incoming customer returns that started with receipt and review of the customer's letter requesting the return, approving the return, and sending the customer a return authorization with shipping instructions. As customers started communicating electronically with the company and using overnight delivery more frequently, the process became more difficult to manage. There was never a system in place to revisit and review the customer returns process and adjust for these different events. Management just took a stubborn attitude and said we spend a lot of money on this process. Make it work!

Worksheet A

What kinds of problems do you encounter with your coworkers, team members, suppliers, and customers that impact your performance and affect customer value?

Enterprise Level **Enterprise Linkages**	We have difficulty sharing information with our suppliers and customers. Our organization is not set up for effectively communicating outside of our company.
Customer Interfaces	Our customers (distributors) tell us that we are difficult to deal with: Our salespeople aren't knowledgeable enough; they seem always to have to go back to their organization to get an answer or make a decision; and they don't listen very well.
Organizational Level **Organizational Design**	We're very structured. Management likes the old style of command and control and discourages people from speaking out. Management says we need rigid structure or else there will be chaos in the organization.
Policies and Procedures	Our policies haven't been updated in years. Everything we do is defined by a policy or a procedure. Sometimes we feel like it's more of a prison than a paint factory.
Alternative Structures	We just landed a big account at one of the top department stores. It has a certain process for ordering that we must adhere to. We seem to be having extreme difficulty figuring out how to organize ourselves. Things just take too long to get done!
Individual Level **Teams/Tasks/Design**	Last month sales informed management that customers were looking for brighter and longer-lasting colors. Management has done nothing, even though some of the workers told management they have a solution.
Empowerment	We suggested that looking at different transportation carriers could save us money and improve service. Instead of letting us form a project team the department head tried to do all the work himself. After two months, he hasn't had time to start the project.

Figure 5–16. Developing an Agile Structure

Worksheet B
What could be done to better the working environment that would also result in improved customer value?

Enterprise Level **Enterprise Linkages**	We need to establish communication links with our partners and suppliers at the enterprise level that allow us to share information effectively and enable teams to work together as if they were in the same room.
Customer Interfaces	Our salespeople need to be more customer-focused. They have to listen to our customers and have information available that provides answers to questions as well as information that would enhance our relationship.
Organizational Level **Organizational Design**	More and more companies are organizing around business processes. We need to figure out how to do that and do it quickly or else our customers are going to find other suppliers who satisfy their needs.
Policies and Procedures	Our policies and procedures need to be at the macro level, not the micro level. People can be more effective if empowered to make decisions and also have boundaries that ensure they don't go away.
Alternative Structures	Management isn't doing anything. If we could have worked together during the past month in cross-functional teams, we would have figured out how to manufacture brighter and longer-lasting colors.
Individual Level **Teams/Tasks/Design**	We know how to solve the problem. We can have a new paint line running in 30 days, yet management won't let us get involved. The last time something like this happened, it was six months before the first gallon of paint rolled off the manufacturing line.
Empowerment	Management must delegate authority and responsibility. We know our jobs and we do them well. It's a matter of trust. They don't trust us. How much do our customers trust our management?

Figure 5–17. Developing an Agile Structure

6. DEVELOPING SUPPORTING SUBSYSTEMS— 105 MINUTES

The next exercise builds on the first. The group breaks into the same teams and, with the help of the facilitator, discusses the supporting subsystems and how they complement an agile structure. Figure 5–18 is a sample of the exercise instruction sheet the facilitator shows to the group. Each team looks at the same level that it focused on in the previous exercise, answering the same questions but focusing on supporting subsystems. At one session the facilitator used Figure 5–9 and the team's completed worksheet from the previous exercise as the focal points for the thirty- minute discussion. Again, the facilitator needs to gauge the awareness of the group and may have to spend more time *leading* them to an understanding of the concepts behind supporting subsystems.

Developing Supporting Subsystems

1. Break into the same teams as in the previous exercise.

2. The facilitator assigned to your team will lead you in a *30-minute* discussion in which you will explore the benefits and customer value of a specified level of the agile structure.

3. During the next *30 minutes* you will use the attached worksheet and answer the following questions, designed to determine the use and effectiveness of your assigned level:

   • What kinds of problems do you encounter with your coworkers, team members, suppliers, and customers that impact your performance and affect customer value?

   • What could be done to better the working environment that would also result in improved customer value?

4. Be prepared to present the findings to the rest of the group.

Figure 5–18. Sample Slide: Team Exercise Instructions

Below are the consolidated worksheets, Figures 5–19 and 5–20, that three teams prepared in a workshop for the paint factory. As you can see, the teams did a good job of identifying specific situations in their company that negatively impacted their work performance and affected the value the company as well as its customers received. They also identified possible approaches to improving the supporting subsystem elements.

When the teams return to the main meeting room, each takes five minutes to present its results. As in the previous exercise, the facilitator engages the group in a discussion to try to determine if participants truly understand the concepts. Open-ended questions are best here because they require individuals to think about the answer. At one workshop the facilitator asked participants if they knew of any other companies that had elements of the customer-centered organization. One person had just moved to the area and had previously worked for a competitor on the East Coast. She told the group:

> Management seemed to really understand the value of people. They never called their structure a customer-centered organization but they had many elements of

what we are learning about today. For example, I would meet with my supervisor once a month over lunch, which she paid for, and we just shared ideas and thoughts about the company. I really felt great about that. It also gave us an opportunity to address certain performance issues that each of us wanted to speak about. The annual performance review meeting was nothing more than a review of all the monthly meetings we had, and guess what! There were no surprises.

The facilitator should encourage comments like these because they lead into the section of the workshop that immediately follows the break.

Worksheet A

What kinds of problems do you encounter with your coworkers, team members, suppliers, and customers that impact your performance and affect customer value?

Enterprise Level **Recognition and Rewards**	Management doesn't do much to reward us. We punch in, do our jobs, punch out, and go home.
Managing Information	I had to send a paint specification sheet to one of our suppliers. It took two hours to find it on our system, print it, copy the data onto a floppy, and mail it.
Knowledge Management	Our supervisor always gives the difficult jobs to Joe, who has the expertise to do the job. He never shares his secrets and it always makes the rest of us look bad.
Organizational Level **Staffing Systems**	Last year we had a special rush paint order from one of our largest customers. It took three days to find the right group of people to do the job.
Two-Way Communication	Every time my supervisor wants to see me it's a one-way conversation. She never asks me what I think or if there is anything I want to talk about.
Performance Measurement	My boss keeps telling me to produce quality, yet at the same time he tells me to do my job as quickly as possible—quality control will catch any errors.
Individual Level **Career Development**	I returned to college two years ago. I've asked personnel six times if I can better myself at our company. I never see any tangible evidence that they care.
Education and Training	Every once in a while we have some training class, but there is no formal process that helps us improve our skills. We've got to do that ourselves.
Compensation Systems	It's the same scene every year. I sit down with my supervisor, he gives me my raise, and the meeting is over. We never speak about my performance.

Figure 5–19. Developing Supporting Subsystems

Worksheet B

What could be done to better the working environment that would also result in improved customer value?

Enterprise Level **Recognition and Rewards**		All we want is some recognition. If management could put in place some reward system it certainly would provide us more incentive to perform better.
Managing Information		We would be a lot more productive if we had an information system that enabled us to get the data we need when we want it, very quickly.
Knowledge Management		Each of us has a specialty. If we had a system that captured everyone's knowledge we would all be more skilled and productive. Management and our customers would certainly benefit from this.
Organizational Level **Staffing Systems**		We need a process that captures the skills from all 500 employees. In this way, we could quickly find the right person for the right job.
Two-Way Communication		If management and the supervisors were better coaches and mentors they would start listening to what we have to say. We have ideas that can really help our company grow.
Performance Measurement		We all need to be dancing to the same drumbeat. We should look at our measurement systems and make sure they link to our business strategies.
Individual Level **Career Development**		If we had a career development program we wouldn't be losing so many good people to other companies for better jobs. Our company is growing and we should hold onto good people just like we want to hold onto good customers.
Education and Training		Management should ask us about training that would help us to be more productive and efficient. Management, the customer, and the employees would benefit from it!
Compensation Systems		We need to have ongoing reviews of our work so that if we are doing something wrong we don't have to wait for the once-a-year meeting to hear about it.

Figure 5–20. Developing Supporting Subsystems

7. BREAK—15 MINUTES

The afternoon break is always the most difficult to control. Facilitators will probably be needed to ensure that the group reconvenes at the right time. Like with other breaks, the facilitator should announce the current time and the time participants are expected to return to the main meeting room.

8. NEXT STEPS—30 MINUTES

In this workshop the team exercises feed the next-steps segment very nicely. In each of the two exercises the teams identified ways to better the working environment within the company to improve customer value. Figures 5–17 and 5–19 identify actions management should take. The facilitator makes acetates from the consolidated worksheets and displays them on an overhead projector. He then asks the group to go a step further and define more specific actions for each recommendation. This becomes a nice list to present to management.

9. WORKSHOP DEBRIEF—45 MINUTES

Like the other workshop debriefs, a short description of how the workshop helped can be captured in a grid, which makes a good takeaway. At one session a participant told the group that she had all the workshop debrief grids framed and hanging on a wall in her work area. "They are wonderful reminders of how valuable these workshops have been for me and my coworkers."

Agile structures link the enterprise.	Agile structures help us provide value across the enterprise.	The agile structure enables teams to perform better.	I now better understand the needs of my coworkers.	Business partners and suppliers are part of the structure.
The individual level of an agile structure affects people.	Breaking down the framework into three levels is unique.	Supporting subsystems enable people to succeed.	Subsystems help employees perform better.	Empowerment is critical if we are to be customer-focused.
Two-way communication is very important to our success.	Leadership is a very important element of the framework.	Management better get on the bandwagon.	A customer-centered organization provides value.	I learned that sharing ideas leads to better ideas.

Figure 5–21. Lessons Learned

10. GROUP DINNER—120 MINUTES

The group dinner is another opportunity to explore issues addressed during the workshop. At one such event the facilitators made copies of the lessons learned slide and had each person at the table explore his comment in more detail. This enabled more discussion, more thought, and more buy-in. Take every opportunity to have people learn while they are having fun!

ENDNOTES

1. Interview with a LEGO manager, May 1996.

2. Interview with a LEGO Group executive, June 1996.

3. Special supplement to the 1997 LEGO Group Annual Report.

4. Telephone interview with Robert J. Bailey, December 1995.

5. This area is gaining more attention, as the amount of information becomes too large to manage. Tom Davenport, James Martin, Professor Dick Nolan, and others have written extensively on these concepts.

6. "Wanted: A Few Good CEOs," *BusinessWeek,* August 11, 1997, p. 64.

PART II

PERCEIVE YOUR MARKETPLACE

CHAPTER 6

HOW YOUR CUSTOMER PERCEIVES VALUE

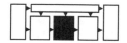

I'm proud of what I've done with the company. But it would not have been possible had I not listened to my customers.

Chris Martin
Chairman of the Board and CEO
The Martin Guitar Company

In 1989 Xerox won the prestigious Malcolm Baldrige National Quality Award and in 1990 and 1991 customer satisfaction ratings peaked. Revenues and profits were up and management was delighted that the company was becoming the one that others sought to emulate when implementing quality programs in their own organizations (see Figure 6–1).

The euphoria, however, was short-lived. During the following few years customer satisfaction ratings started to decline not only at Xerox but also at its competitors Kodak, Canon, and Sharp. Xerox was still leading the pack but management became concerned that unless it did something quickly market share and the company's leadership position would be affected.

Year	Revenues (billions of dollars)
1990	13.2
1991	13.4
1992	14.3
1993	14.2
1994	15.1
1995	16.6
1996	17.4

Figure 6–1. Xerox Corporation: 1990–1996 Revenues[1]

In July 1995 management commissioned a team to find out what was happening in the marketplace. Employees, customers, suppliers, former customers, and noncustomers were interviewed about their perceptions of Xerox. What Xerox heard was not pleasant but eye-opening. A former customer said, "Xerox is only looking for the big accounts. Smaller companies like ours were not even within your range." A current customer said, "You are more concerned with making a sale than listening to what my needs are." A third customer, who was thinking of switching to Xerox, said, "I like your product but the paperwork to close the sale is mind-boggling. It seems that management doesn't understand the word *simplicity*." A former customer switched to Kodak because "it was easier to do business."[2]

After a few months of hearing how difficult it was for customers and former customers to do business with Xerox, the Xerox team studied other companies' customer service programs to find out what could be done to help create a distinct customer satisfaction advantage and recognition for Xerox in the marketplace. After a few weeks the team developed a strategy that it hoped would reverse the downward customer service satisfaction rating. As Peter Garcia, Xerox's director of customer satisfaction, said, "We needed to develop an approach that captures the hearts and minds of the employee so they can capture the hearts and minds of our customer."[3] The team developed a theme that was easy to articulate but challenging to implement. Employees, suppliers, and everyone along the value chain, no matter how far removed from the customer, was asked to put the customer first in every action they perform, behaving as if they were in front of the customer at all times. Thus the *Customer First* program was born. It has changed the way 85,000 Xerox employees all over the world think and act every day of the week.

During most of 1995 Garcia and his team worked hard at creating a program that would articulate the essence of the Customer First program (see Figure 6–2).

VISION: Our customers recognize Xerox as the best company in the industry and talk about the extraordinary things we do to satisfy their requirements and earn their loyalty.

OVERALL STRATEGIES: Clearly understand customers' requirements and satisfy them quickly and cost-effectively. Prioritize doing what's right for the customer above all other objectives.

SUPPORT STRATEGIES	ENABLERS
• Customer-focused people	• Senior managment behavior and actions
• Customer-oriented marketing	• Communications
• Customer-focused processes	• Training
• Customer-focused measurements	• Recognition and reward
	• Standards and measures
	• Organization structure and roles

Figure 6–2. Xerox Customer First Framework

Employees were to listen to their customers, understand their requirements, prioritize them, and satisfy them quickly and cost-effectively. To implement the overall strategy the Customer First team developed a set of support strategies.

Garcia and his team realized that if the program were to be successful, executive management would have to lead these efforts. Senior managers had to articulate their commitment to the program in their behaviors and communications. Companywide communications would integrate the Customer First theme supported by a training program for all Xerox employees. Recognition and reward programs that reinforced positive Customer First behaviors would be established and widely communicated. Finally, Customer First measures would be fully integrated into business plans, operating plans, and annual objectives to ensure a systematic approach to customer and loyalty improvements. The measures Garcia and his team developed were represented by the expression *3R+V,* which stands for Reliability, Responsiveness, Relationship, and Value. *Reliability* means that customers can count on employees anytime and anywhere. *Responsiveness* means that employees are quick to help their customers. *Relationships* require Xerox to truly care about its customers. *Value* means that Xerox provides the solution that fits the needs of customers.

In December 1995 the Customer First team was feeling comfortable that they had a good plan in place. Barry Rand, executive vice president, presented the plan to Paul Allaire, chairman and CEO, and his staff. He didn't have to say much. He told them, "The Customer First Program brings together all the resources, all the innovation, all our energy from across the entire corporation and focuses it on the customer."[4] He provided an overview of the strategy and with their support a half-day workshop was conducted for the entire 170-member senior management team in early 1996 to explain the high-level strategy and get feedback from the group on the priority of the initiatives required for the program to be successful.

It was now time to broaden the Customer First team. Offices were established in each business unit to oversee the training and champion the program. In the Xerox Business Services (XBS) organization the Customer First program office includes five dedicated workers. Kay Burkin, Customer First program manager, is really excited about her job. "Within XBS 85 percent of our employees touch the customer. This means we have the opportunity to really know our customers, get close to them and build strong, long-lasting relationships with them."[5] The XBS Customer First program office customized the training to fit its particular business needs. All XBS employees participate in a half-day workshop with their manager where they identify, learn, and practice how to treat customers with the kind of care that builds solid relationships and leads to long-term customer loyalty. First, the session provides an overview of the program and why it is important to focus on customers. Second, it teaches how to create the right impressions with customers. Third, participants experience what it is like to receive poor service. Fourth, they create statements and action plans about what they plan to do differently to carry out the principles of Customer First. Follow-up training is conducted in small groups to reinforce learning and share Customer First experiences. A Customer First Advisory Board within XBS consists of twenty-three professional-level XBS employees who act in an advisory role to champion and support the Customer First process.

Customer Hero awards are given to employees who exhibit Customer First behaviors. Charles Alexander, a lawyer at Xerox, is one of them. He and his team worked at simplifying complex legal documents that were as long as forty pages and used to baffle customers. Now they are four pages long and dazzle customers with their straightforwardness. Alexander says, "I think we are all connected to the customer. That may sound hokey, but I think it's true. I don't day in and day out walk out and shake the hand of a customer. But I do create a document that the customer sees every day."[6]

In Rochester, New York, Xerox factory workers never see a customer but they, too, care about customer service. When copiers come off the assembly line they are packaged, stored, and shipped to customers. One day a worker wondered what happens when a customer opens up the crate and unpacks one of the machines. Within a week a new activity was started; a team simulates the actions that customers take when they receive a machine. A completed copier is now picked at random and moved around the factory on a forklift to simulate the activity at the customer's site upon delivery. Team members unpack the machine, load it with paper, and test it. "This has really helped me understand what customers do when they receive one of our machines. Now, when I work each day I don't just see metal, I see a group of people at a customer site unpacking the machine and testing it to make sure it functions the way it is supposed to."[7]

The American Society for Quality Control (ASQC) has completed two annual customer service surveys (1995 and 1996).[8] It tracked customer satisfaction in more than two dozen manufacturing and service industries and several public-sector functions representing about 40 percent of U.S. gross domestic product. Despite a lot of talk about putting the customer first, the results show that U.S. companies satisfied their customers *less* in 1996 than in 1995. The decline was most noteworthy in the computer industry, where the American Customer Satisfaction Index fell by 3.8 percent.

Focusing on your customer is not a luxury; it is a necessity if you want to profitably grow your business. Research by the consulting firm Bain & Company indicates that an increased retention of 5 percent of customers can improve profits by 25–100 percent. British Airways views each customer as a lifetime customer. Instead of looking at the average for a one-off trip, it looks at the $25,000 of potential lifetime revenue. Hertz also has identified the expected lifetime revenue from frequent customers at $50,000. It is no wonder they are serious about providing superior value for every one of their customers. Representing this shift in focus, the prestigious Baldrige award now allocates 30 percent of its scoring to customer value.

THE BUSINESS NEED TO FOCUS ON CUSTOMERS

When the Ford Motor Company built the Edsel its customers were not included in the process, and when it hit the market they thought it was the ugliest car they had ever seen. The result was the biggest automotive fiasco in history. When Ford designed the Taurus thousands of customers were contacted to provide input on the design, its interior, its style, and comfort factors. The result has been a financial bonanza for Ford.

Figure 6–3 reflects the historical change in focus that has occurred in the competitive marketplace. In the 1960s companies focused on producing products as fast as they could to keep up with nearly insatiable consumer demands. In the 1970s management was still internally focused, but this time on the cost issue, as foreign competition encroached on markets that American companies never thought would be lost. By the 1980s everyone was on the quality bandwagon as the customer began to enter the equation. The focus, however, was very much on the factory floor.

By the beginning of the 1990s customers' appetite for products was supplemented with a new desire for service. Hertz created its #1 Club Gold Service in 1989 as a result of customers telling it that they didn't want to wait in line to fill out the paperwork associated with the car rental process—they wanted to get to their cars as quickly as possible. Suddenly customers found more value in the services being offered than in the product itself. Customers could get the same car at the same price at other car rental companies, but they chose Hertz because they could get to the car more easily and leave the parking lot more quickly than at its competitors.

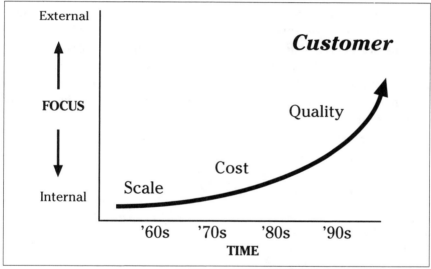

Figure 6–3. The Evolution Toward Customer Focus

Research indicates that about 25 percent of customers will switch to competitors every year. This can result in significant revenue and profit opportunities. Sears lost sight of its customers and ceded market share to companies like Wal-Mart that satisfied customers with new and competitively priced products. Frederick Reicheld, a business consultant, studied the concept of customer retention and loyalty in the banking industry. He found that "retail banks typically find that the branches with the highest customer-retention ratios are also the most profitable."[9] The reason is that it costs at least six times as much to attract new customers as it does to maintain existing customers. When customers are happy, they come back to purchase more products and services; this offsets the continuing cost of acquiring new customers.

The time to acquire new customers and benefit from their first purchase is longer than the time it takes existing customers to re-purchase your product or service. This means that your revenue stream is affected by the loss of customers. The concept is obvious but often ignored. Existing loyal customers provide a continuous revenue stream. Customers who switch to other companies provide a discontinuous revenue stream. Each time a customer switches, time is required to acquire a new customer. The revenue stream stops until the new customer is acquired. This is represented in Figure 6–4 by the horizontal areas between the *A* and *B* points on the curve. When a new customer is acquired, the revenue stream begins again, as represented by sloped areas between the *B* and *A* points.

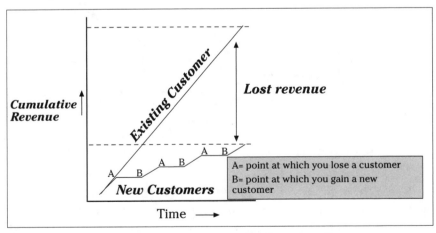

Figure 6–4. The Profit Motive for Keeping Customers

PERCEIVING CUSTOMER NEEDS, WANTS, AND DESIRES

Every customer defines value based on needs, wants, and desires. *Needs* means the product or service that the customer urgently re-quires. *Wants* define the characteristics of the product or service they need. *Desires* indicate the need independent of any customer constraint. For example, a young couple *needs* to move from a cramped apartment into a house and can afford a price of about $75,000. They *want* their house to have a minimum of two bedrooms and two baths with a small yard for their young child. Their *desire* is for a four-bedroom home in the country on an acre of land.

Noncustomers as well as customers provide insights into their needs, wants, and desires. When Rainbow Discovery Center in Allentown, Pennsylvania, opened its child-care facility, management was keen on identifying the needs, wants and desires of parents in the community. During the first years of business the director spoke to parents at great length to understand more about their child-care needs. She wanted to know why parents chose the child-care provider they used. She also asked parents to identify the child-care characteristics they were looking for and how they would design a program that would meet their needs if they had the opportunity to do so. As a result of listening to both customers and noncustomers, Rainbow developed a quality program that has kept it in business for fifteen years; it enjoys a reputation for small class size and excellent teachers.

British Airways regularly interviews noncustomers to find out with whom they fly and why, to identify their needs, wants, and desires. When noncustomers talked about their need to have ethnic food on flights from Asia, BA started offering Asian food choices for these flights. When Burger King interviewed noncustomers it found that people wanted to purchase a meal quickly and not have to order a hamburger, then some fries, and then a soft drink. So it started the Value Meal program, where customers can order a Whopper, large fries, and medium soft drink by just saying, "I'll have a Whopper #2 Value Meal."

Some companies are able to take customers' desires and turn them into lucrative businesses. Ikea, the Swedish manufacturer of home furniture, recognized a tremendous market for customers who wanted quality furniture at an affordable price. Ikea leveraged this knowledge by entering into a coproduction relationship with its customers. This relationship combines basic assembly skills with well-thought-out written instructions. The concept of coproduction of quality furniture has been the key to Ikea's success.

Taco Bell turned a customer monitoring program into tremendous growth. Sales increased from $1.6 billion in 1988 to $3.9 billion on 1993. Earnings rose from $82 million in 1988 to $253 million in 1993. It went from a generic fast-food business offering convenient, inexpensive, reasonably satisfying meals and snacks, to a company that monitored its customer base and exploited every conceivable opportunity. Taco Bell previously identified its target market as high-frequency fast-food users (HFFFUs)—a single broad category. Management decided to monitor customers and noncustomers and divided the potential customer base into three distinctive patterns—customers who visit Taco Bell at least once a week, people who visit as little as once a month, and people who never patronize Taco Bell because they don't like Mexican food (these noncustomers could be turned into customers if Taco Bell offered them alternative food choices). Analysis indicated that the most promising customers from these three groupings were penny-pinchers—18- to 24-year-olds who visit frequently but spend their money on low-priced menu items, and speed freaks—generally two-income families concerned about quick service, ease of use, and taste of food. These groups represented only 30 percent of the traffic but accounted for 70 percent of the company's volume. By focusing in on these market segments and developing products and services to satisfy their particular needs, Taco Bell generated substantial growth and profits.[10]

As we have seen, companies that take the time to perceive their customers' and potential customers' needs, wants, and desires reap the benefits.

For six generations the Martin Guitar Company has made quality acoustical guitars, but this Steinway of guitar manufacturers has not had it so easy competing in a tumultuous marketplace. In fact, in the mid-1980s it was losing money, and a financial planning consultant hired by the company recommended that it be liquidated. By perceiving its customers' needs, wants, and desires, however, Martin transformed its business. Today it is a robust $47 million company that competes in 67 foreign countries, is growing at a 10 percent annual rate, and shares its profits with all 500 employees.

Chris Martin, a sixth-generation Martin, is current chairman of the board and CEO. When he was faced with the recommendation to liquidate his company, he thought long and hard before deciding to continue and rebuild the business. First, he looked at the history of the Martin Guitar Company. The pear-shaped design of the acoustic guitar—named the Dreadnought after a large class of World War I British battleships—was invented by the company but never patented. It became the standard for acoustic guitars, especially among country music performers, who look for the deep bass response that the shape evokes. Gene Autry, Johnny Cash, Bob Dylan, Peter, Paul, and Mary, Paul McCartney, and a host of other famous performers have used the Martin guitar. Chris Martin realized that the heritage of his product and its quality should be the cornerstone of his company's transformation.

Because he was convinced the company did not adequately perceive its customers' needs, Martin's next step was to find out what motivated dealers and what consumers thought about his guitars. The dealers complained about the price. The popularity of the acoustic guitar had resulted in strong competition as Gibson, Guild, Taylor, and Collins as well as foreign competitors tried to copy the Martin style. Although these competitors could never copy the quality, many customers could not afford the average Martin price tag of $1,800 and higher.

To hear firsthand what guitar customers thought Martin held customer clinics at dealer locations. He talked about the history of the guitar and the various models that the company manufactured. He brought along company employees, some of whom were excellent guitar players and who performed on a variety of Martin guitars. Others were there to observe and listen. He used this forum to capture comments and concerns. He wanted to make sure he and his colleagues could personally observe how customers held the guitar, how it fit in relationship to the individual, and the individual's expression when he played the guitar. Among the comments he heard were: "It's the best darn guitar in the whole world but I just can't afford it," and "It's too big. I can't take this size guitar camping and hiking. I'm afraid I'm going to damage it." A number of women loved the guitar but had difficulty holding it.

Martin also started company tours that allow his staff to observe people as they tour the plant. The guides explain the history of the Martin guitar, show the visitors the manufacturing process, and listen to their questions and comments. When visitors were shown some of the famous guitars that Martin manufactured, like the Jimmy Rodgers series, the tour guides would hear them say, "I love the guitar but could never afford $25,000."

As a result of listening to customers and noncustomers, the Martin Guitar Company embarked on a new strategy. To satisfy the needs of customers who loved the guitar but couldn't afford one, the company initiated a cost improvement program. Without compromising its high quality standards it developed a series of Martin guitars starting as low as $849, a price that most guitar enthusiasts are willing to spend. To satisfy the customers who wanted a guitar that could travel, Martin developed the Backpacker series, which features sleek guitars that are easy to carry, have a richness of sound synonymous with Martin guitars, and sell for a few hundred dollars. To accommodate the female customers who had difficulty with the fit of the standard Martin guitar, a new model was designed named Woman in Music. To satisfy the desires of those who want to play the older guitars, which have risen significantly in value, the company designed the Vintage series, which consists of copies of the originals at a price tag of about $2,000 each, around 10 percent of the original models.

Today the Martin Guitar Company is achieving success that Chris Martin's forebears would be proud of. He doesn't, however, sit on his laurels. He realizes that customers have constantly changing needs, wants, and desires, and that the customer listening process is not a static event. The company continues to pursue new products that satisfy the ever-changing demands of its customers.[11]

INTERACTIVE LISTENING AND LEARNING SYSTEMS

Management can seek customer information through channels that I call listening and learning systems. Of the three types of systems, the first is *interactive* (the others are *one-way* systems and *electronic* systems). Interactive systems allow you to communicate directly with customers, in nonelectronic form, to perceive their needs, wants, and desires.

British Airways uses focus groups to identify customer profiles. It periodically gathers existing customers, noncustomers, and employees to study specific issues. This interactive approach led to the development of BA's European business-class services, which improved both customer service and retention and contributed greatly to the company's preeminence in the European business travel market.

Many companies use focus groups as a means of gathering customers together for a specific purpose and to help pinpoint data. Automotive companies use them to measure participants' responses to existing or planned advertising. Airlines use focus groups to flush out issues that can help develop new services. Companies use focus groups to help build allegiance to their products. Binney and Smith, maker of Crayola crayons, conducts regular focus groups with children as young as eight.[12] Sony uses focus groups to help identify what its customers are looking for in the way of new products and services.

BA conducts thousands of interviews per year with arriving passengers. The ten-minute interview takes place at the baggage claim area as passengers await their luggage. They are asked for subjective responses to questions including:

- While you were checking in, did the staff treat you as a friend and an individual or as a number?

- While you were checking in, was the staff warm and friendly or superior and aloof?

- Were the cabin staff attentive and ready to help you?

- Did the cabin staff anticipate your needs and willingly offer assistance?

- Did the cabin staff stand around or disappear when they could have been doing something to help serve you better?

Hilary Rickard, head of market research at BA, says that these personalized questions elicit true customer feelings about the behaviors of the staff. "These questions are specifically designed to identify the *behaviors* of BA service personnel. This is quite different than other surveys. If we can isolate the behaviors that create value for our customers then we can focus on those behaviors in our training program." BA also talks to both noncustomers and ex-customers. "We need to talk to people who have moved away from us," says Rickard. "We need to identify regular business flyers and why they do not fly BA. Identifying these barriers will help improve our customer retention and attract former and new customers."[13]

One of the best ways to find out what your customers want is to spend a day with them. The experience can generate new insights into business opportunities, act as a catalyst for change, and reawaken managers to the realities of the marketplace. Wireline is a division of Schlumberger, a major player in the petroleum services industry. The company offers a wide array of specialized services to the oil industry and is known for its expertise and punctuality. Technicians in fully equipped trucks visit customer sites prepared for any challenge. When market share dropped management didn't know why. They spent time with customers and discovered that they felt Wireline performed unnecessary tests and its service calls were too expensive. Customers who drilled shallow wells and didn't need a full array of technical services had switched to competitors whose costs were lower. In response, Wireline redesigned its service vehicles and trained technicians to focus on customer relationships.[14]

Company tours also offer the opportunity for a business to cultivate a relationship. Harley-Davidson and Martin Guitar are swamped with visits by the public to tour their plants. These companies also sell their products at the plant, as well as memorabilia with company logos.

Automotive companies including Toyota, Ford, and GM have customer advisory boards. This interaction provides management with a constant flow of customer information. Ford, in addition integrates the customer into research and development efforts in an effort to identify customer needs and build loyalty. Toyota has been doing this for years, and the payoff is well worth it.

Most companies view trade shows as a one-way process of selling, but they can also be a venue for collecting information during interaction with customers, noncustomers, and competitors. The next time your company exhibits at a trade show, plan for the event. Get a profile of the expected participants, determine the information you would like to gather, and develop a process for doing so. A selected group from a consulting firm, for example, wanted to find out the depth of competitors' service offerings. Companies who would be exhibiting at and attending a trade show were identified and individuals from the consulting company given assignments about who to see, what questions to ask, and what information to convey. After the trade show they analyzed the information obtained, which was invaluable in developing a strategy to learn more about potential client needs.

Forging partnerships is a good method for understanding customer wants and needs. Chrysler, Ford, and GM all built partnerships with companies in different parts of the world in order to find out more about customers. In addition, alliances with competitors can help fill a gap in a particular competency that your customers are seeking. To build an electric car, the Big Three auto companies formed a project partnership that harnessed the energies of all three.

Interactive listening systems are effective because they involve people speaking to people. Management should pursue these opportunities as often as possible so it can capture, analyze, and interpret the information to create value.

ONE-WAY LISTENING AND LEARNING SYSTEMS

One-way systems are those where there is no overt interaction with customers or company personnel. Sometimes you have to observe customers to find out what they are really thinking about. "The best way to understand customers is to study them under normal, natural conditions," says Larry Keeley, president of Doblin Group, a Chicago consulting firm. Steelcase was designing a new product specifically for work teams. Rather than seek customer feedback, the company set up cameras at customer work sites to observe how teams worked together. They were "watching for patterns of behavior and motion that customers don't even notice themselves."[15]

Urban Outfitters is a Philadelphia-based chain of twenty stores that is growing fast. A key to its success has been observing customers. In fact, it has conducted only two interviews in the last twenty-five years and has not used focus groups at all. It obtains customer profiles by videotaping and taking snapshots of customers in its stores. It also observes customers in their local neighborhoods. In New York it might be the East Village; in Philadelphia, it might be South Street. Observers look for what people are wearing. This provides the company with a feel for the target market and allows management to make quick decisions on merchandise.[16]

Companies use listening posts as a means of understanding consumer behavior. LEGO Group uses its theme parks and its global village on the Internet to capture the needs, wants, and desires of its customers. Yamaha has a listening post in London; musicians from all over the world visit the store to try out musical instruments. These experiences help to develop new and innovative products that have been functionally defined by the customers rather than by an engineer in a lab. Sony lets kindergarten children play with its newest toys in order to determine the products' attractiveness and usefulness. Clearly, an additional benefit to Sony is that it captures customers at an early age.

Mystery shoppers are used by many national department store chains to find out how sales personnel treat customers as well as to find out what customers think. They act like regular shoppers and interact under this guise with other shoppers and with salespeople. The difference is that they are there for information. How do salespeople behave? How do shoppers react to new merchandise? The mystery shopper is a potentially valuable aid in your toolkit for obtaining information about customer wants, needs, and desires.

Advertising is a means of communicating with the customer and capturing customer profile data. More companies are using videocassettes as a means of enticing customers to call the company. Automotive companies use videotapes as a means of advertising, but only if the customer contacts the company to request a specific video. This provides an opportunity to capture customer profile data. Colleges and universities use videos in the same manner. Travel agencies use them as a means of informing prospective travelers about specific travel destinations. To get information, customers have to provide information of their own to the company.

Surveys and questionnaires are excellent methods of obtaining customer information. A survey is an analytical tool, whereas a questionnaire can provide basic information. Businesses use surveys to analyze their customers, markets, employees, and a host of other subjects. Hotels use surveys all the time. The problem is to get people to fill them out and to provide accurate information. Most people hate surveys. Anything greater than a 2–3 percent return rate for a mailed survey is considered good. However, even when people fill them out they may not take the time to answer the questions correctly. To address these problems *Fortune* magazine notifies customers that it will make a contribution to charity if they take the time to participate in a survey. The reasoning is that when individuals read that a contribution will be made to a good cause they may feel more inclined to fill out the survey, and to fill it out accurately.

Red Lobster is a billion-dollar business and the largest seafood dinner house in the United States, serving nearly 70 million pounds of seafood each year. Management realizes that customer profile information is one of the key ingredients of this successful business. Mailing 15,000 questionnaires to customers each month provides management with information on taste patterns, menu preferences, and so on. New patterns emerging from the customer database result in almost overnight changes to the Red Lobster menu.[17]

One-way listening and learning systems provide a time-tested approach to capturing customer and noncustomer information. This is the first type of system that was so used, and it is the most prevalent today.

ELECTRONIC LISTENING AND LEARNING SYSTEMS

Electronic systems are becoming more popular as the cost of capturing information drops precipitously and the amount of information available grows exponentially. Electronic systems help companies gather, analyze, and distribute customer information across the world.

Kiosks allow customers to interact with you electronically and enable you to satisfy their individual wants and needs. Anderson Window increased sales by allowing customers to interact and collaborate with trained sales staff in a multimedia kiosk, dubbed the Window of Knowledge, in order to better satisfy individual expectations, needs, and competencies. This interaction provides

Anderson customers with a way to design their own window specifications and the company with customer information that can be used in future selling opportunities.[18] OfficeMax is considering the use of this same concept in its stores.

The Internet is an excellent way to obtain customer information. Every time you log onto a Web site you provide information to its owner. Your Web address, the type of computer you have, which pages of the site you look at, how much time you spend on each page, and so forth are all captured. This mode of communication is a whole new territory for companies and is growing rapidly as a source of customer information.

One executive recently told me that when a business problem arises, instead of calling in an expensive consultant he types a note on the Internet asking for expert advice. He receives numerous responses that help resolve the problem. It seems the world is full of specialists who are willing to help others at a fraction of the cost of a Big Six consulting firm.

Point-of-sale systems help companies find out about customer buying habits quickly. When a customer buys merchandise at any Benetton store, the transaction is relayed to a central database. The type of merchandise sold, its color, and other transaction and customer information is relayed and captured electronically. This provides Benetton with buying patterns for each store and enables it to allocate inventories based on actual geographic buying patterns that reflect current activity.

The automotive companies made EDI (Electronic Data Interchange) a household word. Companies instantaneously communicate their orders, and suppliers their shipments and invoices, over electronic networks. Companies and suppliers thus learn about each other's needs quickly. Today, all the automotive companies and major retailing chains, including Wal-Mart, use EDI as a common means of communication.

Inter-Design is a private company in Solon, Ohio, with annual sales of more than $10 million. Inter-Design sells plastic clocks, refrigerator magnets, soap dishes, and similar products to major retailers including Wal-Mart, K-mart, and Target. Its business tripled in the twelve-year period ending in 1993. Bob Immerman, president of Inter-Design, says, "In the seventies, we went to the post office to pick up our orders. In the early eighties, we put in an 800 number. In the late eighties, we got a fax machine. In 1991, pressured first by Target, we added Electronic Data Interchange."

The smart card is an emerging technology that will allow large amounts of customer transaction data to be captured quickly and efficiently. Smart cards are credit-card-size devices with a central processing unit (CPU) and (as of summer 1995) up to 32 kilobytes of random-access memory (RAM) for storing information. The newest generation of smart card is known as the contactless smart card, or CSC. The CSC is additionally equipped with a radio-frequency (RF) transmitter and receiver that makes it unnecessary for the card to be swiped through a reader or inserted into a slot. The card is read and written to by an RF beam that also powers the electronics embedded in the card. As a result, the cards can be read and written to while they remain in a wallet or purse, at distances of up to tens of feet.

In Hong Kong, contactless smart cards are used by commuters to pay for transit services, whether they travel the ferry, subway, bus, or train systems. Travelers can purchase prepaid fares from a kiosk and have the cost charged directly to their bank account. When the commuter enters a subway platform or surface vehicle, the smart card is awakened by an RF beam and automatically relays the customer number, date and time, and transit entry point to a central data clearinghouse. Later, when the traveler leaves a station or vehicle, the fare is calculated based on the distance traveled and deducted from the balance remaining on the card. When the balance becomes less than the current fare amount, the card is automatically recharged, again from the customer's bank account.

The possibilities are endless; clearly, the use of these cards can easily be extended to cover a wide range of high-volume, low-value purchases such as taxis, fast food, and even the contents of vending machines. The types of data that can be stored on the smart card are limited only by the imagination. Names, addresses, and telephone numbers of customers, product or service purchased, time of service, dollar amount per transaction—such information is invaluable, and its availability will quickly lead to the implementation of many new customer loyalty programs. As smart cards and the equipment designed to read them proliferate, customer profile information will be easily obtained.

CUSTOMER RELATIONSHIP SYSTEMS

Individual, Inc., is a Burlington, Massachusetts, company that supplies information to a user base of 30,000 that comprises 4,000 accounts. It enjoys a customer retention rate of 85–90 percent. Instead of customers having to sort through magazines, newspapers, and conference proceedings to find information, an editorial manager assigned to the account learns about the customer's needs through understanding his or her objectives. A SMART system (System for Manipulation and Retrieval of Text) using a customer profile of needs, wants, and desires sorts through 400 sources containing more than 12,000 articles for a match. Every week the customer is supplied with the appropriate articles or abstracts by fax, mail, or electronic means. The learning takes place as the customer rates each article as not relevant, somewhat relevant, or very relevant. Over a three-week period, the hit rate of very relevant articles increases from approximately 40 percent to over 80 percent, the result of Individual, Inc., learning from its customers. The system learns what the reader considers very relevant and further defines the rules for sorting specific matches.

Cultivating relationships with your customers will bring in an ongoing and profitable revenue stream. Customers who value your products or services don't have to be sold; they are already aware of the value and keep coming back for more. Saturn has done an excellent job of developing relationships with its customers by developing a listening and learning system that exploits the customer relationship. Saturn uses every opportunity to learn from its customers. At first, the relationship may be at arm's length. As company and customer become more dependent on one another, true learning occurs. Saturn recognizes that most of its customers don't know how to take care of a car. By inviting them to Saturn showrooms and demonstrating how to maintain cars, the company has developed a listening and learning system. This interaction helps customers learn how to take care of their automobile while at the same time enabling Saturn to learn more about its customers' needs, wants, and desires.

Kraft General Foods, Inc., has information provided by each of its thirty million customers as a result of coupons and other KGF offerings. It uses this database to keep track of customers' needs, wants, and desires. The more information customers have about a product, the more they will use it—for instance, "Use Miracle Whip instead of butter for grilling sandwiches." Management at Kraft and similar companies recognizes that identifying customer preferences and needs is not a one-time occurrence but an ongoing process that results in the development of a learning relationship. These relationships teach management about the needs of customers and improving the value delivered to the customer.

In 1992 General Motors joined with MasterCard to offer the GM credit card. The resulting database of twelve million GM cardholders is constantly surveyed to determine the kind of vehicle customers are driving, when they plan to buy their next car, and what kind of vehicle they would like to own. GM then sends cardholders information about their choice and forwards their names to the appropriate GM division. Blockbuster Entertainment Corp. uses its thirty-six-million-household database and two million daily transactions to help its customers find the movie of their choice. Its objective is to capture as much information about customers as possible and determine their needs, wants, and desires. To help identify the individual customer's needs and wants, the company is testing a system whereby customers will receive a list of ten recommended movies based on their prior rental history. Customers who choose movies not on the list are indicating a change in past behavior patterns. They are conveying their desires for different types of films.

Even casinos like Claridge's are getting in on the action. In the early days pit bosses at casinos would keep handwritten lists of frequent players. Now computers keep tabs on visitors who use and frequent the casinos. Claridge's CompCard Gold has 350,000 members to whom it offers discounts and tips on upcoming events. This helps target its efforts on frequent customers.

Airlines use the travel reservation system to capture the habits of its customers—where they like to sit, what type of meals they like, when they like to travel, whom they travel with, and so forth. Domino's, Pizza Hut, and others are capturing buying patterns as well. When my daughter, Danielle, calls Domino's the employee answers the phone with "Domino's Pizza. May I have your name please?" When she replies, he asks, "Would you like your regular order of one medium cheese pizza today?" Domino's maintains a customer order history and uses it to *personalize* the order process.

The electronic capture of reservation and other guest information allows Ritz Carlton to satisfy individual wants and needs. When guests call the Ritz Carlton reservation system, information such as type of room booked, and whether they are traveling for business or pleasure is held over for future reservations. Special requests such as feather pillows and ice for the room are also entered on the customer database. When the guest travels to her next Ritz Carlton a bucket of ice and feather pillows will be in her room.

With technology rapidly advancing, the amount of information that can be captured is almost endless and cost keeps dropping every day. The future is in transforming customer and noncustomer information into customer value.

CHOOSING LISTENING AND LEARNING SYSTEMS

In deciding which listening and learning system to use, the choice is not an exclusive one between one system and another but rather is about combinations of systems and depth of use. Each business must determine what mix of systems is best for them. All are appropriate and can provide enormous amounts of information. Following are guidelines for selecting the right combination of listening and learning systems.

1. Select a cross-functional team whose members represent the areas of the company that touch your customer. The team should be no larger than twelve or fifteen people.

2. Have the team select a cross-section of customers to include in the group. Choose among suppliers, distributors, intermediate customers (manufacturers), and end-user customers (the customers' customers). The customer team should include no more than eight people.

3. Use basic team-building concepts to help the group to bond.

4. Have the team identify the information that should be captured from the marketplace and why it is important. Answering the following questions will help the team identify what matters to the customer.[19]

   • Which product and service *characteristics* are important in the eyes of the customer?

   • What is the *relative* importance of each of their needs, wants, and desires?

   • What *level* of performance of each product and service characteristic will meet the customers' expectations? What will exceed the expectations?

5. Identify the current listening systems and the information being captured.

6. Assess the effectiveness of the current listening systems and identify their shortcomings. Use a simple rating system—for example, low, medium, and high.

7. Select the appropriate listening and learning system(s) to capture the information identified in Step 4.

8. Discuss the best means of deploying the listening and learning systems.

9. Use the customer team members as a pilot group for deployment.

10. Develop an action plan that reflects times, actions, and responsibilities of team members.

11. Regularly measure the effectiveness of the listening and learning systems deployed.

Where to locate listening and learning systems is an important factor in generating useful information. Hertz, for example, is dedicated to capturing customer complaints and identifies specific business activities during which they can be elicited. One such activity is the ordering interaction, during which the customer service operator can sense or be explicitly told about concerns the customer has. A customer might say, "The last time I was given a two-door vehicle and I had a problem getting to the back seat, where I had my sales materials." The customer sales representative can capture this information and enter "customer requires four-door vehicle" in the computerized personal profile for use when the customer makes the next reservation.

First, determine what specific type of information you are trying to capture. Second, choose the listening and learning system that can help you capture that information; use Figure 6–5 as a guide. Last, use Figure 6–6 to help you identify where in your enterprise you would want to employ these systems to provide the greatest impact.

QUESTIONNAIRE: MEASURING THE EFFECTIVENESS, EFFICIENCY, AND ADAPTABILITY OF YOUR LISTENING AND LEARNING SYSTEMS

The efficiency of your listening and learning systems is dependent on the competency of the people in your organization, how accessible they are to customers, how courteous they are when they interact with customers, and how securely they maintain the information you provide. The adaptability of your listening and learning systems is dependent on how well you communicate with your customers and how responsive you are to their needs.

Figures 6–7, 6–8, and 6–9 are self-tests you can use to determine how effective, efficient, and adaptable your company's listening and learning systems are. Following the tests is a section that explains how to score your results.

System	Benefits
Interactive	
Focus Groups	Gather data for specific purpose.
Interviews	Determine needs, wants, desires/ complaints.
Spend a day with customers	Generate new insights/business opportunities.
Company tours	Build relationships/capture information.
Customer advisory boards	Provide constant flow of customer information.
Trade shows	Capture customer/competitor/market information.
Partnerships/alliances	Understand customers in unfamiliar markets.

Figure 6–5. Choosing a Listening and Learning System

One-Way

Observation	Learn about customers in natural environment.
Listening posts	Watch customers use products.
Mystery shoppers	Identify how customers are treated.
Advertising	Test new ideas/measure customer perceptions.
Surveys/Questionnaires	Identify customer information.

Electronic

Kiosks	Provide/capture/interact with marketplace.
Internet	Provide/capture/interact with marketplace.
Point-of-sale systems	Capture customer buying patterns in real time.
EDI	Transmit information across value chain.
Smart Card	Enable customer transactions/capture information.

Customer Learning

Credit cards	Capture buying patterns/customer information.
Customer profiles	Capture/use information in future customer interactions.
Coupons	Identify buying patterns/customer information.
Travel reservations	Learn about customer/noncustomer tastes.
Customer purchase histories	Learn about customers.
Customer relationships	Continuous opportunity to learn about customers.

Figure 6–5. (continued)

Company-Initiated Activities	Customer-Initiated Activities
Manufacturing	Ordering
Logistics	Payment
Billing	Information
Collection	Complaints
Delivery	Product repair
Marketing	Reading publications
Product repair	Speaking to friends
Research	Testing product/service
New product development	Comparison shopping

Figure 6–6. Locating Listening and Learning Systems

Measuring the Effectiveness of Your Listening and Learning Systems

Instructions

1. Below are three capabilities that measure the effectiveness of your company's listening and learning systems.

2. Each capability is defined.

3. For each capability have the customer rate the extent to which your company's listening and learning systems match the statements, using the following scale.

1=Never   2=Sometimes   3=Often   4=Always

Dependability

The capability to deliver what was promised in a consistent and reliable manner, the first time and every time. Products and services are delivered when required, and the company honors its commitments to customers—and the customers know it.

1. The products and services I purchase accomplish their purpose.

2. The company's products perform as promised.

3. The company always honors its commitment to quality, service, and performance.

4. Company facilities and equipment reflect the latest technology.

Subtotal

Understanding Knowledge of the Customer

Knowing the individual needs, wants, and desires of individual customers. Caring about customers and treating them as individuals rather than as part of a group.

1. I always feel I am being treated as an individual and not as part of a group.

2. My needs, wants, and desires are understood.

3. A relationship is fostered based on trust.

4. The company desires to learn from me.

5. I feel confident that my needs are being anticipated.

Subtotal

Figure 6–7. Measuring the Effectiveness of Your Listening and Learning Systems

Trustworthiness

Acting in the best interests of the customer by being honest and credible. The operative word is *confidence*. The customer has confidence that you are trying to service his needs and provide the best and most cost-effective solution. This might include explaining the various services and offering choices for the customer; discussing the cost and the options for payment; informing the customer of the product and service options available; and providing the customer with what you think would best meet his needs.

1.   I have confidence in the company.

2.   I have confidence in the personnel I deal with.

3.   I am convinced that my interests are being looked out for.

4.   I am always provided with options.

5.   I am never pushed to make a decision.

Subtotal

TOTAL EFFECTIVENESS SCORE

Figure 6–7. (continued)

Measuring the Efficiency of Your Listening and Learning Systems

Instructions

1.   **Below are four capabilities that measure the efficiency of your company's listening and learning systems.**

2.   **Each capability is defined.**

3.   **For each capability have the customer rate the extent to which your company's listening and learning systems match the statements, using the following scale.**

1=Never   2=Sometimes   3=Often   4=Always

Competence

Having the skills and knowledge required to perform the service. This measurement must thread through the entire organization, not just exist at the point where there is customer contact. Remember, a chain is only as strong as its weakest link.

1.   The personnel I deal with have the knowledge and skills required.

2.   Whenever I contact other organizations within the company, the personnel have the skills and knowledge required.

Figure 6–8. Measuring the Efficiency of Your Listening and Learning Systems

3.   The company always searches for additional skills and knowledge from outside the company, if required to meet my needs.

	Subtotal

Accessibility

Being easy to contact. Services are easily accessible by telephone, by computer, or in person. You don't have to wait for a long time for service, and the hours of operation, as well as locations of service, are convenient for the customer (delivery to your home, office, or other locations where you will be).

1.   When I telephone for service, the company agent always answers by the second ring.

2.   Services are available outside normal business hours, making it convenient for me to use the company's services.

3.   The company has locations that are easily accessible for all my affiliate organizations.

4.   All locations are easily accessible and clean.

5.   I feel confident that my needs are being anticipated.

	Subtotal

Courtesy

Being respectful to, and considerate of, customers. This is most important for personnel who are in frequent contact with customers (receptionists, bank tellers, and front-office staff, for example). Having a neat and clean appearance is important to customers; repair people who clean up after their work gain a lot of respect from customers.

1.   Personnel are always courteous to me.

2.   Personnel are always attentive to my needs.

3.   Personnel always appear professional.

	Subtotal

Security

Conveying to customers that they are personally protected at all times, and any personal belongings, such as stock certificates, are safe. Customers also want the assurance that confidentiality will not be breached (on financial transactions, insurance claims, and so on).

1.   I always feel that my confidence will not be breached.

2.   I always feel safe, secure, and free from harm.

3.   I am confident that my interests come before those of the company.

	Subtotal

	TOTAL EFFICIENCY SCORE

Figure 6–8. (continued)

Measuring the Adaptability of Your Listening and Learning Systems

Instructions

1. **Below are two capabilities that measure the efficiency of your company's listening and learning systems.**

2. **Each capability is defined.**

3. **For each capability have the customer rate the extent to which your company's listening and learning systems match the statements, using the following scale.**

1=Never   2=Sometimes   3=Often   4=Always

Communication

Using language that is understandable by customers. Different language or dialect capabilities are required for customers of different ethnic groups within an area or in different parts of the globe. Level of customer expertise is also a consideration. The more experienced and educated customer should be communicated with differently than the novice customer.

1. Organizational personnel communicate with me using words that are simple and easy to understand.

2. Affiliate organizations in different parts of the world can communicate with the company using their native language.

3. Personnel in my organization with varying levels of education can always converse with the company using words they can understand.

Subtotal

Responsiveness

The willingness to help customers by providing prompt service on the customer's terms (for example, arriving on time for appointments or sending documentation as promised). Calling your customer back as promised.

1. Personnel are always responsive to my needs.

2. Services are always performed in a timely manner.

3. Products are always available in the time I require.

4. When I leave messages they are always returned promptly.

Subtotal

TOTAL ADAPTABILITY SCORE

Figure 6–9. Measuring the Adaptability of Your Listening and Learning Systems

Record your score at the end of each test. Copy the scores into the Total Score column in Figure 6–10. Then,

1. Divide your *Total Scores* by the adjustment factor of 1.40 to convert your score to a 100 percent scale and record the number in the *Adjusted Score* column of Figure 6–10.

2. Circle the corresponding score on Figure 6–11 to see the relative degree of proficiency for each attribute.

3. Review each attribute and determine what actions need to be accomplished for you to improve your customer listening and learning systems. For this exercise to be effective you should rank the attributes in order of importance to determine which will have the most impact on your business. You can then evaluate your scores and focus on the attributes that make the most sense for your business.

Attribute	Total Score	Adjustment Factor (to convert to a 100-percent scale)	Percentile Score
Effectiveness		1.40	
Efficiency		1.40	
Adaptability		1.40	
TOTAL OVERALL SCORE			

Figure 6–10. Scoring Your Results

Adjustment Factor: The total maximum score is 140:

Effectiveness	= 14 Questions x 4	= 56
Efficiency	= 14 Questions x 4	= 56
Adaptability	= 7 Questions x 4	= 28
	Maximum Score	140

Maximum Score of 140 divided by 1.40 = 100%

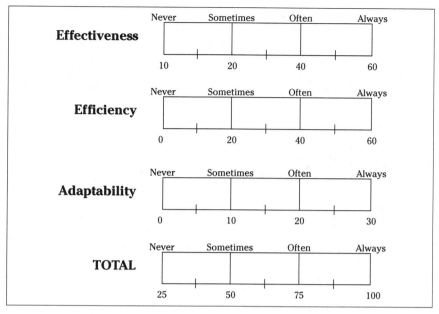

Figure 6–11. Measuring Your Customer Perceptions

WORKSHOP: PERCEIVING CUSTOMER VALUE

Developing a perceive capability is a continuous, never-ending process. Companies cannot ignore the customer if they want to attain market leadership. However, perceiving your customer cannot occur in a vacuum. A machine cannot accomplish it, only people can. This workshop focuses on building a set of skills within your workforce for perceiving customer needs, wants, and desires. Understanding each of these elements in relationship to your company strategy will help your workforce concentrate on those areas that will provide the greatest positive business impact. If you perceive your customers effectively, efficiently, and adaptively, you will provide value your customers will pay handsomely for, maintain a high customer retention rate, and achieve the profitability and market leadership you strive for.

Table 6–1. Perceiving Customer Value

Agenda
9:00 AM – 9:00 PM

Time Frames	Time Allotted	Workshop Exercises	Facilitator	Objectives
1. 9:00–10:00	60 min	Set the Stage	Patrick S.	Discuss the learning objectives and capture participants' expectations.
2. 10:00–10:30	30 min	Warm-Up Exercise	Chelsea K.	Identify customer needs, wants, and desires.
3. 10:30–10:45	15 min	Break		
4. 10:45–12:00	75 min	Identifying Customer Information That Will Help Achieve Our Business Strategies—*Team Exercise*	Stephen L.	Identify the information required for each business strategy to ensure success.
5. 12:00–1:00	60 min	Lunch		
6. 1:00–3:15	135 min	Identifying Customer Listening and Learning Systems That Will Capture Required Customer Information—*Team Exercise*	Chelsea K.	Identify the customer listening and learning systems that will capture the customer information needed to achieve our strategies.
7. 3:15–3:30	15 min	Break		
8. 3:30–4:00	30 min	Next Steps	Stephen L./ Chelsea K.	Identify necessary actions to ensure development of an effective customer listening and learning system.
9. 4:00–4:45	45 min	Workshop Debrief	Chelsea K./ Stephen L.	Capture and share the benefits of the workshop.
10. 7:00–9:00	120 min	Group Dinner		

Lead Facilitator: Patrick S.   Facilitators: Chelsea K./Stephen L.

In the Strategy Awareness Workshop in Chapter 2, a group of employees at a toy company explored business strategies. In this workshop we will use those same strategies to help illustrate how employees can identify the types of customer information and customer listening and learning systems that will help achieve them. Again, it is important to have the right mix of participants. The Assessing Readiness for Change Workshop in Chapter 3 will help you accomplish this.

The subject of customer information and how to perceive it is difficult to convey in a one-day workshop. Participants should prepare for this workshop by reading materials on customer needs, wants, and desires, as well as customer listening and learning systems, which should be provided by the company. Materials from this chapter or similar articles would be adequate. Table 6–1 is the agenda that was used for the toy company.

1. SET THE STAGE—60 MINUTES

The facilitator provides an overview of the workshop, its objectives, and, using Figure 2–8 as a guide, has participants introduce themselves. There are two objectives for this workshop. The first is to help participants understand customer information within a framework comprising needs, wants, and desires. The second is to identify the customer listening and learning systems best suited to capturing the required customer information. As in the previous workshops, the facilitator shows slides to convey these objectives.

Participants are required to review the reading materials in advance in order for the workshop to have maximum value. It is common knowledge that such readings aren't always reviewed. The solution to this problem is to engage the group in a discussion about the material by asking a few questions. This provides them with some of the information they need to participate in the rest of the workshop. At the toy company workshop the facilitator asked the group the following questions and engaged the group in a 20-minute discussion before proceeding to the warm-up exercise.

1. Why is customer information important to the success of a company?
2. What types of customer information are important to capture?
3. What framework can be used to categorize customer information?
4. How can customer information be captured?

2. WARM-UP EXERCISE—30 MINUTES

Warm-up exercises not only get participants relaxed but also can convey important information. This warm-up exercise helps participants understand the difference between customer needs, wants, and desires using quotations captured during various customer interactions. By using actual customer quotations participants deal with real events. If actual customer quotations cannot be obtained, true customer feelings can be approximated in constructed comments. Figure 6–12 presents the instructions used for the toy company workshop.

Identify Customer Needs, Wants, and Desires

1. The attached worksheet includes customer comments that have been captured from a variety of sources (complaints, ordering process, distributors, etc.).

2. In the next *15 minutes* identify each customer comment as either a need, want, or desire and your reasons why, recording your responses on the attached worksheet.

3. Be prepared to review your responses with the rest of the group.

Figure 6–12. Sample Slide: Warm-Up Exercise Instructions

Customer Comment	Need (N) Want (W) Desire (D)	Reason
"My daughter wants a toy all her friends have. Do you have any stock?"	N	It is an <u>immediate</u> requirement.
"If your catalogue were clearer and easier to read, you would have more customers."	D	This is a <u>future</u> requirement.
"Does this toy come in red?"	W	A special color is a <u>characteristic</u> of a paint color that was required immediately.
"I've been looking through your catalogue for two hours and I am having difficulty finding what I need."	N	Customer wants to order something <u>now</u> and is having difficulty.
"You should have more kinds of toys."	D	This is a <u>future</u> need.
"It would be great if someday I could order electronically via the Internet."	D	This represents a comment regarding a <u>future</u> desire.
"My son sprained his wrist and the doctor says he should play with a toy that exercises his wrist. Can you help?"	W	This is a <u>characteristic</u> of an actual ordering process.
"I have a large order from a distributor in Japan that must be delivered on time or I will lose the business."	N	It is an <u>immediate</u> requirement for the order, not something in the future.
"Is there an easier way for me to order this product?"	W	This is a <u>characteristic</u> of the ordering process.

Figure 6–13. Customer Needs, Wants, and Desires

The facilitator reads the instructions to the group and asks for any questions. After answering them she tells the group to start, writing the start and finish times on a flip chart for everyone to see. The facilitator announces when only five minutes remain and calls the group to order at the end of the fifteen-minute period. The facilitator then asks for volunteers to share their comments. Discussing disagreements helps participants to explain to their peers the differences between needs, wants, and desires, and reinforces the concepts to the rest of the group. The facilitator then writes down the answer that the group agrees to on an acetate overhead for everyone to see. Figure 6–13 is the completed worksheet for the toy company workshop.

3. BREAK—15 MINUTES

As with all breaks, participants should be reminded of the time the break starts and the time they are expected back in the meeting room. Facilitators can remind participants of the time and guide them back to meeting room as the end of the break approaches. The next exercise utilizes the reading materials. At the toy company workshop the facilitator announced the following to the group:

> Before we start the break I wanted to let everyone know that the next exercise will use the workshop reading in the first fifteen minutes of discussion with your team. If any of you would like to review the materials, this would be an excellent time to do so. If any of you do not have the materials, please see me and I will provide you with an extra copy.

4. IDENTIFYING CUSTOMER INFORMATION THAT WILL HELP ACHIEVE OUR BUSINESS STRATEGIES—75 MINUTES

The objective of this team exercise is for participants to identify the customer information that would help achieve each business strategy. The facilitator reviews the exercise instructions with the entire group using an overhead projector. Figure 6–14 contains the in-structions for this exercise.

Identifying Customer Information That Will Help Achieve Our Business Strategies

1. The team facilitator will lead the team in a *15-minute* discussion on listening and learning systems, using the reading materials as a reference.

2. For the next *30 minutes*, work as a team to identify the customer information that will help achieve your company's business strategies, recording your responses on the worksheet provided.

3. Be prepared to share your findings with the rest of the group in a *5–10 minute* presentation.

Figure 6–14. Sample Slide: Team Exercise Instructions

The facilitator reviews the instructions with the group and an-swers any questions. He reminds participants that when they break into teams the team facilitator will use the reading material as the basis for the 15-minute discussion and that they should take their materials with them. The team facilitators have extra copies just in case.

Facilitators are instructed that they should not assume that par-ticipants understand the concepts in the reading material just be-cause they have read them. The facilitator, therefore, uses basic ex-amples of customer information. At one workshop the facilitator asked the group, "If my objective were to make sure that we wanted a complete address and phone number for each customer who called our order entry department, what kinds of information would I ask for?" This type of question gets the team members to discuss the concepts of customer information. Before moving on, the facilitator addresses questions with the help of other partici-pants. During the next thirty minutes the facilitator lets the team discuss and complete the exercise, guiding them in the right direc-tion if needed.

When the participants return to the main meeting room the facil-itator asks each team to present its findings to the rest. After all the teams have completed their presentations, the facilitator spends about fifteen minutes discussing the findings from all the teams. In most cases there is a comment about how the information is going to be captured. At one workshop a participant said, "We will never be able to get that information from our customers." The facilitator responded:

> We should not be constrained about how we will capture the information. We will address the how in the next exercise. This exercise is to identify the types of information we need to achieve our business strategies. By being openminded we will do a better job of defining the types of information we need.

Figure 6–15 is a completed worksheet from one of the teams.

What customer information should we listen for and learn from our customers if we are to be successful at implementing our business strategies?

---

1. Understand our customers and translate their needs into new and innovative products and services.

- We have to categorize our customers between channel (K-mart, Wal-Mart, etc.) and final customer (consumers).

- We will have to understand what our customers (both channel and consumer) want, need, and desire.

- We must find ways of capturing their decision criteria when they make a purchase.

---

2. Provide products that are safe and nonviolent and that encourage creativity, expand minds, and promote physical development.

- We need to understand what our customers consider safe products.

- We need to have a better understanding of child development patterns, both physical and mental.

- We must use observation techniques to identify how our customers use our products.

---

3. Provide prompt and accurate delivery of all products and services.

- We need to find out what our customers' delivery requirements are.

- We need to measure our own delivery and accuracy processes.

- We need to assess the delivery process to determine what best-in-class practices are.

Figure 6–15. Team Exercise: Completed Worksheet

4. Provide marketplace with complete information about our products and services so existing and potential customers can make informed purchasing decisions.

• We need to find out what product and service information our customers use in making purchasing decisions.

• We need to look at ways we currently provide information and benchmark best-in-class companies.

• We need to identify the types of services that would provide value to our customers.

5. Build long-term relationships with our customers, who will continue to purchase products and services from our company.

• We need to find out what will attract customers to purchase additional products.

• We need to offer our customers those products and services that will result in repeat business.

• We need to find ways to provide our customers ongoing product/service information that maintains links with our company.

Figure 6–15. (continued)

5. LUNCH—60 MINUTES

Lunch can be used to reinforce learning points from the morning session. An excellent technique is to have each of the facilitators sit at a different table and pose a question to the group. At one workshop the question was, "Today there is an enormous amount of customer information. What information should you focus on? How do you go about capturing it?" The objective of this question is for participants to begin a dialogue that will prepare them for the afternoon exercise. The facilitator should have a copy of the reading at the table in case participants want to use it during the discussion points. At one workshop the facilitators decided to ask the following questions.

How do you determine if the customer information you are capturing has value and should be implemented? For example, let's assume that 150 customers in a survey requested an electronic interface with the company to find out about new products and order products. What do you do? How do you go about determining if an electronic means of communicating with your company is effective?

Open-ended questions that force people to discuss, analyze, and ask new questions help to dig into the underlying issues that face many businesses today.

Lunch is also a good opportunity to remind participants that the afternoon exercise will utilize the reading materials and that participants should spend a few minutes reviewing them. Facilitators can give copies to attendees who have forgotten theirs at the beginning of the lunch.

6. IDENTIFYING CUSTOMER LISTENING AND LEARNING SYSTEMS THAT WILL CAPTURE REQUIRED CUSTOMER INFORMATION—135 MINUTES

This exercise builds on the first. Participants will identify the listening and learning systems best suited to capturing the customer information identified in the first team exercise. The facilitator reviews the instructions with the entire group and answers any questions before the teams move to their break areas. Figure 6–16 is the instruction slide used for this exercise.

Identifying Customer Listening and Learning Systems That Will Capture Required Customer Information

1. The team facilitator will lead the team in a *30-minute* discussion on listening and learning systems, using the reading materials as a reference.

2. In the next *30 minutes* the team will identify at least three listening and learning systems and benefits that would help perceive the customer information required to achieve the company's business strategies (identified in the previous team exercise), recording responses on the worksheet provided.

3. The team will be prepared to share findings with the rest of the group in a *5–10 minute* presentation.

Figure 6–16. Sample Slide: Team Exercise Instructions

As in the previous exercise, the facilitator uses the reading materials as a basis for the thirty-minute discussion. Again, the facilitator doesn't assume that everyone has read the materials and asks the following questions to help get the discussion started:

1. What do we mean by a customer listening and learning system?

2. How do we learn from a listening system?

3. What are some categories of listening and learning systems?

4. What are some examples of listening and learning systems?

The facilitator reviews the previous team exercise because it will be used as part of this one. The facilitator stays more involved as the team members work to complete the worksheet, as this is such a new area for everyone. Figure 6–17 is a completed worksheet from one of the team meetings.

The Customer Listening and Learning Systems We Should Use to Capture Customer Information

1. Understand our customers and translate their needs into new and innovative products and services.

- Categorizing customers: Order entry systems and interviews during market research, ordering, and bill payment business activities.

- Customer wants, needs, and desires: Interviews, focus groups, listening posts, complaints capture, and other systems during all business activities.

- Identifying decision criteria: Observation, videotape, order entry, complaint systems during business activities that interact with the customers.

2. Provide products that are safe and nonviolent and that encourage creativity, expand minds, and promote physical development.

- Safe products: R&D, partnerships/alliances, trade shows, customer interviews, and complaint systems to identify safety needs and trends.

- Child development patterns: Observation, videotaping, and customer advisory and focus groups to understand child development patterns and needs.

- Identifying product use: Customer visits, complaints, observation, focus groups, and interviews to identify how customers use our products.

3. Provide prompt and accurate delivery of all products and services.

- Identifying customer delivery requirements: Order entry, focus groups, company tours, complaints to identify customer delivery requirements.

Figure 6–17. Team Exercise: Completed Worksheet

---

3. Provide prompt and accurate delivery of all products and services. *(continued)*

- Accuracy of our own delivery processes: Observation, videotape, records review of business activities that affect customer delivery.

- Identify best-in-class delivery process: Observation (benchmarking), R&D, trade shows, and partnerships to help us determine best of class.

---

4. Provide marketplace with complete information about our products and services so existing and potential customers can make informed purchasing decisions.

- Identifying required product and service information: Order entry, interviews, focus groups, and point-of-sale systems to find out what customers need.

- Best-in-class methods to provide information: Observation, videotape, trade shows, and focus groups to identify most effective means of delivery.

- Identifying services that provide customer value: Interviews, focus groups, observation, electronics, customer advisory boards to identify value services.

---

5. Build long-term relationships with our customers, who will continue to purchase products and services from our company.

- New methods to attract customers: Observation, interviews, focus groups, and other systems that identify attributes to attract new/existing customers.

- Products/Services that result in repeat business: Customer focus groups, surveys, company tours, and complaints to identify value services.

- Providing product/service information: Focus groups, surveys, complaints, R&D, and trade shows to identify information techniques.

Figure 6–17. (continued)

When the teams have completed their presentations, the facilitator engages the group in a discussion about customer listening and learning systems. He asks the group if anyone has been the object of a customer listening and learning system. At one workshop a participant answered:

> Yesterday I was at the local supermarket and an employee greeted customers inside the store. One young girl approached me and asked if I would mind answering a few brief questions about my shopping habits. During the next five minutes I answered a series of questions. Why did I shop at the store? How often, on average, did I shop at the store? What did I like about the store? Did I shop at other supermarkets, and how often? What changes would I make to the store that would make it more convenient for me?

Another participant pulled out *BusinessWeek* magazine and held up a page to show to the rest of the group. "I saw this ad in last week's *BusinessWeek*. Knowing I would be attending this workshop, I brought it with me to share with everyone." He said the advertisement talks about how Microsoft technology helped Hallmark Cards build a Web site that helped "collect valuable information to help provide their customers with ever-improving products and services." The facilitator then asked the participants why they thought Hallmark was doing this. He asked a number of other questions to help the group explore the reasons Hallmark is using this technique and the type of information that Hallmark is seeking to capture as a result of the Web site.

The facilitator should make sure that the participants have a sound understanding of the basic concepts of listening and learning systems. The experience of the facilitator will help in determining if more discussion is needed. If so, additional questions should be asked until the facilitator feels confident of the group's comprehension. It is not a matter of concern if the segment runs over in time; there is no hard rule that a session can't be extended. There is enough time between the end of the workshop and dinner to accommodate fifteen to thirty minutes of additional discussion if necessary.

7. BREAK—15 MINUTES

The afternoon break is always the most difficult to control. Facilitators will most probably be needed to ensure that the group reconvenes promptly. As at other breaks, the facilitator should announce the current time and the time the group is expected to return to the main meeting room.

8. NEXT STEPS—30 MINUTES

The next steps come right out of the previous exercise. The facilitator should refer to the completed worksheets and ask the group what they believe the next steps should be. At the toy company workshop, the facilitator asked participants to rank each of the strategies in order of importance and then to rank those that created the greatest area of opportunity. One participant said that providing prompt and accurate delivery of all products and services was currently the one strategy that the company needed to work on the most. "We need to measure where we are deficient and what our customers consider excellent delivery." The group agreed, and the facilitator wrote the strategy on the flip chart with a number one next to it. Another participant said, "Our marketing organization keeps telling us that safety and child development is an up-and-coming topic in the marketplace. If we don't capitalize on it we will miss the boat and sales will suffer." Again, the group agreed, and the facilitator wrote the strategy on the flip chart with a number two next to it. For the remainder of the thirty minutes the facilitator engaged the group in a discussion focusing on the specific listening and learning systems that most need to be implemented and on developing an action plan of tasks that need to be accomplished. By the end of the segment the group had a high-level plan that they could refer to in later meetings to implement customer listening and learning systems in their company.

9. WORKSHOP DEBRIEF—45 MINUTES

Like the other workshop debriefs, a short description of how the workshop helped can be captured in a grid. The procedure is to go around the room and have each participant think of a few words that represent the value the workshop provided them. It's acceptable for a participant to pass and then in another round provide input. The participants usually like this part of the session because it summarizes the day's output.

Listening to customers is very important.	Capturing customer needs is important to being successful.	The guidelines for selecting listening and learning systems can be very effective.	Identifying customer needs helps to determine immediate requirements.	Customer retention leads to improved revenues.
Capturing customer desires helps to plan a successful future.	Listening and learning systems can be categorized.	Customers express themselves by their needs, wants, and desires.	There are different ways to listen to customers.	Observation is a terrific technique to capture customer actions.
Wants reflect characteristics of the immediate customer requirements.	Think in terms of lifelong revenue versus one-off revenue.	Spending a day with the customer provides firsthand customer information.	Customer expectations must be captured and measured.	Perceive means to listen, analyze, and create enduring customer value.

Figure 6–18. Lessons Learned

10. GROUP DINNER—120 MINUTES

The group dinner is an excellent venue for reinforcing the lessons learned from the workshop in a relaxed atmosphere. Like the other workshop dinners, it helps for the facilitator to seed questions at the table to help stimulate discussion. At one workshop the participants explored the team exercise worksheets in more detail by asking each person at the table to comment on the value the team exercises had to each participant's daily responsibilities. Any other method that results in participants exploring new ground and learning new concepts is acceptable.

ENDNOTES

1. Data provided by Peter Garcia, director of customer satisfaction, Xerox Corporation, in interview with author, June 1997.

2. *Customer First Program,* Xerox Corporation training video.

3. Garcia, June 1997.

4. *Customer First Program.*

5. Interview with Kay Burkin, June 1997.

6. *Customer First Program.*

7. Ibid.

8. Thomas A. Stewart, "After All You've Done For Your Customers, Why Are They Still Not Happy," *Fortune,* February 5, 1996.

9. Bradley Gale, *Managing Customer Value,* New York: Free Press, 1994.

10. Jonathan Berry, "Database Marketing," *BusinessWeek,* September 5, 1996, p. 56.

11. Interview with Chris Martin, May 1997.

12. Richard C. Whitely, *The Customer-Driven Company,* Reading, MA: Addison-Wesley, 1991.

13. Interview with Hillary Rickard, April 1994.

14. Francis J. Gouillart and Frederick D. Sturdivant, "Spend a Day in the Life of Your Customers," *Harvard Business Review,* January/February 1994.

15. Don Peppers and Martha Rogers, *The One-to-One Future,* New York: Currency-Doubleday, 1993.

16. Thomas A. Stuart, "Welcome to the Revolution," *Fortune,* December 13, 1993, p. 66.

17. Berry, p. 56.

18. Ibid.

19. Whitely, 1991.

CHAPTER 7

YOUR MARKET AND THE COMPETITIVE ENVIRONMENT

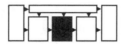

When we looked at trends in the power industry and at what our competitors were (and were not) doing, it changed how we viewed ourselves. Instead of being just another generating company, we created a gas and electricity commodity business with global potential.

James E. Rogers
President and Chief Executive Officer
Cinergy Corporation

Northwest Airlines, with $10 billion in sales, is the fourth largest airline in the United States. In the three-year period ending in 1992, it lost $1.8 billion as cheap ticket prices, together with higher fuel prices and a recession, devastated industry profits. By analyzing its markets and competitive environment, Northwest developed a strategy that resulted in a turnaround, with 1994 profits of over $300 million, 1995 profits of $400 million, and 1996 profits of $500 million.

Northwest was flying short routes of less than 750 miles from at least six hubs in the United States as well as transcontinental flights. The hubs were divided into two distinct markets. Group 1 hubs represented transcontinental markets and markets serviced from the hubs in Milwaukee, Washington State, and Seoul, Korea. Group 2 hubs represented markets served from hubs in Minneapolis, Detroit, and Memphis. Management looked at the competitive strength of the company in each of the markets as well as the profitability of each group. What it found is depicted in Figure 7–1.

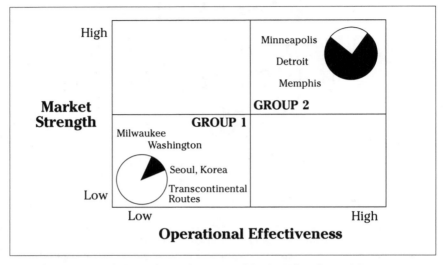

Figure 7–1. Northwest Airlines, Market Analysis Matrix—Major Hubs

Group 1 hubs competed vigorously with competitors yet were only minor players with slight market penetration. They were also very unprofitable. The circle representing Group 1 hubs is positioned in the lower left-hand corner of the matrix, where low operational effectiveness and poor market strength coincide. Hubs represented by Group 2 had little competition, customers were loyal, and the routes were highly profitable. Therefore, Group 2 hubs are positioned in the upper right-hand corner of the matrix, which represents a high level of operational effectiveness. The large shaded area of the circle for Group 2 signifies the large market share. The sizes of the circles in Group 1 and Group 2 hubs indicate the different market sizes. Group 1 had a smaller market size than Group 2.

New low-cost airlines like Nations Air, Reno, and Kiwi are among the seventy new airlines that have been launched since 1991. These airlines tripled their revenues to $1.4 billion in the two-year period ending in 1996. Because these new entrants were focusing on markets of less than 750 miles into densely populated areas, Northwest decided to concentrate on longer routes, many into sparsely populated areas. Looking at the strengths and weaknesses of Group 1 and Group 2 hubs made their decision much easier. It closed hubs in Group 1—Milwaukee, Washington, Seoul—and fortified the hubs in Group 2—Minneapolis, Detroit, Memphis—as well as expanded the Tokyo hub for the Far East market. With additional aircraft, more flights, and strong marketing clout, Northwest reduced its costs and increased profitability in these hubs. It also developed a successful alliance with KLM Royal Dutch Airlines in 1993 that by May 1997 resulted in a $150 million bottom line impact for KLM and $50 million for Northwest.

Northwest reduced its domestic-cost-per-available-seat-mile to eight cents, one of the lowest in the industry. Only Southwest, at about seven cents, is ahead of Northwest. Other major carriers increased their cost-per-available-seat-mile in 1994 over 1993; Northwest was the only carrier to actually reduce these costs. Its on-time performance beats competitors. It upgraded business-class service with improved food, more leg room between seats, personal video terminals, and easier ways to make reservations and to check in for departing flights. Northwest bet on its strengths. By perceiving the market and the competition, it was able to strengthen its existing markets and expand in selected areas.[1]

DETERMINING YOUR MARKET AND COMPETITIVE PROFILE

How well you perceive the direction your market is heading and the strengths and weaknesses of your competitors plays an important role in determining your future success because these signal future opportunities. If you fail to take advantage of them, others will, and your market share will erode and competitors pass you by. Figure 7–2 presents the results of a short questionnaire that a senior management team of a consumer goods company self-administered with the help of a consultant hired by the CEO. The questionnaire was designed to show the importance of perceiving markets and competitors.[2]

Table 7–1. Market and Competitor Profile Questionnaire

For each characteristic, rate the extent to which the statement is true about your organization, using the following scale:

1=not at all   2=to a small degree   3=to a modest degree   4=to a large degree   5=to a great degree

MARKETS

New markets are emerging every day and if we do not constantly search out new markets, our competitors will.

1.	We are sensitive to the local customs, preferences, and cultures of our customers.	**3**
2.	We know the markets we serve.	**2**
3.	We know the markets we don't serve.	**1**
4.	We are aware of emerging markets we could serve in the future.	**2**
5.	We know how to rapidly create new markets for our products and services.	**3**
6.	We are constantly scanning the world for information about new opportunities.	**2**
7.	We have an established global network of alliance partners that helps us search for new opportunities.	**1**
	Total your score	**14**
	Divide your score by 35	**40%**

COMPETITORS

We must respect our competitors and the industry we compete in.

1.	We know our industry and use strategies that influence our competitive supremacy.	**2**
2.	We identify, capture, and analyze our competitors' strengths, weaknesses, opportunities, and threats.	**3**
3.	We constantly monitor our industry and our competitors' activity.	**1**
4.	We know why customers are attracted to our competitors.	**2**
5.	We constantly strive to differentiate ourselves from our competitors, even if it is only in the services provided, and communicate this to our customers.	**2**
6.	We understand how quickly a noncompetitor can become a competitive threat.	**3**
7.	We are able to recognize the shifting boundaries of our industry.	**2**
	Total your score	**15**
	Divide your score by 35	**43%**

After asking each question the consultant asked a series of follow-up questions that helped the senior management team answer realistically. He tested their answers by looking for specific examples. Asked to rate the statement "We know the markets we serve," the group gave the company a 2—to a small degree. The group cited an example of a new product the company had launched in Europe. Because it was familiar with the market it was able to counter heavy competition and establish a local presence. However, group members felt the company was lucky in this instance because the product manager knew the market very well. The consultant asked if the example was a pattern or a one-time event. A one-time event would indicate a score of 1, a casual occurrence of 2. A continuing pattern of this type of company behavior would indicate a score of 3 to 5 depending on the degree of sensitivity. For this example the group felt that it was more of an exception than the rule. The consultant agreed that a score of 2 was reasonable.

The responses were then quantified with marketing data the consultant had compiled on the company that indicated growth areas, historical trends, and competitive information. He reviewed market share statistics with group members and asked if there was any correlation with their answers to the questionnaire. This added reality to the process. During the next twelve months the consultant worked with the organization to improve its perceive capability. He worked with the marketing department and other personnel to better understand the meaning and implications behind each of the questions. One manager told the consultant, "It's not just understanding what each question means but how to develop the organizational behaviors that will result in a perceive capability." Within a year market penetration began to improve and by the end of two years the company had gained 10 percent of the market and was taking advantage of its competitive strengths.

Because of the revolution in communications technology, companies both small and large have had to rapidly acclimate to the new global marketplace. Companies that compete in the microelectronics, biotechnology, telecommunications, utilities, civilian aircraft manufacturing, machine tools and robots, and computer hardware and software arenas are finding new markets in these fast-growing industries. Companies like Intel and GE can compete any-where in the world because of their sheer size, but small companies like Powerwave Technologies, Inc., which manufactures power am-plifiers for cellular phones, are also succeeding. Chosen as the fifth hottest-growing company by *BusinessWeek* and earning most of its revenues from overseas markets, Powerwave is selling its wares to BellSouth Cellular Corporation to boost U.S. sales. President Al-fonso G. Cordero's ten-year-old company is enjoying phenomenal growth in the past few years, with revenues and earnings increasing at the rate of 70 percent a year.[2]

The following four-step process shows how companies are taking advantage of new opportunities, expanding their markets, forming strategic alliances, and exploiting technology.

1. TAKING ADVANTAGE OF NEW OPPORTUNITIES

Companies need a perceive capability to identify new opportuni-ties, whether global or local, in their traditional market or one that has just opened up. For instance, companies like Cinergy, Southern, and Pennsylvania Power and Light (PP&L) are identifying new global opportunities in the newly deregulated utility industry.

Electric companies were always considered asset-based compa-nies because they are primarily producers of electricity delivered to customers through wires owned by the company. Today they are redefining their business. Deregulation is already in full swing in Eu-rope and in the United States the timetable is being moved up very quickly, says George Lewis, senior information specialist at PP&L. "The last two years have been very exciting. We are entering a new era within an industry that previously was very structured and is now marketing its products and services all over the world. We must prepare ourselves to better understand this marketplace and our new competitors."

In California residents can start choosing their electric supplier beginning January 1, 1998, with all customers having a choice by the beginning of 2000. In Pennsylvania one third of PP&L's one-third share of all customers can start choosing their electricity supplier every year for the next three years starting in 1998. Deregulation fever is impacting every part of the country as electric utilities are looking at new opportunities in three distinct business segments—as manufacturers, distributors, and marketers of electricity.

Automotive superstores are redefining the marketing of automobiles. New companies are starting that provide the technology for people to effectively browse the Internet. The Internet is enabling other companies and industries to market their products in entirely new and creative ways. In the one-year period ending April 1996, the capitalization of Internet-related companies like Yahoo! and Netscape rose from near zero to almost $10 billion. Champion Enterprises is catering to a whole new market of homeowners who can't afford on-site construction but can surely afford CEO Walter Young Jr.'s factory-built homes. He's exploited the opportunity and reinvented the housing industry.

2. EXPANDING YOUR MARKETS

Cinergy Corporation was formed in 1994 from the merger of the Cincinnati Gas & Electric Company and PSI Energy, Inc. It services 1.4 million electric customers and 440,000 gas customers in a 25,000-square-mile area of Ohio, Indiana, and Kentucky. Cinergy returns 15 percent to shareholders while the industry average is about 5 percent. Its market-to-book ratio of 2.04 is the highest among the 25 largest electric utilities. As a leader in the new electric industry, Cinergy is redefining the utility industry by expanding current markets.

James E. Rogers, president and CEO, views himself as an entrepreneur and is looking at the electric utility business with a new lens and a thirst for creating innovative products and services that will make his company a leader in the twenty-first century.

> We have organized into four separate business units: Energy Commodities; Energy Delivery; Energy Services; and International. We didn't reshuffle utility functions, but created new businesses. Energy Services is the marketing of end-use products and services to customers and will operate in increasingly competitive markets, while Energy Delivery—the operation of the pipes and wires—will remain essentially a regulated, asset-based business.

People who live in New Hampshire and want to participate in a customer choice program can buy their electricity from Cinergy even though they are separated by a thousand miles. The actual electricity is manufactured by Ontario Hydro and distributed through the power grids of the New Hampshire Power Company. Consumers purchase the electricity through a customer choice company called Wheeled Electric. Cinergy services customers as far east as the U.S. Military Academy at West Point, in New York State. It supplies PSG Industries and Wal-Mart in Illinois and has even added customers in Idaho and Washington State. Breaking traditional vertically integrated utilities into the three components of the value chain—manufacturer, deliverer, and marketer of electricity—enables companies like Cinergy to expand their markets.

Today global markets are within reach of almost every company, both large and small. We've seen how small companies such as Powerwave Technologies compete globally. The explosive growth in the Far East is opening up tremendous opportunities for large companies as well. Companies such as Raytheon, which competes in the construction industry, Intel in electronics, and Motorola in manufacturing, are all enjoying enormous growth as expansion into global markets opens up tremendous opportunities.

3. FORMING STRATEGIC ALLIANCES

The new global marketplace provides many opportunities to form new business relationships with companies around the globe. These relationships are strategic because such companies better understand their own regional markets and the customers within them. AT&T has partnered with sixteen companies in thirty-one countries. Deutsche Telecom, France Telecom, and Sprint have formed a joint venture called Global One. Microsoft is investing $1 billion in the cable company Comsat as a way to push the development of high-speed Internet access and interactive television. BMW has partnered with Chrysler to build shared engines in Brazil. CNN has partnered with NBC Television. Telephone companies are partnering with computer companies. Computer companies are partnering with other companies where opportunities exist. Everyone is joining in the dance because it makes good business sense.

When Cinergy purchased a stake in the English electric utility Midlands Electricity, it did so for a variety of reasons. Deregulation is moving along more quickly in the UK than in the United States. Cinergy's involvement in the UK helps it perceive these new markets and learn many lessons that can be transferred to the U.S. market. PP&L's alliances through its subsidiary, PMDC, enable it to pursue market opportunities that it otherwise would not be able to pursue. Through a consortium, PP&L is building hydroelectric plants in Portugal, Spain, and Peru. In the telecommunications industry the alliance between British Telecom and Sprint enables both companies to leverage their resources and pursue new market opportunities by better understanding each other's markets.

Figure 7–2 shows how the new electronic marketplace and the computing, communications, and content industries are converging.

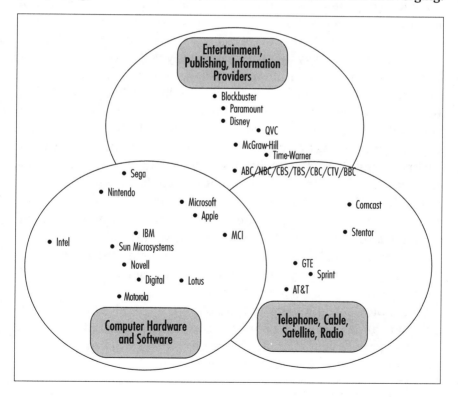

Figure 7–2. The Convergence of the Electronic Marketplace

Adapted from Don Tapscott, *The Digital Economy,* New York: McGraw Hill, 1997, p. 220.

4. EXPLOITING TECHNOLOGY TO CREATE NEW PRODUCTS AND SERVICES

Everyone is touched by technology today. Every new car, computer, telephone, and appliance includes technology developed within the last year and the pace of change is so quick that a product you buy today will be outdated within a year. Technology makes our lives simpler and enables us to enjoy product features, attributes, and services never before imaginable. It has even affected the way electricity is delivered to our homes and businesses.

Cinergy is exploring new technologies that can be exploited to generate new products and services in its industry. The electric and gas company formed a joint venture with Trigen Energy Corporation, a French-owned company that is using the world's most advanced cogeneration and trigeneration technology to win major industrial customers, hospitals, and universities. Trigen has developed a technology that generates local power for creating district heating and cooling systems. Because they will have to stop using freon-based systems within a few years, municipalities, hospitals, airports, universities, and industrial complexes will have to find alternative methods for cooling and heating. Trigen has developed a self-contained system that uses high-powered chilled water and high-powered steam to cool and heat from a centralized system. Cinergy's first use of this technology will be a joint project for a centralized chilled-water air-conditioning system for downtown Cincinnati. Elizabeth K. Lanier, vice president and chief of staff at Cinergy, calls this "cannibalization strategy" a means to offer new energy alternatives to customers. "We realize that we are offering our customers an alternative that will reduce or eliminate the need to buy electricity from Cinergy, but we have to offer our customers an alternative or else our competitors will."

Technological innovation is enabling the development of new products and markets. It's hard to predict the future but if the past few years are any indication, the next five years will bring yet more innovations that will change the way we live.

PERCEIVING THE COMPETITIVE ENVIRONMENT

Today competitors are springing up so quickly that time to market is now measured in months instead of years. There are many techniques to use. One simple yet effective technique focuses on three activities:

1. Identifying your competitors.
2. Analyzing their strengths and weaknesses.
3. Comparing their competitive profiles.

Competitors are not always who you think they are. The U.S. Postal Service thought it had a monopoly on mail delivery until Federal Express came along and showed the world how to deliver mail overnight. The cable television companies never thought of the phone companies as competitors. The electric companies always thought they had a monopoly on their markets until they found a way to sell electricity across state lines. When AT&T wanted to enter the cellular phone market it was faced with having to build an infrastructure. Its purchase of McCaw not only eliminated an existing threat but provided it with an immediate electronic infrastructure. Identifying current and potential competitors is not a difficult process, although it takes resources and time. This should not be a one-time event but an ongoing process that provides the intelligence to help plan your future. Where to look to identify competitors and what to look for is summarized in Figure 7–3.

Existing customers are an excellent source for finding out about competitors. Any effective salesperson should be able to sense if a competitor is moving in on her territory. If sales are dropping, ask your customers why. They may be buying from another competitor. They may have reengineered their internal manufacturing processes and no longer require your product. This is why companies who sell to the manufacturing industry try to develop relationships with the engineering and new product development staff. In this way they can help design in their own products and design out their competitors' products. Sometimes management reorganization can affect the buying patterns of a company. A senior vice president or department manager may have a connection with another company. Customers will probably tell you if they are using another competitor or just aren't using your product or service.

Where to Look	What to Look For
Customers	Sales Trends, New Products, New Management
Employees	Information, New Trends, Research Activity
Publications	Competitors' Ads, Changes in Ads, New Names
Trade Shows	New Products, New Faces, New Concepts
University Research	Existing Competitors, New Competitors, New Ideas
Consortiums	New Research, Industry Activity, Potential Competitors

Figure 7–3. How to Identify Competitors: A Checklist

Management should pay attention to the knowledge of the company's employees. They are one of the best sources of activity in the competitive marketplace because they have the knowledge and experience to provide insight on activities that affect your competitiveness. For instance, when a manufacturer of refrigeration equipment was losing market share it hired an outside consulting firm to help discover why. Three months later, at a cost of over $100,000, a report was issued that didn't provide much insight. Then an assembly worker wrote a letter to the president telling him that his wife shopped at a local supermarket where one of the company products was used to refrigerate vegetables. At regular intervals a fine spray of cold water covered not only the vegetables but also the shoppers. As a consequence of the faulty equipment, the supermarket was losing business. This example shows that solutions to problems are sometimes closer than you think. You hire employees for their skills and experience; don't ignore them as a source of information about industry activity. Also, encourage them to join industry organizations and subscribe to industry publications because the more they know, the more they will be able to help you.

Corporate publications are excellent places to identify potential threats. Companies love to tell consumers what they are doing. Trade magazines and weekly publications are also excellent resources for identifying activities of existing and new competitors. When leafing through publications, look for new competitor advertisements. These might indicate new strategies that are affecting the way they market their products. Look for advertisements from companies you have never seen before and keep track of them. They could be your next major competitors. Finally, look for research articles that identify how innovations in science and technology are being applied in your industry.

The trade show is an excellent venue for finding out what is happening in your industry. It's the place where everybody advertises and the latest and greatest is shown to the consumer. Meet with personnel who will be going to the trade show and assign people different kinds of information to capture. Are there new faces you haven't seen before? Do you see familiar faces with new products? Are there any new networking groups your company can join?

University research is a good indicator of developments in the marketplace. Many new ideas germinate from research conducted by academics at leading universities. This is why relationships with universities are so important. Xerox Corporation and Fuji Xerox established the Xerox Distinguished Professorship in Knowledge at the University of California at Berkeley, Walter A. Haas School of Business with a million-dollar grant in May 1997. This is the first-ever professorship dedicated to the study of knowledge and its impact on business. In speaking about the professorship, Dan Holtshouse, director of knowledge work initiatives and corporate business strategy at Xerox Corporation said:

> Businesses today are dependent more than ever for a constant supply of new knowledge to create the innovative products and services needed to grow and be competitive. The university environment, with its rich diversity of disciplines in technology, cognitive science, and social/behavior studies can bring a rigorous approach to understanding the underlying complex processes in knowledge creating environments. We call

this management *for* knowledge and it deals with the *creation* of *new* knowledge.

A tool manufacturer uses faculty at selected universities for research and development. This opens up a communication channel with leading metallurgic scientists who can help identify new materials or new processes for cutting, forming, and heat-treating metal.

Find out if any of your competitors have relationships with universities. This will help you to identify some appropriate institutions to associate with.

Consortia offer a double return. Not only are they an excellent vehicle for identifying potential competitors, they also are vehicles for identifying new products and services that will help rejuvenate your industry. Thirty-five steel companies from the International Iron and Steel Institute are part of a $20 million project to design an ultralight car. Germany's Porsche Engineering Services is doing the design work and steelmakers are funding the venture. Many consortia research new ideas and concepts and are brokered through universities. Look for consortia in your industry and investigate them thoroughly. If you can't find one start one of your own. Do your competitors belong to consortia? If any of your known competitors are consortium members, you can be assured they are investigating new ideas and concepts. Find out which consortia they belong to and join the bandwagon. Don't forget to look at organizations, research reports, and conferences. These are good places to investigate and identify competitor activity.

BENCHMARKING YOUR COMPETITORS

Every four years athletes set new Olympic records. During the intervening years athletes train endlessly practicing what the Japanese call *donastru*—striving to be the best of the best. Their goal is to set new records for others to break. Companies also strive to be the best through a process called *benchmarking*. Companies feel that competitive advantage is only a few short steps away if they can perceive best practices and replicate them in their own company. Andersen Consulting boasts a global best-practices database that can help clients become the best of the best.

The art of benchmarking was born at Xerox in the early 1980s and documented by Robert Camp in the bestseller *Benchmarking: The Search for Industry Best Practices That Lead to Superior Performance.* Companies were on a benchmarking craze but soon found that copying others doesn't make one a market leader. "Nothing remains a best practice for very long; you either change or quickly fall behind," says Frederick W. Smith, chairman of Federal Express. At best, benchmarking allows you to catch up. The mistake companies make is thinking that a business process can be followed like a recipe. It is, however, much more complicated because business processes are implemented by individuals in an organizational culture; both are always almost impossible to copy.

What follows is a high-level overview of benchmarking and how I have used it to help companies create superior customer value. I like to define benchmarking as a process that sparks new ideas and insights (see Figure 7–4).

Gaining insight and knowledge of how other organizations perform specific processes in order to spark new ideas that create superior customer value.

Figure 7–4. Benchmarking Redefined

In addition, the knowledge gained is used to provide new customer value.

Benchmarking in its simplest form is a three-step process. Step one is to plan for success. You define the objectives, harness the resources, identify potential companies to benchmark, and develop the plan. Step two of the process is to collect data. In this phase you identify methods to use, set up appointments with companies to visit, and collect and summarize the data. The final step is to analyze the data. Here you review the objectives, align the findings, prioritize the results, and prepare the final report. To properly plan your benchmarking effort you first need to decide on your objective. You can then use benchmarking to get to know yourself better, understand your competitors, gain knowledge learned by others, and improve your organizational capability. A sample of processes, activities, and measurements you can benchmark is shown in Figure 7–5.

Customer Service	Plant Production	Layout

Customer Service
- On-time delivery
- Customer satisfaction index
- Billing errors
- Abandonment rate of incoming calls
- Order fulfillment cycle time
- Customer complaints vs. total orders (%, #)
- Backorders ($, %, time)
- Promised delivery time vs. actual delivery time
- Customer defection rate vs. industry standard

Production/Inventory Management
(Individual and across supply chain)
- Inventory replenishment time
- Excess inventory
- Order backlog
- Inventory accuracy
- Cycle counts

Organizational Effectiveness Measures
- Organizational levels
- Empowerment capability
- Management layers
- Training dollars as percent of sales
- Training time per employee
- Number of active teams

Plant Production
- Yield (e.g., raw material to finished steel)
- Safety record (lost time due to accidents)
- Efficiency/Productivity/Utilization
- BTU/Ton
- Environment waste per 1K labor hours

Financial
- Sales revenue
- Operating income
- ROA
- ROI
- ROE
- Sales growth
- Sales $/Employee (total sales, direct labor)
- S, G, & A as percent of sales
- Shareholders growth

Quality
- Defects/1,000
- Customer complaints
- Service cost as percent of sales
- Warranty costs

Layout
- Travel distance between workstations
- Repeat visits to a process
- Material handling: cost, people
- Space for growth

Financial
- Lead time vs. total processing time
- Queue/backlog time
- Value added vs. non-value added
- Direct vs. indirect labor
- Overtime as percent of total hours

Supply Chain Management
- Number of suppliers
- Delivery performance/Supplier
- Rejected lots/Parts incoming/Supplier
- Supplier certification program
- JIT delivery (synchronized schedules)
- Paperless ordering systems
- Number of information management systems processing complementary data

Figure 7–5. Sample Processes, Activities, and Measurements

The four types of benchmarking are internal, competitive, functional, and generic. Following is brief description of each.

1. INTERNAL BENCHMARKING—KNOW YOURSELF BETTER

Companies that compete in national or global markets usually have several physical locations, some of which perform the same functions and processes. Understanding how different divisions, manufacturing plants, and business offices perform particular processes can help improve operating efficiencies. For example, Motorola, with plants all over the world, constantly benchmarks specific functions or processes so it can get to know itself better. When a department store chain in the South was experiencing a downturn in telephone sales it decided to perform an internal benchmark. The vice president of sales received numerous letters from customers about poor telephone service, so he organized a team to benchmark the telephone sales process. As a result of the effort the telephone process was completely redesigned for quicker response and new ordering methods were introduced—kiosks, Internet, and personalized shopping valets. Within six months sales improved by 40 percent. Customer satisfaction improved dramatically and the benchmarking team was rewarded with a one-week Caribbean vacation.

2. COMPETITIVE BENCHMARKING—UNDERSTAND YOUR INDUSTRY

Myopic business practices are a sure way to end a flourishing business. Therefore, you should have a better understanding of how your industry is performing in order to survive and flourish. Competitive benchmarking can help you compare advantages and disadvantages. Today there are no secrets but many ways to uncover what practices are used at your competitors. Third parties who represent you anonymously, vendors, consultants, and publications are some of the ways management can find out the happenings at its competitors. The president of a mid-size consulting firm purchases one share each of his competitors' stock so he can receive all their shareholder reports.

3. FUNCTIONAL BENCHMARKING—GAIN KNOWLEDGE LEARNED BY OTHERS

Everyone tends to focus on the activities of competitors to improve a specific process. This is not the only course of action available to you. Companies that want to improve their logistics operations, for example, can find a number of companies that would be happy to share their knowledge with others. Federal Express and L. L. Bean constantly entertain requests from companies all over the world. Publications are filled with stories of how companies excel and therefore it is not difficult to uncover possible sources. Functional benchmarking is more accessible than competitive benchmarking because companies are more comfortable sharing data with someone who isn't a threat.

4. GENERIC BENCHMARKING—IMPROVE YOUR ORGANIZATIONAL CAPABILITY

Certain processes are industry independent. Order entry, for example, is a critical process in every business. Regardless of your industry you can learn about the order entry process from bench-marking companies in other industries. Generic benchmarking can help fuel innovative thinking. An insightful senior manager at a pharmaceutical firm sent the director of logistics to a major bank to investigate check-clearing procedures. The director viewed this as a waste of time but during his visit he was shown how the bank sorted 400 bills per minute using a digitized process that determined if the bill was a good bill, a mutilated bill, or a counterfeit bill. This process intrigued the director because he had a similar identification prob-lem sorting packages in the packaging department that currently had a maximum speed of 100 packages per minute. The wasteful trip turned out to be a gold mine for the pharmaceutical company.[3] Generic benchmarking opens up the mind to observe, listen, and learn from others, and helps to stimulate the creative juices.

ANALYZING COMPETITORS' STRENGTHS AND WEAKNESSES

Consumers look for the best value for their money. Value, which once was defined by price, is today defined by a new set of capabil-ities that include speed, consistency, acuity, agility, and innovation. Each capability represents a different dimension of customer value. By analyzing your competitors' strengths and weaknesses in each of these five capabilities you will be able to determine your relative position in the competitive marketplace.[4]

1. SPEED

We all know the story of the tortoise and the hare. We also have heard that it is not how hard you work but how smart you work. In today's competitive marketplace it's the combination of speed and wit that will make you a market leader. Being first to market is great, but, if no one will buy your product, being first is the same as being last. Coca-Cola got to market early with its new version of Coke. It wanted to regain the market share Pepsi had grabbed, but forgot to ask the customers if they liked the product. "New" Coke was a dis-mal failure even though it got to market very quickly. The business benefit of speed is that it allows companies to recover their investment more quickly. Therefore, a new measurement called *concept* to cash (the time it takes from conceiving an idea until cash flows into the company as a result of sales) allows a company to determine the actual business benefit of speed.

2. CONSISTENCY

Consistency used to be measured on the factory floor as a quality metric. Today we have moved this measure into the hands of the customer and have included service in the formula. The overnight letter and package business is booming, yet Federal Express is always the winner because it combines consistent quality—always getting the package to the addressee on time as promised—with a level of service that has no equal.

3. ACUITY

The ability to identify customer needs, wants, and desires depends on listening and learning systems that continuously monitor the competitive landscape. Sony has acuity and is brilliant at it. For example, Sony supplies toddler classrooms with toys so it can observe how children play as well as their needs and wants. The company doesn't sit back and wait for the market to define its needs; it seeks them out.

4. AGILITY

In today's marketplace change is a reality and those companies that can be agile and harness the necessary skills, capabilities, and knowledge to profitably respond will be successful. The days of rigid market boundaries and rules of market entry are over. The global marketplace is open to anyone and those who thrive on the change and uncertainty that prevail will achieve success. Companies like Motorola, Texas Instruments, and GE are agile companies that lead the way for others to learn and profit from. They train and motivate their employees to be empowered, responsible leaders. They instill a set of business behaviors that help employees focus on the key business issues needed to achieve market success. Organizations with these characteristics are true market leaders and agile companies.

5. INNOVATION

The ability to innovate value is one that few companies have. Sony created the electronic piano as a result of this ability. 3M, with its 60,000-plus products, creates a culture of innovation in the organization by encouraging its employees to spend creative time each day. It also sets performance goals that drive innovation. Thirty percent of revenue must be derived from new products introduced within the last four years. Hewlett Packard has also demonstrated innovation by generating 50 percent of its revenues from products developed during the last two years.

The process of perceiving the competitive landscape by measuring a competitor's five customer focus capabilities consists of three basic steps. The first step is to gather data about your competitors. The second step is to summarize your findings. The final step consists of analyzing your results. All these steps are explored in the workshop for this chapter. You must constantly monitor your market and competitive environment along the five customer focus capabilities if you want to compete successfully. Those companies that do it well will succeed and enjoy the benefits of market success.

When Ford manufactured the Edsel, it gathered information from customers and noncustomers. Market research indicated that the public wanted a bigger car. Instead of finding out exactly what the consumer wanted in a big car, Ford simply designed the big car they thought the consumer would like. Ford guessed wrong! In contrast, it solicited the input of customers before building the Taurus, knowing that the information would be used to create customer value. It collected detailed information about color, style, configuration, and a host of other automobile attributes that customers wanted. Ford incorporated almost 5,000 customer suggestions in the original Taurus and profited handsomely because of it.

Companies like Hertz, Ritz Carlton, and Disney have developed an extremely effective perceive capability. Others can learn from these market leaders and make it a practice to understand, embrace, and constantly perceive their customers, markets, and competitors.

WORKSHOP: PERCEIVING THE COMPETITIVE LANDSCAPE

This workshop is most effective for a project team about to begin a competitive analysis of competitors' customer focus capabilities. It can also be used as a general awareness-builder for employees. Reading materials that cover concepts from this chapter are distributed in advance to help participants understand the basic principles and be better prepared for the workshop. The company's competitive information is an important element of this exercise. If the company has not conducted competitive analysis projects recently, this would be a good time to obtain information about each of its major competitors. Table 7–2 is the agenda for a workshop conducted at a construction fastener company.

Table 7–2. Perceiving the Competitive Landscape

Agenda
9:00 AM – 9:00 PM

Time Frames	Time Allotted	Workshop Exercises	Facilitator	Objectives
1. 9:00–10:00	60 min	Set the Stage	Glen S.	Discuss the learning objectives and capture participants' expectations.
2. 10:00–10:30	30 min	Warm-Up Exercise	Kevin P.	Explore the meaning of each of the customer focus capabilities.
3. 10:30–10:45	15 min	Break		
4. 10:45–12:15	90 min	Perceiving Competitors' Customer Focus Capabilities—Team Exercise	Julie P.	Complete customer focus capabilities questionnaires for competitors.
5. 12:15–1:15	60 min	Lunch		
6. 1:15–4:30	195 min	Assessing Competitors' Customer Focus—Capabilities—Team Exercise (includinging 15-min break)	Kevin T.	Summarize competitors' customer focus capabilities and analyze data to determine market opportunities.
7. 4:30–5:00	30 min	Next Steps	Kevin T./	Identify necessary actions to ensure development of an effective customer focus capabilities.
8. 5:00–5:45	45 min	Workshop Debrief	Julie P./ Kevin T.	Capture and share the benefits of the workshop with colleagues.
9. 7:00–9:00	120 min	Group Dinner		

Lead Facilitator: Glen S.   Facilitators: Julie P./Kevin T.

1. SET THE STAGE—60 MINUTES

The facilitator provides an overview of the workshop, its objectives, and has participants introduce themselves. The objective of this workshop is for the participants to understand the customer focus capabilities and learn how to apply them in a competitive analysis. The facilitator shows a slide similar to the ones used in the previous workshops to convey the main learning points of the workshop.

2. WARM-UP EXERCISE—30 MINUTES

The ideas may be new to many of the participants. The warm-up exercise can help them with new vocabulary and concepts. At a workshop for a construction fastener company located in the Southwest, the senior vice president was concerned that his company was not focused enough on customers and wanted to understand better how his competitors were performing in that area. These ideas were very new to the organization and especially the project team that was assigned the responsibility of performing the competitive analysis, so a customer focus capability workshop was held exclusively for the team. To help team members become familiar with the concepts, the facilitator used an LCD panel to display a 5 x 4 grid. On the top line of the grid were the five customer focus capabilities. Under each capability were three boxes. The facilitator asked each participant to choose a few words that represented the capability and typed each phrase identified. When all the grids were filled in the facilitator went around the room again and asked the participants to identify a particular event that illustrated the phrase. This helped the participants correlate each phrase with an event (see Figure 7–6).

3. BREAK—15 MINUTES

As with all breaks, the facilitator should remind the participants of the time the break starts and the time they are expected back in the meeting room. Facilitators can remind participants of the time and guide them back to meeting room as the end of the break approaches.

SPEED	CONSISTENCY	ACUITY	AGILITY	INNOVATION
Doing your job quickly.	Continually doing the same thing well.	Sensing what is needed.	Being flexible.	Being clever.
Bringing products to market quickly.	Quality/ Quality/ Quality.	Anticipating the future.	Adapting to unforeseen situations.	Being creative.
Responding to customer needs quickly.	Doing the right things intuitively.	Having a sixth sense.	Being able to do many things at the same time.	Always thinking about new ways to do things.

Figure 7–6. Customer Focus Capabilities: Warm-Up Exercise

4. PERCEIVING COMPETITORS' CUSTOMER FOCUS CAPABILITIES—90 MINUTES

The objective of this team exercise is for participants to complete customer focus capability questionnaires about the company's major competitors. In the fastener company workshop the facilitator explained to the group that a consulting firm had been hired the previous year to perform a competitive analysis but that it did not address customer focus capabilities directly. The consultants did, however, conduct enough customer interviews to draw some conclusions.

The facilitator reminds the group that this exercise is meant to identify the customer focus capabilities of each of the competitors and determine the degree of competency for each. After lunch the team exercise will focus on how to analyze the data. Figure 7–7 is the instruction slide used for the team exercise.

The team facilitators should be briefed in advance and have read all the consultant reports. At the fastener company the facilitators even completed their version of the questionnaire so they would be better able to help their teams. The facilitators have to be careful not to give the teams answers but lead them as they work through the ninety minutes assigned to this segment of the exercise. For instance, one team at the fastener company workshop was having difficulty assessing acuity capability and the facilitator had to show them where the information could be found in the consultant's report. (This illustrates another reason why the team facilitators need to review materials before the workshop.)

Perceiving Competitors' Customer Focus Capabilities

1. The facilitator will assign participants to each of the three teams.

2. For the next *90 minutes* each team will review the consultant report for the competitors that the facilitator assigns. Ten competitors as well as our own company were evaluated by the consulting firm. Two teams will be assigned four companies and one team will be assigned three.

3. After reviewing the consultant reports the team will complete a Customer Focus Capability Questionnaire for each competitor and record the scores on the summary table provided.

4. The teams will return to the main meeting room prepared to review their findings with the rest of the group in a *5–10-minute* presentation.

Figure 7–7. Sample Slide: Team Exercise Instructions

Each team uses the questionnaire shown in Table 7–3 to record its collective assessment and records each competitor's score on the summary table. When the teams have completed their assessments they return to the main meeting room and present their findings. At the fastener company one of the facilitators recorded each team's assessments on a master summary table and showed it to the group using the computer display. Table 7–3 is the summary table for all the competitors and the fastener company.

At the fastener company, workshop participants recorded their data on electronic spreadsheets. This was done so the lead facilitator could sort all the data electronically by total score so the competitor with the highest total score would be first and the competitor with the lowest would be last (see Table 7–4).

Table 7–3. Competitive Analysis: Customer Focus Capabilities Summary Table

CAPABILITY	DESCRIPTION	METRIC	FASTENER FIRM	A	B	C	D	E	F	G	H	I	J
Speed	Rate at which an organization profitably responds to customer or market demands.	Concept to cash	7	5	5	11	9	5	11	9	5	3	11
Consistency	Development and delivery of a product/service that continuously satisfies customers.	Customer satisfaction	5	5	9	13	5	13	5	3	7	5	9
Acuity	Ability to perceive the competitive environment and identify customer's wants, needs, and desires.	Effective listening systems/processes	9	6	5	4	9	3	7	11	3	5	9
Agility	Flexibility with which an organization can respond to changing market conditions.	Organizational responsiveness	5	3	3	3	4	5	5	3	3	3	3
Innovation	Ability to generate new ideas that produce value to customers.	New product/select revenue as a percent of total product/service revenue	9	3	9	5	13	5	11	9	7	3	5
		TOTALS	35	22	31	36	40	31	39	35	25	19	37

Table 7–4. Customer Focus Capabilities Summary Table

(Sorted by Total Score)						
	Total Score	**Speed**	**Consistency**	**Acuity**	**Agility**	**Innovation**
D	40	9	5	9	4	**13**
F	39	**11**	5	7	**5**	11
J	37	**11**	9	9	3	5
C	36	**11**	**13**	4	3	5
Your Company	35	7	5	9	**5**	9
G	35	9	3	**11**	3	9
B	31	5	9	5	3	9
E	31	5	**13**	3	**5**	5
H	25	5	7	3	3	7
A	22	5	5	6	3	3
I	19	3	5	5	3	3

The facilitator asked the group for initial observations. One individual said, "It's obvious from the data that our company is fifth on the list based on total scores. The second thing I see is that our company didn't rank first in any capability." The facilitator told the group that the exercise after lunch would help identify the specific gaps between the fastener company and its competitors.

5. LUNCH—60 MINUTES

Adding learning to the lunch hour adds to the value of the workshop. At the fastener company workshop the facilitator at each table asked, "As consumers, what are some examples that you have seen where companies have exhibited any of the five customer focus capabilities?" As each person provided examples, the facilitator recorded them onto a formatted overhead slide. If participants had difficulty identifying examples the facilitator helped by providing personal examples from a list prepared prior to the workshop.

6. ASSESSING COMPETITORS' CUSTOMER FOCUS CAPABILITIES—195 MINUTES

This exercise helps the participants understand how to analyze the data they developed in the first team exercise. To begin, the facilitator shows the group the Customer Focus Capabilities Summary Table from the previous exercise. At the fastener company, the facilitator reminded the group that when he showed the summary scores at the end of the last team exercise it was hard to analyze the data because, as one individual said, "There's too many numbers on the page." The facilitator then showed a slide that displayed the data of companies A and B using a graphic technique called a spider chart (see Figure 7–8). A spider chart, sometimes called a radar chart, plots data from a central point along as many radii as you need, rather like spokes from the hub of a wheel. The points are then joined, so that the resulting area can be identified and compared with far greater immediacy and ease than other graphs allow.

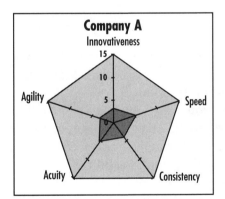
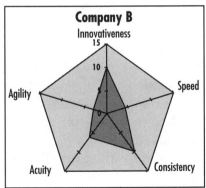

Figure 7–8. Spider Diagram Comparison Technique

The facilitator explains that the objective of the next team exercise is to analyze the data collected in the first team exercise, using the spider chart technique to represent the data. At the fastener company each team was supplied with a laptop computer and the software required to prepare the spider diagrams. (Microsoft Excel or any electronic spreadsheet program will suffice. If computers are not available the participants can draw the spider charts as best they can by hand.) Facilitators should know how to use the software application so participants need not worry if they don't have the skill. The facilitator then reviews the team exercise instructions with the group (see Figure 7–9).

Perceiving Competitors' Customer Focus Capabilities

1. Participants will work in the same teams as before.

2. For the next *60 minutes* each team will prepare spider charts for each of the competitors using the data from the Summary Table developed in the first team exercise.

3. After that, each team will summarize its analysis of the data for *60 minutes.*

4. Teams return to the main meeting room prepared to review their results with the rest of the group in a *5–10-minute* presentation.

Figure 7–9. Sample Slide: Team Exercise Instructions

The facilitator should mention to the group that break time is included in the three hours allotted to this exercise. Each team should choose a fifteen-minute period to break.

At the workshop at the fastener company, only the team facilitators had the skills to prepare the spider charts. They helped the team prepare them by coaching them through the process, not by actually doing the work. This is why a full hour is spent on this portion of the exercise—to allow the teams to practice the skill.

The teams return to the main meeting room to present their findings. While this is going on the lead facilitator is merging the three electronic files that he received from each of the teams. After the presentations the lead facilitator displays a consolidated electronic file containing all the spider diagrams via a computer overhead display. Figure 7–10 shows the spider diagrams from the fastener company workshop.

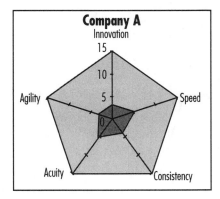

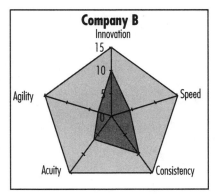

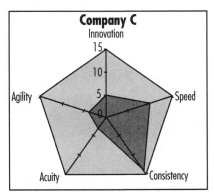

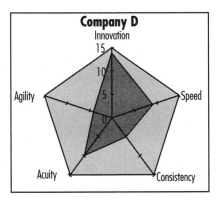

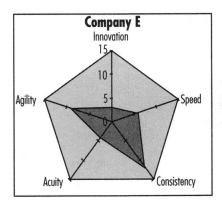

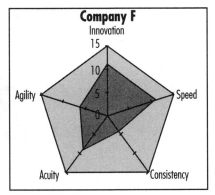

Figure 7–10. Spider Diagrams

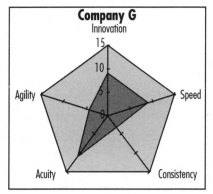

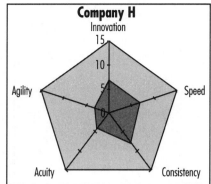

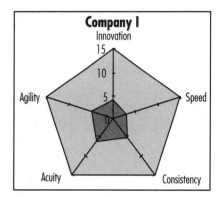

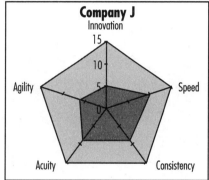

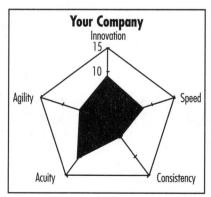

Figure 7–10. (continued)

The facilitator asks the group what conclusions could be drawn from the spider diagrams. At the fastener company workshop, one person said, "Most of the competitors are strong in one or more areas. Visually, our company seems to be sort of in the middle of the pack." Another participant raised her hand and said, "I just noticed something interesting. If company F merged with competitor C the resultant company would be very strong on four of the five customer focus capabilities." The lead facilitator should elicit as much input as possible in the time allotted. The objective is for participants to articulate their observations and realize that the spider chart technique is a good way to analyze data. The facilitator concludes the segment by telling the group that next they will discuss what steps their company should take to improve its position relative to its competitors.

7. NEXT STEPS—30 MINUTES

The next steps come right out of the previous exercise. The facilitator asks participants to look at the spider charts as well as the summary tables and suggest courses of action that would help their company. At the fastener company the participants decided that it would be difficult to identify specific steps needed for each capability but agreed to the following points:

- The company needs to improve in all five customer focus capabilities.

- The priority for improvement efforts should be based on those capabilities whose enhancement has the greatest impact on the achievement of business strategies.

- The company should investigate what its competitors are doing in each of the customer focus capabilities so it can be more creative and outperform them in the marketplace.

- The company should establish a project team to focus on these areas.

8. WORKSHOP DEBRIEF—45 MINUTES

Below is the lessons learned slide from the fastener company workshop.

Perceiving markets and competitors is very important.	Customer focus capabilities is an interesting concept.	Benchmarking should spark new ideas, not copy old ideas.	Market opportunities can generate huge revenue impacts.	Technology is redefining our markets.
Don't forget to identify your competitors.	Competitors can be anywhere in the world.	Perceiving your market and competitors is a full-time job.	There are different ways to listen to customers.	Marketing boundaries are disappearing.
Define specific roles for your benchmarking team.	Choosing your objective in benchmarking is very important.	Perceiving your competitors is not a one-time event.	Don't ignore your employees when perceiving your competitors.	Perceiving requires different skills.

Figure 7–11. Lessons Learned

9. GROUP DINNER—120 MINUTES

As with the other workshops the group dinner can help reinforce the learning points. The facilitator should judge whether the group could tolerate more "work." At the fastener company workshop the facilitator felt that the group worked hard and dinner should just be used for eating and relaxation. At another workshop the facilitator felt that a table discussion around a specific question would be valuable. The question she chose was, "What percentage of time should your company spend on perceiving its competitors and its markets?" This is not only an open-ended question but it sounds out people's ideas about the marketplace and the competitive environment.

ENDNOTES

1. Susan Chandler, "Nothing But Blue Sky at Northwest," *Business-Week,* October 17, 1994, p. 72.

2. Larry Armstrong, "Hot Growth Companies," *BusinessWeek,* May 26, 1997, p. 102.

3. Bradley T. Gale, *Managing Customer Value,* New York: Free Press, 1994.

4. These five capabilities first appeared in the following article as five dimensions along which companies should compete: George Stalk, Philip Evans, and Lawrence E. Shulman, "Competing on Capabilities," *Harvard Business Review,* March/April 1992.

PART III
PROVIDE SUPERIOR VALUE

CHAPTER 8

HOW TO BUILD CORE CAPABILITIES THAT PROVIDE VALUE

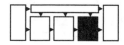

Companies that focus on core capabilities can compete in a remarkable di-
versity of regions, products, and businesses and do it far more coherently...
and be able to come out of nowhere and move rapidly from nonparticipant
to major player and even to industrial leader.

George Stalk, Philip Evans, Lawrence E. Shulman
"Competing on Capabilities"

At a military base in the United States during the Gulf War a private
began his day at 8:00 AM. His first task was to process transfer pa-
pers for soldiers being sent overseas in support of Desert Storm. As
he looked frantically through the drawers of his file cabinet, he re-
membered that he had used the last form the day before and forgot
to order more. The paperwork for the dozen transferees had to be
completed by 3:00 PM, which precluded his ordering the forms
through the regular process, which took at least three days. The private informed his sergeant that he was going to the forms supply
warehouse and would be back as soon as possible.

The base covers almost 300 square miles and employs 55,000 soldiers and civilians. The private drove 75 miles without exceeding

251

the 45 mph speed limit and arrived at the warehouse in one hour and forty-five minutes. It was now 10:00 AM. He entered the building, picked up two packs of forms—the limit, drove back to his office, and worked for the next two hours filling out the transfer forms manually. At 2:00 PM the private requested permission from his sergeant to leave for an hour to have lunch.

The Defense Automated Printing Service (DAPS) is responsible for the consolidated printing, duplicating, and document automation resources for the Department of Defense (DoD) and has almost 200 sites around the world. This means that every form the DoD uses is printed by DAPS and distributed to all DoD agencies throughout the world. Until Vice President Gore's Reinventing Government initiative sought to turn bureaucratic departments into performance-based organizations, DAPS operated like any other government bureaucracy. Now DAPS is a profit center and has to go out and find customers who are willing to pay for its services. As a consequence, the DAPS management team had to reinvent its business to create superior value that customers would pay for.

When the managers looked at their operation and interviewed their customers, what they found was surprising to DAPS but old news to users: Service was terrible. As one user said, "Sure, you guys are good at the technical things you do but why do I have to drive 75 miles to get a form? This is ridiculous." At about the same time a consulting team from Xerox Professional Document Services approached DAPS to help it rethink its strategy. The Xerox team proposed that instead of thinking of the business as printing and distribution, DAPS should start thinking of itself as a print-on-demand business. "Why have your customer come to you when you can go to the customer?" said one of the consultants. That thought sparked a whole new way of doing business.

DAPS started by looking at what it did well, which was printing, duplicating, and warehousing. It then decided that its main strategy should be to provide customers what they need, when they need it, from any location where forms are used. Managers started by mapping the current process from beginning to end and realized that it was not only filled with barriers that affected its efficiency but also lacked processes that would enable customers to use the services effectively. The problem was the delivery mechanism. Because

DAPS had been the only game in town it never focused on delivering service; it paid attention to the technical side of the operation only.

DAPS identified its current processes as well as potential constraints. The next step was to develop the high-level processes that would enable the organization to reverse its current business. Instead of printing forms in centralized facilities and distributing through a complex warehousing network it would provide customers the technology and supporting processes to print any form, any time, from any location.

Aided by Xerox consultants, DAPS worked on a software architecture that would electronically store all documents in a mainframe computer. These documents could be accessed from any location through local area networks connected to the main computer. Personnel who have to fill out a form can access it electronically, fill it out with a few keystrokes, and print it locally. As DAPS explored this concept more fully it realized that not only could it improve value for its customers, it could also develop new businesses. Many forms that are filled out have to be processed through a complicated routing system. By combining imaging of documents along with the print-on-demand feature, DAPS can now help customers process the completed forms more efficiently. In addition, it is contemplating developing Internet and intranet access so that personnel at any base around the world can communicate with one another.

DAPS had to exploit its core capabilities to design new processes with added value for its customers. It did so by becoming more focused on the delivery of services. Now, instead of driving 75 miles to pick up packs of forms, personnel can access a needed form on a computer, complete it, and distribute it electronically. By developing a core capability in the access, completion, and distribution of documents DAPS created a way to provide value to its customers.

THE OUTSOURCING REVOLUTION

During the postwar boom of the 1950s through the 1970s, companies expanded explosively. People could find jobs almost anywhere as the thirst for products required companies to hire more people and build larger factories. Before anyone realized what was happening, management was spending as much time focusing on the nontraditional side of business as it was in those areas that made the profits. Cafeterias were large; payroll, maintenance, and security services grew to the same size as some manufacturing departments. Even receptionist and typing pools became powerful as their managers were rewarded for the number of employees in their departments.

In the 1970s Japanese imports started squeezing American profits and management started focusing more on traditional business activities to reduce costs. American Restaurant Associates (ARA) grew rapidly as it managed food services for businesses more economically than the companies could themselves. Soon most company cafeterias were being managed by an outside service. Management started looking at other areas of the organization that could be managed more economically by outside services. Security, payroll, and groundskeeping were the next services that management decided to let out of its grasp.

By the beginning of the 1980s global pressures forced companies to start focusing on their key business areas as foreign competition encroached on protected markets. Businesses started looking at yet more activities that could be better managed by an outside service. Travel reservations, training, payroll, and even maintenance departments were handed over to outside services. As management required more detailed cost reports to manage the business, data processing departments grew dramatically. In 1962 Ross Perot founded Electronic Data Systems (EDS) with a $1,000 investment and a dream that he could build a company that could help businesses manage their information centers more efficiently. In 1963 EDS sold its first five-year facilities-management contract to commercial customer Frito-Lay at a monthly fee of $5,000. The rest is history. Today EDS, has 100,000 employees and revenues of more than $14 billion. It services companies in financial services, energy, travel and transportation, manufacturing, retail, communications, government, and health care. In 1994 EDS signed the largest information technology contract ever awarded—$3.2 billion—with Xerox. The success of EDS is based on its ability to perform data processing functions economically as well as manage data operations centers efficiently.[1]

In the early 1990s American industry coined a new word—*outsourcing*—to represent the management and operation of business activities by a third party. The outsourcing revolution in operational activities started to take hold in high levels of the organization. Logistic services, including inventory control, packaging, shipping, freight forwarding, and traffic, were soon managed by third parties. Then came the customer focus revolution and call centers (toll-free numbers) were being managed by third parties. Billing, invoicing, purchasing, document reproduction, and printing soon followed as management let go of these sacred cows in order to focus on the critical parts of the business—those that enabled it to provide differentiating value to customers.

In today's dynamic marketplace management time is a precious commodity. In the 1970's activities were measured in weeks, today in seconds. As a result, management needs to focus its activities in those areas that are critical to the company's success. This is what drove the outsourcing revolution and led to the tremendous success of EDS.

More and more companies are looking at parts of their information technology (IT) as strategic to their business while others can be outsourced. The *Washington Post,* for example, outsourced its legacy systems to Computer Aid, Inc. "We did this so we could focus more of our attention on using IT to accomplish our primary organizational goals," says Gordon Adler, director of application services for the *Post.* Paul Smith, Computer Aid's general manager for the Lehigh Valley, believes that strategic outsourcing enables organizations to redeploy their own people, who typically have more knowledge about the business than outsiders and can thus add significant value. "If the entire IT organization were outsourced we would have to retrain the staff who might be on another assignment next week at one of our competitors," says Adler. Joe Hessmiller, general manager for the Midwest region, believes strategic outsourcing is the new trend. "Why should a company have to bring in very expensive outside talent who they have to train, when their own personnel are the most knowledgeable and talented? By only outsourcing the part of the IT organization that is more generic, such as software development and mainframe maintenance, the IT organization can start focusing on creating strategic value for its company."

By identifying those parts of the business that are strategically important, management can focus its energy where it will yield the greatest return. It is, therefore, imperative for management to understand how to identify those areas within its business that are important to its success.

CORE COMPETENCIES VERSUS CORE CAPABILITIES

Core competencies are the technical skills such as engineering and product design that underlie your products and services. In turn, these outputs must be delivered to the consumer with superior service using a set of *core capabilities* in the form of business processes that in their own right create customer value. This is what drives mergers and acquisitions; companies need to improve either their core competencies or their core capabilities. NBC News had the core competencies to gather news but recognized that it needed to become part of the information revolution. It merged with Microsoft to gain the latter's core capability to broadcast over the World Wide Web; thus MSNBC was born.

Today's dynamic marketplace requires companies to focus carefully on the elements of their business that provide customer value. Success can quickly turn into failure if management doesn't concentrate on core competencies and capabilities. Sony and Honda are examples of companies that have stayed clearly focused and profited because of it. Honda's ability to manufacture an engine or power train is a core competency. The company recognized that this skill had no value unless it was integrated into products that customers would pay for. Its ability to develop products that use its engines in motorcycles, cars, lawnmowers, watercraft, and other products is a core capability. Sony has a core competency in its ability to miniaturize almost anything. Like Honda, it recognized that unless this could be integrated into marketable products it would remain an unprofitable skill. Sony's core capability to transform its competency into miniature radios, motors, television sets, and digital readouts generates enviable revenues.

Developing Sustainable Core Competencies

Core competencies have strategic value to your company. A skill or technological expertise must pass two thresholds to be considered a core competency. First, it must create access to several markets and, second, it must be extremely difficult for others to copy. When companies examine their value in today's customer-driven marketplace they sometimes discover core competencies they didn't know they had.

---

1. Creates access to worldwide markets.
2. Cannot be mirrored by other companies.

Figure 8–1. Core Competency Attributes

According to the Xerox Corporation annual report, the company posted revenues of $17.4 billion in 1996. It employs 85,000 people and operates in more than 130 countries. Since Chester Carlson made the first xerographic image in his makeshift laboratory in New York City on October 22, 1938, Xerox has made his copying process a core competency in terms of the global marketplace.

Unfortunately, in 1980 Xerox discovered the second attribute of core competencies. Canon successfully challenged Xerox in the marketplace, not only duplicating the xerographic process but also incorporating it into copiers that sold worldwide at a lower price. Xerox's sales dropped dramatically until it realigned its cost structure to compete more favorably with Canon. Xerox's competency was no longer core to its business because Canon could *mirror* it.

During its search for best practices that resulted in a more competitive cost structure, Xerox learned that it had developed knowledge about documents: how people used them, how to identify critical company documents, how documents should be designed, how they should be printed, and so on. It established the Palo Alto Research Center, known as PARC Labs, in the early 1980s to study how people work together and the role of the document in the work environment. Sociologists, anthropologists, computer engineers, scientists, and technicians work side by side in this endeavor.

Xerox found that it was developing a new core competency and, as a result, adopted "The Document Company, Xerox" in 1994 as its corporate signature. It even redefined the word document to mean *information that is structured for use by people in any form or medium*. Soon Xerox was developing technologies that enabled information to be captured, analyzed, managed, and distributed enterprisewide. Its glyph technology translates hundreds of pages of information into electronic digitized form, somewhat like a bar code, that can be stored in a one-inch area of a page. Now insurance companies add glyphs to insurance policies and other documents that contain client information. Xerox always was in the information business but had never realized it. By developing core competencies that enabled access to worldwide markets and that could not be mirrored by competitors, Xerox developed a sustainable core competency that will lead it to new heights in the twenty-first century.

Core competencies are an important element in any business strategy. Every company needs to have a specific skill that underlies its products or services. A local grocery store that always has fresh fruit and vegetables has developed a competency in its ordering process. A travel agent who can always provide the latest fares and travel insights has developed a core competency in obtaining information. These core competencies, however, will not by themselves provide value to customers. Core capabilities have to be developed that deliver the competencies to the customers.

DEVELOPING CORE CAPABILITIES THAT PROVIDE SUPERIOR CUSTOMER VALUE

Core capabilities are the processes that provide value to customers. They have high visibility and consistently deliver value. The new product development capability in companies like Intel, 3M, and Toyota brings innovative new products quickly to market. Underlying a core capability is a set of supporting business processes graphically presented in Figure 8–2.

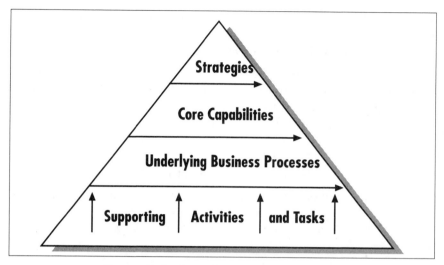

Figure 8–2. Core Capability Alignment

Business processes move horizontally across the enterprise and extend beyond organizational boundaries. Business activities, on the other hand, are the manageable tasks assigned to individuals and teams that are normally performed within specific organizations in the enterprise.

Federal Express has a core capability in its delivery processes because it consistently provides customer value by delivering packages on time. Supporting services contribute to on-time deliveries. By calling customer service or communicating via computer you can track your package anytime, anywhere, and from any location. The sophisticated support processes that Federal Express employs and their links with other processes, such as the effective training of customer service representatives, result in superior customer satisfaction almost every time there is a customer service representative–customer interaction. Wal-Mart's core capability in order replenishment is composed of its continuous replenishment process (CRM), warehouse/store location layout, and its vendor relationships. It integrates vendors into the entire process so that products are on the shelf when and where they are needed.

A core capability has three distinct characteristics, as shown in Figure 8–3. First, it must be visible to the customer. For instance,

guests at Ritz Carlton hotels cannot escape the visible superior customer service of the employees. Second, it must successfully
deliver superior value to your customers. Ritz Carlton guests consistently rate customer service as superior. Third, it must score
high in the five customer focus capabilities (speed, consistency,
acuity, agility, and innovation). Ritz Carlton guests score the chain
high in each of these areas.

1. Visible to customers. 2. Successfully delivers value to customers. 3. Scores high in customer focus capabilities.

Figure 8–3. Core Capability Attributes

New product development, sales and fulfillment, and customer
support are examples of potential core capabilities. Companies that
fail usually do so because they don't have a core capability or let
their existing core capability deteriorate. People's Express was an
airline that competed on price. It succeeded until it tried to develop
a core capability in service. It failed miserably and went out of business. As long as it competed on price the public tolerated the bare-
bones service, but when it raised its prices and couldn't deliver on
the service component, customers fled. The U.S. Postal Service is
beginning to develop a capability in customer service. For years it
was a government monopoly; if you wanted a letter or package delivered anywhere in the United States or abroad you had to use its
services. With Federal Express, Airborne Express, DHL, UPS, and
others entering the marketplace, the Postal Service had to do something to retain customers. It started by developing an express delivery service that costs less than the competition but does not
provide quite the same level of speed.

Core competencies and core capabilities are important concepts
to understand in providing value to your customer. Customers always see core capabilities and their underlying business processes
because these are the delivery arms of products and services. Core
competencies can only be seen inside the product but would never
get to the customer without the core capability. This is why companies are so focused on reinventing their business processes—these

are the channels that connect the company with the customer. With effective business processes you can lead the market. Without them the market will pass you by.

REDESIGNING BUSINESS PROCESSES

Business process redesign became popular in the early 1990s when Michael Hammer and James Champy crafted the notion of reengineering for dramatic performance improvements. In their book *Reengineering the Corporation,* the authors write, "The book you are holding describes a conceptually new business model and an associated set of techniques that American executives and managers will have to use to reinvent their companies for competition in a new world."[2] In the early 1990s companies all across America grabbed onto the reeningeering concept as a means to improving their competitiveness. Unfortunately, many failed. In James Champy's 1996 book *Reengineering Management,* he writes, "Reengineering is in trouble. It's not easy for me to make this admission. I was one of the two people who introduced the concept."[3]

The problem with reengineering is that management forgot some basic principles. First, every business process has two components: one is a company component that affects internal activities and one is a customer component that affects customers during interactions with company personnel or services. Reengineering in the early nineties focused primarily on the internal business components, and companies made radical changes with a zest and vigor American industry hadn't seen in years. Management thought it improved process. Unfortunately, both the workers, who lost their jobs, and the customers, who were ignored, suffered. Now these companies have come full circle and are asking the same question they did a few years ago: How do we provide profitable value in the marketplace? While some strides were made in improving customer processes, most activity centered on the internal components of business processes, whereas profitability derives from providing superior customer value.

IDENTIFYING COMPANY AND CUSTOMER PROCESS COMPONENTS

Every business process has a business and a customer component. Look at the bill payment process. It wasn't that many years ago when people wrote checks for electricity, oil, gasoline, taxes, and department store purchases and mailed them in preaddressed envelopes. At each destination a clerk opened the envelope, removed the check and statement from the envelope, and recorded the payment. The check and the payment information was then handed off to other clerks who would process the check, post the payment to the customer's account, and perform other functional tasks that could take up to a week. Companies reengineered the company component of the process by automating almost every activity. Costs were reduced but the customer received no benefit; she still had to write the check, insert it in an envelope, and mail it. The process could have been improved for customers by allowing them to make payments by credit card, through automated check-writing systems, or via the Internet. These are the features that add true value to the process. Improvements to the company component impact costs; improvements in the customer components affect value.

It is important that you identify both company and customer components for each business process (see Figure 8–4). If you don't, your internal cost structure might be affected favorably but your customer satisfaction rating may not. There are three steps to identifying customer and company components to the business process:

1. List all the processes and associated activities that affect the business problem you are trying to solve.

2. Identify the departments that participate in the process.

3. Highlight each activity within the process that customers are directly involved with. These highlighted areas represent the customer component of the business process, where value is transferred to the customer. These intersection points were sometimes called moments of truth by former Scandinavian Airlines CEO Jan

Carlzon because this is where the customer interacts directly with the company through a process or individual.

IDENTIFYING PROCESS CONSTRAINTS

A six-point checklist for identifying process information can help you put your finger on potential process problems (see Figure 8–4). Below are the six areas to look at followed by a more detailed description of each.

Location	Where and how is the work performed?
Time	When is the process performed?
Sequence	What are the activity flows?
Responsibility	Who does what?
Resources	What resources are required?
Equipment	What equipment is required?

Figure 8–4. Process Information Six-Point Checklist

Location. Understanding where the process is performed can be important. A Fortune 500 computer company relocated its accounts payable processing to the Midwest because of lower costs there. Then they had a problem finding qualified help in an area where most people made their living in the agriculture industry. Where work is performed can impact the effectiveness of the process. An activity that can only be performed in one work location is not as flexible as an activity that can be performed in numerous locations.

Time. When an activity is performed can indicate a potential problem. In today's business world sending an overnight package via Federal Express, Airborne, or UPS is easy, but if your package isn't ready by around 6:00 pm you will have to find a local drop box or branch office rather than enjoying the convenience of having it picked up.

Sequence. The sequence and flow of work can be a real constraint to an otherwise efficient process. Activities that occur serially versus concurrently are always sources of potential problems. In today's hectic environment an individual who is responsible for reviewing, assigning, or authorizing activities can in fact be a constraint if the backlog of work increases. Having customers wait in line at a bank while two or three tellers reconcile their daily transactions impacts customer service.

Responsibility. We have all heard the line "Go see Joe–he's the only one who can help." Whenever you hear this, stop and ask yourself what will happen if Joe gets sick. Even worse, what happens if he leaves the firm? Allowing individuals to have an exclusive hold on a specific activity is like signing a death warrant. Be on the lookout for actions that can only be accomplished by specific individuals.

Resources. We've all had the experience of calling an insurance company and waiting on the phone for what appears to be forever. The customer service representative listens to your question and then tells you, "Please hold on for a minute while I look up the necessary information." The resources are not efficient.

Equipment. We've all seen the line form at the copy or fax machine. Take a look at the equipment required to perform an activity. A broken scanning machine at a supermarket can slow checkout lines. A computer system that has more downtime than uptime is a definite constraint.

Every process has constraints that impact effectiveness, efficiency, and flexibility. Lines that are too long at the supermarket impact customer satisfaction. Waiting for a bank teller to find your account information before posting your deposit creates frustration. Waiting too long for a service representative to answer your phone call is annoying. Adding more tellers, phone lines, or operators may initially overcome the problems but if you investigate further there may still be more. Do the personnel have the skills and training to perform the job? Do they have the necessary equipment or access to information that they need?

Within each component of customer and company processes are focus areas that will help you identify potential process constraints. When focusing on the customer component of the process you look for satisfaction, dissatisfaction, and areas for improvement. When you are focusing on the company component of the process you look for work flow, quality, speed, and cost. Figure 8–5 identifies the focus areas.

CUSTOMER FOCUS AREA	QUESTION TO ANSWER
Satisfaction	What do they like about it?
Dissatisfaction	What don't they like about it?
Improvement	What can be done better?
COMPANY FOCUS AREAS	**QUESTION TO ANSWER**
Work Flow	What extra work is created?
Quality	How does this effect quality?
Speed	Does it slow us down?
Cost	How does it increase our costs?

Figure 8–5. Identifying Process Constraints

DETERMINING THE CUSTOMER VALUE OF PROCESS ACTIVITIES

The customer focus revolution is founded on the concept of providing superior and sustainable value. Herein lies the essence of analyzing your business processes. In Chapter 7 five customer focus capabilities (speed, consistency, acuity, agility, and innovation) that management can use to measure a competitor's perceive capability were identified. These same metrics can be used to measure the effectiveness of a business process.

Both the company and the customer want to improve each of them. Customers want to be serviced quickly; companies want to deliver products quickly. Customers want quality; companies want to produce a quality product. Customers want to be able to find out everything they need to know about the company product or service; the company wants to know everything it can about its customers. Customers want the company to respond quickly to their needs, wants, and desires; companies want to respond quickly to changing market conditions. Customers want to use a company's products in a variety of applications; companies want their employees to be innovative in every activity they perform.

These five customer focus capabilities form the cornerstone of determining customer and company value. If you look at the process constraints in analyzing the customer and company focus areas (see Figure 8–4) you can determine their positive or negative impact on each of the customer focus capabilities.

Let's look at the order replenishment process for a department store that was reviewed by a management team. The team identified the major steps of the process and recorded them on a chart in the left-hand column (see Table 8–1). Across the top of the chart are the five customer focus capabilities. Team members spent the next hour talking about each major process and used the customer focus capabilities to make observations about the quality of the process. As you can see from the results, they identified a number of areas to focus on in creating value in the process.

IDENTIFYING ACTIONS THAT CREATE VALUE

When activities within a business process have been identified as not adding value, action needs to be taken to address the deficiency. If a bank teller has to spend time navigating the bank's computer system to find a customer's account number, what should management do to address the problem? There are four possible actions for every non-value-added activity. The easiest course of action is to *eliminate* it. If a clerk is checking someone else's work, there is no need to continue this activity. Each person should be responsible for his own quality of work. The days of having people check other people's work disappeared with mass production thinking. The second course of action is to *automate* the process. It wasn't that long ago that you drove into a gas station, pumped your own gas, and then went inside to pay the attendant. Today this process has been automated so the entire monetary transaction can be conducted at the gas pump. The third course of action is to *simplify* the activity. A salesclerk who has to fill out a complicated sales slip can accomplish the same task with a redesigned form that shortens the task. The fourth course of active is to *integrate* activities. An employee entering expense report information into an automated system, then printing it out for a supervisor's signature is performing several time-consuming actions. If the expense report can be routed electronically to the supervisor, approved, and returned electronically, the process has been streamlined because the activities are more integrated. By looking at each activity with

Table 8–1. Customer Value Analysis: Order Replenishment Process of a Department Store

Process	Speed	Consistency	Acuity	Agility	Innovation
Notifying central inventory control	Only by phone or interoffice mail	Information lost or misplaced	Always ordering when stock is out	Very structured process	Doing it the same way for 10 years
Ordering from supplier	By phone or mail	Fairly accurate most of the time	Difficulty forecasting usage	Same process all the time, even when there is a rush	Same way the last 5 years
Following up on order	By phone or mail	Suppliers late on deliveries most of the time	Vendors never call us to let us know order could be late	Same way all the time	Same way the last 5 years
Receiving of goods	Manual	Miscounts occur	Receiving is sometimes backed up for 2 days or more	Same way all the time	Same way the last 5 years
Forwarding packing list to accounting	Interoffice mail	Slips lost	Not a problem	Same way all the time	Same way the last 5 years
Stocking shelves	Manually, 2–3 days after receipt	Shelves always stocked	Stock clerks never notified of anticipated receipts	Same way all the time	Same way the last 5 years

these four possible actions in mind you can identify methods by which non-value-added activities can be transformed into value (see Figure 8–6).

Action	Description
Eliminate	Entirely do away with the activity.
Automate	Use a machine to perform the activity.
Simplify	Make it easier to perform the activity.
Integrate	Incorporate the activity into another part of the process.

Figure 8–6. Four Ways to Deal with a Non-Value-Added Activity

As companies focus more on their customers than ever before, their business processes reflect new ways of doing business. Creating processes that add value for customers has been beneficial for both the consumer and commercial business. Shell Oil is implementing a process that allows a consumer to drive into one of its stations and pull up to a special pump that automatically opens the gas cap, fills the tank, and bills the consumer's credit card, all without the driver getting out of the car. Instead of waiting in line to buy a ticket or to check in for a flight, airline passengers can purchase an electronic ticket over the telephone or Internet and walk directly to the gate, show a picture ID, and board the plane. The process saves time for both the passenger and airline. Municipalities are using one-person vehicles that automatically pick up specially designed containers of trash. The municipality is happy because the process is efficient and lowers cost, and residents are happy because it lowers taxes.

In today's market-driven economy companies are striving to improve customer value. The customer component of your business processes is an important element to your market success and although core competencies are important, core capabilities are the visible processes that your customers use to measure your true success. Focus on developing core capabilities that provide superior value and your customers will reward you with improved satisfaction ratings, increased revenues, and sustainable profitability.

WORKSHOP: PROVIDING ROBUST PROCESSES THAT DELIVER VALUE

This workshop can be an invaluable tool in helping your workforce understand the concepts behind, and techniques in, creating value-added processes that will dazzle your customers and burnish your bottom line. The objective is for participants to divide a process into its customer and company components, identify potential constraints, and determine the possible actions that can lead to improving its value.

Table 8–2. Provide Robust Processes that Deliver Value

Agenda
9:00 AM – 9:00 PM

Time Frames	Time Allotted	Workshop Exercises	Facilitator	Objectives
1. 9:00–9:45	45 min	Set the Stage	Ken V.	Discuss the learning objectives and capture participants' expectations.
2. 9:45–10:15	30 min	Warm-Up Exercise	Steven O.	Identify the travel and expense process steps.
3. 10:15–10:30	15 min	Break		
4. 10:30–1:00	150 min	Evaluating Travel Expense Process—Team Exercise	Lynne W.	Identify constraints by analyzing customer and company focus areas of the travel and expense reporting process.
5. 1:00–2:00	60 min	Lunch		
6. 2:00–4:00	120 min	Improving the Travel Expense Process—Team Exercise (includes 15-min break)	Steven O.	Evaluate constraints and identify possible changes to process that would improve its effectiveness and efficiency.
7. 4:00–5:00	60 min	Next Steps	Steven O./ Lynne W.	Identify necessary actions to ensure we develop effective customer focus capabilities.
8. 5:00–5:45	45 min	Workshop Debrief	Lynne W./ Steven O.	Capture and share the benefits of the workshop with colleagues.
9. 7:00–9:00	120 min	Group Dinner		

Lead Facilitator: Ken V.   Facilitators: Steven O./Lynne W.

Understanding how to analyze process activities is an integral part of providing value. This workshop will help participants to understand and apply the concepts behind the customer and company dimension of each process, value-added and non-value-added components, and process constraints. The workshop focuses on the travel and expense reporting process because it is one that many employees are familiar with and tend to criticize the most. Employees are actually the customers of the travel and expense reporting process and this tends to add more flavor to the workshop because it is a real event.

The workshop is scheduled for one day but can be extended depending on the knowledge of the participants. At most workshops, management adds a two- to three-hour primer on the concepts of competencies, capabilities, and business processes the afternoon before the workshop proper for participants who may not be familiar with them. This chapter or other appropriate material can be used. Table 8–2 is the agenda for the one-day workshop.

1. SET THE STAGE—45 MINUTES

The facilitator provides an overview of the workshop and its objectives, and participants introduce themselves. The objective of this workshop is for the participants to understand how to divide a process into its customer and company components, identify potential constraints, and determine the possible actions that can lead to improving its value. The facilitator can use some of the time during this segment to review basic concepts of competencies, capabilities, and processes so everyone understands the key points. He can do this by asking general questions to get a dialogue going. This helps to place everyone on the same page and to generate involvement.

2. WARM-UP EXERCISE—30 MINUTES

The concepts of process redesign may not be new to many participants but the concepts in this workshop likely are. Almost everyone has an opinion about a company process. To help get the group warmed up the facilitator asks, "How many have used the travel expense and reporting process?" Usually, most hands get raised. The next question is the one that everyone seems to enjoy the most: "How many feel it is an efficient and user-friendly process?" Not too many participants raise their hands. The next one gets the most reaction. "How many of you would like to change the process?" This is when almost every hand is raised.

To begin, the facilitator asks the group to identify the major activities involved in the travel and expense process. It's not as easy as it sounds. Everyone has an opinion and the facilitator needs to control the group so everyone gets a chance to speak. What works well is to go around the room and start a list of activities. They don't have to be in any order. Just have everyone add to the list. After participants agree that all the activities have been identified they can remove duplications and order the activities by priority. Figure 8–7 is an example of prioritized list of process steps.

---

1. Employee responsible for obtaining travel authorization.

2. Employee responsible for making travel reservations.

3. Employee enters expense data into systems.

4. Employee makes copies of expense statement and forwards it to travel accounting.

5. Employee copies receipts and forwards it to travel accounting.

6. Travel accounting audits expense report matching electronic and mailed copy.

7. Travel accounting forwards discrepancy to employee.

8. Employee corrects discrepancy or obtains supervisor's approval.

9. Travel accounting authorizes payment to accounts payable.

10. Accounts payable issues check and mails to employee via interoffice mail.

Figure 8–7. Travel Expense Reporting—Major Activities

3. BREAK—15 MINUTES

As in the previous workshops, participants should be reminded of the time the break starts and the time they are expected back in the meeting room. Facilitators can remind participants of the time and guide them back to the meeting room as the end of the break approaches. The exercise after the break utilizes the reading materials.

4. EVALUATING TRAVEL EXPENSE PROCESS—150 MINUTES

The facilitator starts the exercise by explaining that this is the most intense part of the workshop but also the most fun. This is where the teams have the opportunity to dissect the travel expense process and identify potential constraints. The facilitator then shows an instruction slide similar to Figure 8–8 and reviews it with the group. (Team facilitators will review the instructions with their respective teams later.) The facilitator also reassures participants that they should not be alarmed at what appears to be a complex exercise and that facilitators will guide them through it step by step.

Participants are assigned to their respective teams and break areas. The team facilitators review the instructions as well as the worksheet template they will use and give the teams a 10-minute tutorial on the elements of the worksheet and their meanings. After answering any questions each facilitator provides a second 10-minute tutorial on the process dimensions and focus areas using a handout supplied to each team member. The facilitator must reassure participants that she will help them and they should not be concerned about not immediately understanding the details of what to do.

The team facilitator then hands out a copy of the travel expense process steps that were identified in the warm-up exercise. Using this as a base, she asks a set of specific questions that helps the team complete the worksheet. At one workshop the team facilitator for the customer view said, "To start the process, focus on location. Ask yourselves where and how is the work performed." One of the team members said, "Reservations can be made only in writing or by telephone." The team facilitator wrote those words on the worksheet. The facilitator then continued asking leading questions until all the dimensions had been reviewed and the process steps identified.

For the next part of the exercise the team facilitator asks the team to brainstorm potential constraints for each dimension by focus area. When the teams are finished they return to the main meeting room; each presents its findings to the other team. After both presentations the facilitator asks the group for suggestions on improving their content. This usually takes ten to fifteen minutes. Tables 8–3 and 8–4 are examples of completed worksheets.

The teams are to identify potential conflict areas. The worksheets are designed to help participants think though the process. For the final half-hour of the segment the facilitator goes around the room asking each participant to identify constraint areas, capturing their comments on an overhead slide, like that shown in Table 8–4.

Travel Expense Process

1. The facilitator will assign participants to Team A or Team B.

2. Team A will focus on the customer view and Team B will focus on the company view.

3. For the next *45 minutes* each team will identify process activities for each of the process dimensions (location, time, sequence, responsibility, resources, equipment).

4. For the following *45 minutes* each team will identify the potential constraints for each process dimension, categorizing them by focus area using the appropriate area of the supplies worksheet.

   - *Company view—work flow, quality, speed, and cost*

   - *Customer view—satisfaction, dissatisfaction, and improvement*

5. Teams will present their findings to the group in a *10-minute* presentation.

Figure 8–8. Sample Slide: Team Exercise Instructions

Table 8–3. Expense Report Process: Identifying Constraints—Customer View

Dimension	Description	Process Steps	Satisfaction	Dissatisfaction	Improvement
Location	Where work is performed	1. Reservations can only be made via telephone or in writing. 2. Entering expenses on system must be on company computer.	Operators are courteous. Computer system is slow.	Reservation response is slow. You have to wait to find out if flights and hotels are available. Entering expenses is slow and cumbersome.	Should be alternate method for making reservations. Entering data should be more user-friendly.
Time	When the process is performed	1. Data can be entered during business hours, 8 AM – 5 PM. 2. Average completion time for expense report is 15–45 minutes, depending on complexity.	Never a friendly experience.	Employees who come into work early cannot enter information. System is overloaded at 8 AM. Not user-friendly.	The system should be available 24 hours a day. It should be easier to enter data.
Sequence	Sequence of activities	1. Go on trip. 2. Upon return from trip, enter information into expense reporting system at local office. 3. Copy receipts. 4. Send via interoffice mail to central processing. 5. Central processing audits report. 6. Central processing forwards report for approval.	During a trip things are fine. It's only when you return that you are faced with this difficult process. The process seems too serial. Have to wait for check.	Organizing receipts upon return is difficult. Entering data is difficult electronically and forwarding receipts physically seems dumb. It takes 3 days for receipts to reach accounting.	There must be an easier way to capture expense information during trip. There should be another way to send receipts to central accounting.

Table 8–3. (continued)

Dimension	Description	Process Steps	Satisfaction	Dissatisfaction	Improvement
Sequence (continued)		7. Upon approval authorization goes to account payable for payment. 8. Accounts payable issues check. 9. Check is mailed interoffice to employee.			
Responsibility	Who does what	1. Employee responsible for obtaining travel authorization. 2. Employee responsible for making travel reservations. 3. Employee responsible for submitting travel expenses. 4. Travel accounting audits expense report. 5. Travel accounting forwards to employee's supervisor for approval. 6. Supervisor approves report. 7. Travel accounting authorizes payment to accounts payable. 8. Accounts payable issues check and mails to employee via interoffice mail. 9. Employee receives check.	It's not a fun process. Employee has to obtain approval for everything.	Travel authorization takes too much time. It takes 3 days for supervisor to approve expense report. Checks are processed once every 2 weeks and mailing takes up to 1 week.	Travel authorization should be easier. It shouldn't take so long to forward receipts, obtain supervisor approval, and receive check.

Table 8–3. (continued)

Dimension	Description	Process Steps	Satisfaction	Dissatisfaction	Improvement
Resources	People	1. Employee. 2. Travel accounting. 3. Supervisor. 4. Accounts payable.	No comment.	Everyone is pleasant and amiable. When there is a discrepancy it is difficult for travel accounting to locate your records.	Travel accounting personnel should be either better trained or have more effective information systems.
Equipment	Materials and equipment needed	1. Computer at office.	Equipment at office works okay. It's the software that is the problem.	Software is slow. Hardware is only available at office.	You should be able to dial in from off site. Software should be more user-friendly.

Table 8–4. Expense Report Process: Identifying Constraints—Company View

Dimension	Description	Process Steps	Work Flow	Quality	Speed	Cost
Location	Where work is performed	1. Reservations can only be made via telephone or in writing. 2. Entering expenses on system must be on company computer.	Entering data twice, only at office. Expense report includes data from reservation.	Errors from original reservations can be made when entering expense reports.	Impacted because data is entered twice.	Employees' time to enter data twice.
Time	When the process is performed	1. Data can be entered during business hours, 8 A.M.–5 P.M. 2. Average completion time for expense report is 15–45 minutes, depending on complexity.	Not flexible. Employees who travel could be entering costs as incurred.	The longer it takes to enter data, the more chance of of error.	Speed is impacted because system is not user-friendly.	Clerical time could be replaced with more value-added work.
Sequence	Sequence of activities	1. Go on trip. 2. Upon return from trip, enter information into expense reporting system at local office. 3. Copy receipts. 4. Send via interoffice mail to central processing. 5. Central processing audits report. 6. Central processing forwards report for approval. 7. Upon approval, authorization goes to accounts payable for payment. 8. Accounts payable issues check. 9. Check is mailed via interoffice mail to employee.	Double-entry bookkeeping. Employee makes reservations and then reenters data into expense report.	When there are many expense receipts, quality suffers. Foreign conversions difficult.	Speed impacted because of double entries and user-unfriendly environment.	Time is money. Employee has to wait 7–14 days to be reimbursed from time receipts that are received by Accounts Receivable.

Table 8–4. (continued)

Dimension	Description	Process Steps	Work Flow	Quality	Speed	Cost
Responsibility	Who does what	1. Employee responsible for obtaining travel authorization. 2. Employee responsible for making travel reservations. 3. Employee responsible for submitting travel receipts. 4. Travel accounting audits expense report. 5. Travel accounting forwards to employee's supervisor for approval. 6. Supervisor approves report. 7. Travel accounting authorizes payment to accounts payable. 8. Accounts payable issues check and mails to employee via interoffice mail. 9. Employee receives check.	Too many steps.	The more steps, the greater the likelihood of errors.	Entering data electronically and sending receipts physically is not logical. Audit cannot start until the receipts have been received.	Mail cost impacted as well as sorting costs of matching receipts with electronic data.

Table 8–4. (continued)

Dimension	Description	Process Steps	Work Flow	Quality	Speed	Cost
Resources	People	1. Employee. 2. Travel accounting. 3. Supervisor. 4. Accounts payable.	Too many hands in the pot.	The more hands that touch the data, the greater chance for error.	Speed impacted while waiting for data. Work in process backs up.	Too costly a process. Too many people, too many activities. Employees have to wait for their money.
Equipment	Materials and equipment needed	1. Computer at office.	Equipment is only at office.	Slow and user-unfriendly process prone to errors.	User-unfriendly system impacts speed.	Employee per-hour cost is greater than equipment cost.

Table 8–5. Travel Expense Process: Summary of Constraints

Dimensions	Consumer View	Producer View
General Summary	Too slow cumbersome, inconvenient	Serial activities, too much cost, too many people involved
Location	• Reservations can be made made only by telephone or in writing. • Data can be entered only in office location.	• Inflexible: only at office location.
Time	• Reservations, data entry, review, and authorization can only be accomplished between 8 AM and 5 PM.	• Speed is impacted because system is overloaded at 8 AM and other peak times.
Sequence	• Activities are serial. • Expenses can be entered only after business trip is completed. • Organizing receipts for data entry is complex. • Systems are not user-friendly. • Process takes a lot of time.	• Double entry of data. • Errors made during data entry because of complexity of systems. • Audit takes too long; difficult to match mailed receipts with electronic data. • Backlog always exists for audit. • Data entered electronically and receipts sent physically.
Responsibility	• Travel authorization takes too much time. • Authorization is serial. • Approval takes too long.	• Resources needed to match receipts with electronic data. • Too many handoffs involved.
Resources	• Reservations and travel accounting personnel are polite but systems are slow and unresponsive to needs.	• Slow. • Software not user-friendly.
Equipment	• Only available at office.	

5. LUNCH—60 MINUTES

Allowing time during lunch for reinforcing the lessons adds to the learning process. At one workshop the facilitators made copies for all the participants of the summary constraints that were identified in the previous exercise. The facilitator at each table asked participants to identify a personal experience for each of the constraints and what they would do to make the process more efficient. They could use an experience from a fellow worker or from a prior employer. This helped build up an information base for the next exercise.

6. IMPROVING THE TRAVEL EXPENSE PROCESS—120 MINUTES

The facilitator explains to the group that this team exercise is designed to help the participants learn to evaluate the constraints and identify changes that might improve the effectiveness and efficiency of the travel expense process. At one workshop the facilitator asked the group, "Did anyone have a problem recently with the travel expense process?" A participant raised her hand. "Yes, I recently returned from a business trip and lost one of the receipts for a dinner. I attached a copy of my credit card statement, wrote a note that I lost the receipt, and sent it along with my travel expense form to travel accounting after my supervisor signed it. Travel accounting said that I needed to submit the original copy of my credit card statement and that copies were not allowed." The facilitator then asked the woman to explain what she did next. "When I got home I had to go through my bills to find the original credit card statement. I then took it into the office, wrote a cover note, and made a copy for my records. I followed up with a phone call about a week later and now three weeks have gone by and I still have not received my payment." The objective is for the facilitator to get a participant to share an unhappy experience and then explain to the group that there is a logical way to uncover the root of the problem and to identify possible solutions.

The facilitator explains to the group that there are two types of questions you can ask to identify possible solutions. The first is a set of *why* questions that are called *implication* questions because they help to uncover the root of the problem, not the surface problem. The next is a set of *what* questions called *rule-breaking questions* because they help to identify the actions you can take to resolve the problem. The facilitator then shows the group a slide, using the overhead projector, that identifies sets of *why* and *what* questions (see Figure 8–9).

Implication Questions	Rule-Breaking Questions
Why are there constraints in the process?	What can we change?
Why was this rule established?	What can be done differently?
Why is extra work created?	What compromises can be made?
Why does it slow us down?	What can be done to automate the rule?
Why are costs impacted?	What can be done to integrate the rule?
Why is quality impacted?	What can be done to eliminate the rule?
Why are customers dissatisfied?	What can be done to simplify the rule?

Figure 8–9. Implication and Rule-Breaking Questions

The facilitator instructs participants to spend twenty minutes with their teams to try to answer the implication questions. They will then return to the main meeting room, where each team will present its answers. The facilitator then repeats the same process, this time focusing on the rule-breaking questions, and allowing the teams sixty minutes to work in their break areas. Figures 8–10 and 8–11 are the result of one group's work. Note: The afternoon break is included in the exercise.

Why are there constraints in the process?

Why was this rule established?	Why are costs impacted?
1. To reimburse employees for business travel.	1. Current process takes too long. 2. Too much time to enter data. 3. Audit process is slow due to antiquated computer system. 4. Receipts have to be photocopied. 5. Information system isn't always available.

Why is extra work created?	Why is quality impacted?
1. Because of having to photocopy receipts. 2. Supervisor has to approve travel authorization and expense report. 3. Travel accounting has to match receipts with expense report. 4. Computer system is slow and breaks down a lot, requiring reentering of data.	1. Computer system is slow and not user-friendly. 2. Poor quality of photocopying creates problems when accounting asks questions about receipts. 3. Auditing is manual, takes too long, and results in errors. 4. Entire process takes away from other important work.

Why does it slow us down?	Why are customers dissatisfied?
1. Travel authorization is by phone or writing. 2. Employee must copy expense receipts. 3. Employee must mail expense receipts to central processing. 4. Audit process is manual.	1. Too much time to enter data. 2. Computer system is not user-friendly. 3. Travel accounting makes mistakes. 4. Checks take too long to issue.

Figure 8–10. Implication Questions Worksheet

What can we change?

What can be done differently?	What can be done to integrate the rule?
1. Entire system can be computerized. 2. Include travel expense budget in travel authorization. 3. Audit can be as simple. If within travel authorization, budget is approved, if not, supervisor can approve electronically.	1. Travel authorization and expense approval. 2. Travel reservation data and entering same data on expense report. 3. Forwarding expense receipts to travel accounting and photocopying. 4. Travel reservations and entering same data on expense report.

Figure 8–11. Rule-Breaking Questions Worksheet

What can we change? *(continued)*

What can be done differently?	What can be done to integrate the rule?
4. Expense receipts can be electronically imaged or stored at local office. 5. Employee can enter expenses while on business trip. 6. Replace manual check with EFT to employee's account.	5. Manual check preparation and mailing.

What compromises can be made?	What can be done to eliminate the rule?
1. Use travel authorization as basis for expense audit. 2. Reservation data automatically updates expense report template. 3. Employee can enter expense data during travel. 4. Manually handle only exceptions to process; everything else is automated.	1. Electronic imaging of expense receipts eliminates photocopying. 2. Expert system can replace manual audit. 3. Approval of travel authorization eliminates approval of expense report if within guidelines. 4. Using EFT eliminates manual checks and improves cycle time.

What can be done to automate the rule?	What can be done to simplify the rule?
1. Travel authorization. 2. Employee travel reservations. 3. The audit process of expense reports. 4. Expense receipts (could be electronically imaged). 5. Issuing employee's check. 6. Notifying employee of expense report discrepancies. 7. Obtaining supervisor's approval.	1. Automate. 2. Handle only exceptions manually. 3. Don't duplicate activities. 4. Improve computer systems.

Figure 8–11. (continued)

7. NEXT STEPS—30 MINUTES

The next steps come right out of the previous exercise. The facilitator asks the group what they would recommend as the next steps based on the two team exercises; this usually leads to open discussion for about five minutes. The facilitator goes around the room asking for specific recommendations and records them on a flip chart. He then asks the group to identify the key ones and prioritize them in an order that makes sense. At one workshop the following were the major recommendations from the group:

1. The current travel expense process is too slow and inconvenient and includes a number of non-value-added activities.

2. The travel expense process needs to be reinvented so it satisfies objectives of the company as well as the customer.

3. A project team should be established to investigate ways to improve the process.

4. Company and customer process objectives should be established at the outset of the project.

5. The project team should use the framework from this workshop to fully explore all the potential obstacles and recommended changes.

9. WORKSHOP DEBRIEF—45 MINUTES

Asking participants to share lessons learned with a few words is a fun exercise. See Figure 8–12 for a lessons learned slide from an actual workshop.

10. GROUP DINNER—120 MINUTES

The group dinner can be a venue where learning points are reinforced. However, this workshop is very draining for the participants. My recommendation is not include any exercises during dinner. The facilitators can, if they feel the group can tolerate it, generate relevant discussion at each table.

Processes are composed of customer and company views.	There is a framework to help identify process improvements.	Location, time sequence, resources, responsibility, and equipment are process dimensions.	Constraints can be summarized in a framework.	Simplifying steps can help improve a process.
Automating a step can help improve a process.	Implication questions get at the root cause of a constraint.	There is a framework to help identify constraints.	Company view includes work flow, quality, speed, and cost.	Integrating activities can help improve a process.
Improving processes requires focus, time, and commitment.	Customer view includes satisfaction, dissatisfaction, and improvement.	Rule-breaking questions help identify what can be changed.	Eliminating process steps can help improve a process.	Improving processes is a team event.

Figure 8–12. Lessons Learned

ENDNOTES

1. Michael Hammer and James Champy, *Reengineering the Corporation,* Harper Business, 1993.

2. Ibid.

3. James Champy, *Reengineering Management,* Harper Business, 1996.

CHAPTER 9

REINVENTING SUPERIOR CUSTOMER VALUE AND DELIGHTING YOUR CUSTOMERS

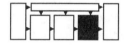

When you provide superior service to your customers you will achieve un-expected benefits for your company.

Robert J. Bailey
Senior Vice President
Hertz Corporation

In 1989 Robert J. Bailey, senior vice president of quality assurance and administration at Hertz Corporation, decided that Hertz needed to reinvent the level of service it provided customers, especially at airports. Bailey realized that most of the customers were business travelers and needed to get to their destinations quickly. The problem was that when customers walked up to the Hertz rental counter, they had to wait while the customer service representative asked a series of questions. "It didn't seem right that customers should have to be delayed when their primary objective is to drive off as quickly as possible," says Bailey. "We should have the vehicle ready." His colleagues argued that it was a nice idea but would lose the company money because 20 percent of customers who make reservations never show up. Bailey felt that providing customer value was worth the costs that no-shows would generate, and he finally convinced operations management that they had to bite the bullet in order to provide this value to their customers.

He did not stop there. Even vehicles prepared ahead of time, customers would still have to locate them in the lot. A customer service representative would tell a customer, "Your vehicle is located in stall #4. It's a blue Grand Am." Customers who were unfamiliar with the location sometimes had difficulty finding their vehicle. Bailey decided to list the names of customers and the stall number where their car was located in flashing lights on a billboard at the drop-off point. He also decided that "the customer's name should also be flashing on an electric sign right above the car with an arrow pointing to the actual vehicle. This would make it easier for the customer to find it." This service was eventually called Hertz #1 Club Gold.

Bailey still wasn't finished. "No matter what we did, some customers were always getting into the wrong vehicle." When they got to the exit gate and the guard informed them that they were in the wrong car, most customers said, "Why can't I just take this car?" Unfortunately, rental companies have to match up the vehicle to the driver. To combat this problem Bailey decided that a third check was needed. When the customer gets into the vehicle, the rental contract, with the customer's name printed in very large block letters, hangs from the rear-view mirror. As a result of these three quality checkpoints, virtually no Hertz #1 Club Gold customer ever gets in the wrong car.

With Hertz #1 Club Gold, all you have to do when you get off the plane is get on the Hertz bus, which drops you right at the electronic billboard. You locate your name on the billboard and walk toward the electric sign that has your name in lights with an arrow pointing to your car. You put your luggage in the trunk, which is already open, get in the car, which is running, drive to the exit gate, show your driver's license, and continue on your journey. The entire process, once you get off the bus, takes less than two minutes.

Bailey had not forecasted an unexpected business benefit of this customer-focused program. The number of no-shows for Hertz #1 Club Gold customers has fallen from 20 percent, before the program started, to 10 percent today. This means 10 percent more business from Hertz #1 Club Gold customers each and every year the program has been in existence.

Reinventing superior customer value is a four-step process that starts by identifying opportunities. Next, opportunities should align with competencies, capabilities, customer value, and business strategies. Then you must analyze the revenue, cost, and risk associated with each opportunity. Finally, you determine the degree of impact each opportunity will have on the five customer focus capabilities (speed, consistency, agility, acuity, and innovation).

IDENTIFYING ENTERPRISE OPPORTUNITIES TO CREATE VALUE

Sources for identifying opportunities exist in three dimensions of the business landscape, as represented in Figure 9–1. The first dimension comprises the competencies and capabilities of your company, the second its markets and competitors, and the third both its customers and noncustomers.

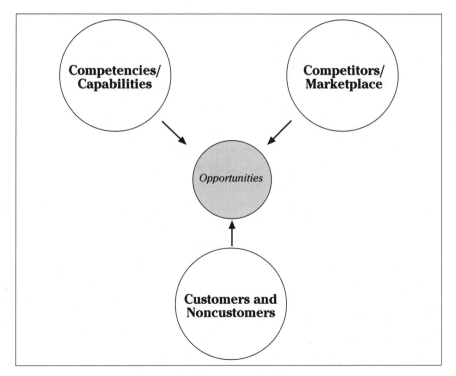

Figure 9–1. Opportunities Sources

At this point in the process it is necessary only to identify opportunities in each area. How they align to the other areas will be
addressed in the next step.

In Chapter 6 we explored techniques you could use to capture
customers' and noncustomers' needs, wants, and desires. In Chapter 7 we identified methods for determining in which competencies
and capabilities your enterprise excels and how to evaluate your
markets and competitors. To help place the three dimensions in a
single business model, you can look at the combination of business
entities, as depicted in Figure 9–2, that make up the value chain of
every enterprise.

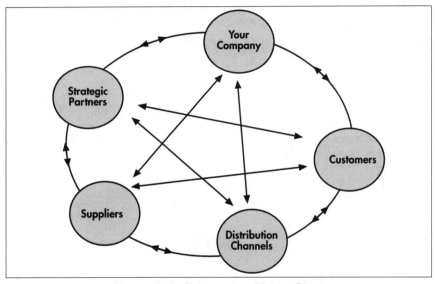

Figure 9–2. Enterprise Value Chain

By evaluating the three business dimensions across the value
chain you can more easily identify potential opportunities to pursue. Figure 9–3 is a template that has been completed for a health-
care provider. As you look at each of the value chain components
you can see where opportunities exist based on competencies and
capabilities, competitors and markets, and customers and noncustomers. Claims processing is a competency for this health-care
provider and represents an opportunity in the *your company* com-

ponent of the value chain. Market research by competitors suggests opportunities that this health-care provider can exploit with its strategic partners. Drug prescription programs offer additional opportunities for customers and noncustomers along the distribution channels value chain component. This technique can be used for any industry and is an excellent method for identifying opportunities to create value.

Value Chain Components	Competencies/ Capabilities	Competitors/ Markets	Customers and Noncustomers
Customers	Medical knowledge	Health statistics	Customer information
Your company	Claims processing	Competitive position	Focus groups
Strategic partners	Medical knowledge	Market research	Doctors/ Hospitals
Suppliers	Medical information	Health information	Extended networks
Distribution channels	Physician networks	Extended networks	Drug prescriptions

Figure 9–3. Health-Care Provider Opportunities

There are many different ways to use these techniques to identify potential opportunities, although project teams in a workshop environment are usually the most effective. The workshop at the conclusion of this chapter will explore the use of the alignment quotient and this technique in more detail.

ALIGNING OPPORTUNITIES FOR BUSINESS SUCCESS

Opportunities identified in the previous step need to be aligned to ensure the maximum value for the enterprise. A market opportunity that requires a competency you don't have and cannot develop should not be pursued. A market opportunity that doesn't help you achieve your business strategy shouldn't be pursued either. An inexpensive airline ticket from New York to Miami is not worth purchasing if you have no reason to go there. The same logic holds true for pursuing business opportunities. You first need to determine if the opportunity makes business sense before you look at its cost. If the business opportunity doesn't improve your company's competencies, enhance a capability, improve customer value, or help achieve a business strategy, it doesn't matter what it costs—it isn't worthy of pursuit. Opportunities aligned to these four areas should be pursued because these will provide the greatest value for your company and have the greatest financial impact.

ITT for many years had a voracious appetite for gobbling up companies for the sake of building an empire. Management finally realized that some divisions didn't really improve the corporation's competitive position in the marketplace. Some businesses required a core competency or capability that ITT didn't have. Others didn't seem to fit into ITT's value chain. Others, although successful in their own right, didn't mesh with ITT's overall business strategy. As a result, corporate resources were being drained to support areas of the business that didn't help the corporation as a whole.

When Snap-on Tools opened for business in the 1920s it relied on its core competency of manufacturing quality tools for its success. It soon realized that this wasn't enough. Although it targeted mechanics and others who valued tools, sales never quite materialized to the expectations of management. Snap-on sold through the normal retail channels but wasn't drawing enough customers to the stores. The problem was that its target customers were passionate about their tools but did not have time to shop for them. So management decided to pursue a strategy that brought the product to the customer. Soon the company became so proficient at it that distribution became a core capability. Snap-on was also able to provide value to customers by guaranteeing that once a week a Snap-on Tools van would pull into their place of work. The opportunity to sell tools to a market segment that was thirsty for quality but unable to find the time to shop enabled Snap-on Tools to grow rapidly during its seventy-five-year history. In fact, the approach has worked so well that revenues have more than doubled since 1986 to $1.5 billion dollars.[1]

Evaluating opportunities along these dimensions results in what I term an *alignment quotient* that can help you focus on those opportunities that may have the greatest positive impact on your business. Table 9–1 is an alignment quotient worksheet that an electronics manufacturer completed for an opportunity it was considering. The company was thinking about forming an alliance with another electronics company that would help it to enter new markets. It hoped these markets would improve revenue and profitability. A group of senior executives met to review a number of companies whom they had been in discussions with and used the alignment quotient worksheet as a tool for evaluating each potential partner.

The group discussed each question before agreeing on a score. For the question on competitive position the group agreed that company *D* could help improve their own firm's competitive position because of the relationships it had developed in overseas markets that their company wanted to enter. When the managers addressed the core competency question they all agreed that company *D* had a core competency in circuit design that their company didn't have. Combining a competency in circuit design with their own competency in manufacturing would yield beneficial results; they felt that the alliance would have a high degree of success in improving the overall competencies of both companies.

When the group discussed the core capability question they agreed that because their company had a well-established distribution network in the United States, the addition of company *D*'s moderately successful network would not impact them greatly. Finally, they felt that the alliance would help their company's goal of selling products in the European market only to a small degree. When they finished their discussion of company *D* the managers added up the scores and divided by five, the number of questions (see Table 9–1).

Table 9–1. Alignment Quotient Potential Opportunity for Company D

Description of Opportunity: Develop an alliance with company *D* that will help us enter new markets.
Description of Benefit: Improve revenue and profitability.

Alignment Dimensions		Response (Insert number that corresponds to your answer)
1=Not at all **2=To a low degree** **3=To a moderate degree**		**4=To a high degree**
A. *COMPETITIVE POSITION*	To what degree would the potential opportunity improve your competitive position in the marketplace?	3
B. *CORE COMPETENCY*	To what degree would the potential opportunity improve or develop a core competency?	4
C. *CORE CAPABILITY*	To what degree would the potential opportunity improve or develop a core capability?	3
D. *VALUE CHAIN*	To what degree would the potential opportunity improve customer value in any one or more points of the value chain elements?	4
E. *STRATEGY*	To what degree would the potential opportunity achieve your business strategy?	3

Calculating Alignment Quotient
   1. Total score for all questions (add responses).   17
   2. Divide by 5. This is equal to the OVERALL ALIGNMENT QUOTIENT.   3.4

When the group finished discussing all five potential partners in the way they tabulated the alignment results. Figure 9–4 represents the completed table that shows company D with the highest alignment quotient of 3.4.

Company	Alignment Quotient
A	3.2
B	2.8
C	2.6
D	3.4
E	2.4

Figure 9–4. Alignment Quotient Summary Table

Evaluating each opportunity helps you determine its business value. You can then determine whether the opportunities with the most favorable alignment quotient have a financial profile that will positively impact the company's operating performance.

ANALYZING REVENUE, COST, AND RISK OF OPPORTUNITIES

Every company has its own algorithm that it uses to evaluate the financial worthiness of an opportunity. I do not propose to rewrite accounting theory but offer a simple framework—revenue, cost, and risk—to help prioritize those opportunities that can be further scrutinized by financial mavens. Following is a brief description of each element.

REVENUE

The source of revenue can be tangible, intangible, or accelerated. Exploring each source will help you to identify potential revenue opportunities you may not have thought of.

Tangible revenue is quantifiable and directly impacts revenue. A new product or service launch will result in customers spending dollars for value received. Investing in laptop computers that allow salespeople to be more mobile and spend more time with their customers, answering questions or helping to resolve problems, will have a direct impact on revenue. Customer service personnel can help customers with their purchasing decisions by being smarter through the use of information technology; this also affects revenue. The key to identifying tangible revenue is its direct link to revenue improvement.

Intangible revenue is qualitative. You can express it in words but cannot directly link it to a specific activity. For example, McDonald's advertises that it focuses on an environmental philosophy, contributes to charities, and hires retired people. This builds market image but it is hard to quantify the specific revenue impact. A McDonald's advertisement that promotes a meal, on the other hand, yields a tangible benefit. It is important to identify sources of intangible revenue because the revenue is real. It is, however, subject to wide variations because it cannot be directly tied to a specific action. How to address this problem will be discussed below.

Accelerated revenue impacts cash flow. The investment in a credit card payment system or electronic payment system affects the receipt of revenues and should not be ignored. An insurance company that receives thousands of payments each day can improve its cash flow by improving the process of receiving, opening, processing, and applying payments from customers.

Revenues can occur as one-time events or be ongoing. The development and implementation of a new order entry system that makes it easier for customers to order products or services will have an ongoing revenue impact. The revenue, however, from a one-time promotion is bound by time placed on the activity. Any opportunity that has a revenue impact bounded by time is a one-time revenue opportunity.

COST

Every potential opportunity has associated costs. In order to properly evaluate an opportunity you must identify the category of cost associated with it. The categories are people, equipment, and technology.

The addition or reduction of personnel obviously affects people costs. There are, however, other costs to think about in this category. Investment in training programs is often overlooked as a cost when installing a new information system or new piece of equipment, or in redesigning a business process. A large pharmaceutical company that purchased an expensive information application underestimated the cost of training by a million dollars. When purchasing any new piece of equipment or designing a new process, answer the following two questions: What will be the effect on the people in the organization? What training or new skills will be required by the workforce?

Most opportunities require an investment in plant and/or equipment. Make sure that you are clear about all equipment that will be required for a turnkey implementation. An air compressor manufacturer tried to save money by managing an expansion project by itself. The $200,000 project management fee saved was eaten up very quickly when the employee who managed the project forgot to include the $700,000 electric generating plant that was required for the expansion. When purchasing equipment, speak to other customers to determine actual maintenance and operating costs so you don't underestimate or overestimate the cost impact.

Investments in technology can be very expensive and should not be overlooked when evaluating the costs of an opportunity. It is very difficult today to invest in anything without using some form of technology. A new order entry system will require investment in computers, local area networks, and monitors. The cost of the software cannot be overlooked either. Site licenses for Microsoft Office, Lotus Notes, and other applications are expensive but can be negotiated. And don't forget about technology support requirements. A computer manufacturer that installed Lotus Notes didn't think about the technology support required for users. Help desks are a necessity and should not be overlooked or underestimated. Contact other companies to determine what the actual costs are. Don't rely on the word of the salesperson; spend the time to find out from other users what their costs are and develop your own estimate.

Costs, like revenues, can occur once or be ongoing. The investment cost for equipment is a one-time cost, less annual maintenance, but ongoing benefits can be derived from savings in labor, rework, improved quality, or a redesigned business process. Remember to consider both one-time and ongoing costs in calculating total costs.

RISK

In today's business environment, where change is the only certainty, we have to look at all possible outcomes to make prudent business decisions.

A software engineering company won a $3 million proposal to develop a new order entry system for a customer. The application required some customer design that the company had never done before but was considered a piece of cake by the software engineers and management. They underestimated the design by a factor of 3 and a $500,000 profit turned out to be a $400,000 loss.

The concept behind measuring risk is probability theory. There is always an upside and a downside to every project. By applying a probability percentage you can calculate the risks associated with any project. Let us take the example of a company considering a new product line. Marketing personnel projected annual revenue increases for the first year to be anywhere from $2 million to $3 million. After evaluating the probability of potential outcomes they prepared a table (see Figure 9–5).

They first identified the downside ($2 million), projected ($2.5 million), and upside ($3 million) revenue for the opportunity. They then estimated the probability for each event. After considering all the issues the team agreed that the downside possibility was 5 percent, the projected possibility was 80 percent, and the upside possibility was 15 percent. The team then multiplied the revenue increase numbers for each of the three possibilities by the probability percentage and recorded the results (see the line titled Projected Outcome in Figure 9–5). They then added the projected outcome dollars for each of the three possible outcomes to arrive at the overall projected outcome of $2,550 million.

Opportunity	Range Of Possible Outcomes ($000)			Projected Outcome $'s[6]
	Downside[1]	Projected[2]	Upside[3]	
Revenue increase	2,000K	2,500K	3,000K	
Probability % [4]	5%	80%	15%	
Projected Outcome $ [5]	100K	2,000K	450K	2,550K

Notes:
1. Worst-case scenario
2. Most probable outcome
3. Best-case scenario
4. Probability percentage of outcome occurring
5. Benefit $'s or each range element multiplied by probability percentage
6. The sum of the downside projected, and upside projected outcomes

Figure 9–5. Determining Projected Revenue
Using Risk Analysis Technique

The overall objective of measuring risk is to understand and quantify the range of possible outcomes. This same process can be used for measuring risks in costs.

Once you have quantified risk you need to identify the factors that contribute to it so you can control them. In this example the major factor affecting the downside projection was the development team's three-month delay in launching the new product. A competitor had already announced a launch date about two weeks ahead of theirs. Inside information indicated that the competitor was in fact further behind and the probability was that the competitor's new product would be launched later than theirs. This is why the probability of the upside outcome is higher than the downside outcome. As a result of this analysis, risk areas were identified and managed. Most times, if risk isn't identified it overtakes the project and management has to react to problems. It is much easier to identify risk and manage it than to react to it. As it turned out, the product was launched a month early and the competitor's launch was three weeks later. Sales increased by $3.2 million dollars the first year.

Every opportunity needs to be analyzed for revenue, cost, and risk. Using the same method of analysis helps you to be consistent in the assessment of each opportunity and also acts as a checklist to ensure that no areas are overlooked. Figure 9–6 presents another analysis the project team prepared.

New Product Line Opportunity Analysis

Element	Description	Description	Revenue/Cost
Annual Revenue			
Tangible	Quantifiable	New products/services	$2,000
Intanigble	Qualitative	General image advertising	$ 500
Accelerated	Improve Cash Flow	Electronic/Credit Card payments	$ 225
		Projected Revenue	**$2,500**
Costs			
People	Additions, reductions training	New product line	$ 550
Plant/ Equipment	New facilities/ equipment	Plant addition to manufacturing facility	$1,500
Technology	Computer/ application	New order entry system	$ 750
		Projected Annual Costs	**$ 550**
		One-Time Costs	**$2,250**

Figure 9–6. Annual Cost and Revenue Summary

The projected revenue of $2.5 million is made up of $2 million in tangible revenue and half a million in intangible revenue. Additionally, the new order entry system that enables electronic or credit card payment is expected to generate $500,000 of additional revenues from customers who will order because it is easier to pay that way. The one-time cost of $2.2 million is the result of additional plant and equipment and the cost of the new order entry system. The annual incremental cost for the new product line is $550,000, which includes additional sales and manufacturing personnel as well as ongoing maintenance costs for facilities and the new order entry system.

Assessing risk is not always about dollars and cents. Companies like 3M learned from its legendary success with Post-It Notes, a "failed" project, that the benefits of failure can be lucrative.

DETERMINING IMPACT ON CUSTOMER FOCUS CAPABILITIES

As a final step, it makes sense to determine each opportunity's potential impact in terms of the five customer focus capabilities we explored in Chapter 7. These capabilities—speed, acuity, consistency, agility, and innovation—represent a set of metrics that focus on customer value. In Step 2 of the process we aligned each opportunity with the company's competencies, capabilities, customer value, and business strategies. This looks at customer value at a high level. At this point we will explore each opportunity more closely in light of each customer focus capability.

Table 9–2 summarizes the benefits for each of the capabilities. You can use the same template and spider diagramming techniques discussed in the Chapter 7 workshop.

Each of the four steps in the process filters out opportunities that are not aligned to the business needs of the enterprise. By following this process you will target opportunities that optimize customer value only (see Figure 9–7).

Table 9–2. Customer Focus Capabilities

Customer Focus Capability	Description	Company Benefits	Customer Benefits
Speed	The rate at which you profitably respond to customer or market demands (Metric: Concept to Cash)	Bring products to market quickly.	Respond to customer requests quickly and effectively.
Consistency	The continued high degree of delivery of quality products and services (Metric: Customer Satisfaction)	Challenge competitors' actions consistently and successfully.	Consistently produce a product/service with unfailing quality.
Acuity	Clear perception of competitive environment and response with profitable value (Metric: Market Leader, Follower, Survivor)	Awareness of competitors' strengths and weaknesses.	Awareness of customer wants, needs, and desires.
Agility	Simultaneous adaptation to many different business environments (Metric: Rate of Responsiveness)	Ability to anticipate/ respond to changing market requirements.	Ability to anticipate/ respond to changing customer needs.
Innovation	The degree to which you can turn new ideas into revenue-producing products and services (Metric: New Product Revenue)	Create new ideas that capitalize on your strengths and exploit competitors' weaknesses.	Incorporate new ideas that create value for customers.

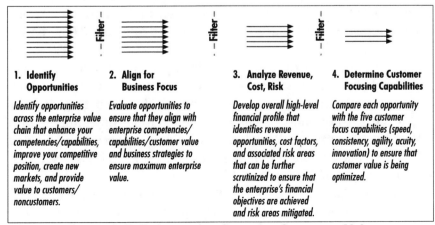

1. Identify Opportunities

Identify opportunities across the enterprise value chain that enhance your competencies/capabilities, improve your competitive position, create new markets, and provide value to customers/ noncustomers.

2. Align for Business Focus

Evaluate opportunities to ensure that they align with enterprise competencies/ capabilities/customer value and business strategies to ensure maximum enterprise value.

3. Analyze Revenue, Cost, Risk

Develop overall high-level financial profile that identifies revenue opportunities, cost factors, and associated risk areas that can be further scrutinized to ensure that the enterprise's financial objectives are achieved and risk areas mitigated.

4. Determine Customer Focusing Capabilities

Compare each opportunity with the five customer focus capabilities (speed, consistency, agility, acuity, innovation) to ensure that customer value is being optimized.

Figure 9–7. Reinventing Superior Customer Value

Each opportunity Hertz pursues focuses on providing customer value. If you look at Figure 9–8, which lists Hertz Firsts, you will notice that it aligns every opportunity with its business needs.

1925—First coast-to-coast network
1926—First charge card
1932—First airport Rent-a-Car location, at Chicago's Midway Airport
1933—First rent-it-here/leave-it-there plan
1950—First European location (France)
1959—First centralized billing system
1962—First booking system for travel agents
1972—First club for frequent travelers, #1 Club
1978—First nationwide emergency road service
1980—First Express Service
1984—First computerized driving directions
1988—First in-car cellular phones
1989—First launched Hertz #1 Club Gold
1995—First introduced on-board navigational system, NeverLost
1996—First launched World Wide Web site

Figure 9–8. Hertz Firsts

In the early years Hertz launched infrastructure services, like a centralized billing system in 1959, then a nationwide road service in 1978. With the launch of its First Express Service in 1980, Hertz developed a series of services that kept adding value to customer interactions. The Hertz #1 Club Gold program capitalizes on the competency of turning vehicles around quickly and getting them ready for the next customer. At Los Angeles International Airport, not too long ago, Hertz set a company record of nearly 3,000 rentals in one day. The centralized billing system developed in 1959 led to a capability built on successful financial business processes. Computerized driving directions provided real customer value. Each new service or process Hertz develops is designed to provide a memorable experience for customers each time they interact with a Hertz representative. Whether it is making a reservation, picking up a car, calling about a bill, or riding in the Hertz bus, every customer interaction is scrutinized for customer value.

Evaluating potential opportunities is an important part of reinventing superior value. The workshop for this chapter will help identify those opportunities that are best positioned to ensure market success. It focuses on two distinct areas: first, identifying a set of opportunities to pursue, and second, aligning those opportunities with enterprise competencies, capabilities, customer value, and business strategies to ensure a business focus and achieve maximum enterprise value.

WORKSHOP: REINVENTING SUPERIOR CUSTOMER VALUE

This workshop will use some of the background materials from the Strategy Awareness Workshop, in Chapter 2 and the Perceiving Customer Value Workshop in Chapter 6, which was illustrated by an actual workshop held at a toy company. Participants should have attended the earlier workshops as prerequisites to this one. The number of attendees at this workshop should not exceed fifteen to allow plenty of interaction and learning. Participants who have not attended the previous workshops should receive an overview of the concepts through other methods. At one workshop participants attended a one-day overview that reviewed the concepts and the actual completed exercises from the previous workshops. Here is the agenda for the workshop.

Table 9–3. Reinventing Superior Customer Value

Agenda
9:00 AM – 9:00 PM

Time Frames	Time Allotted	Workshop Exercises	Facilitator	Objectives
1. 9:00–9:45	45 min	Set the Stage	Julia K.	Discuss the learning objectives and capture participants' expectations.
2. 9:45–10:45	60 min	Warm-Up Exercise (includes 15 min break)	Barbara K.	Identify customer needs, wants, and desires.
3. 10:45–12:30	105 min	Determining Alignment Quotient for Selected Opportunities—*Team Exercise*	Brian L.	Learn how to evaluate opportunities for business focus.
4. 12:30–1:30	60 min	Lunch		
5. 1:30—3:00	90 min	Determining Customer Focus Capability Index for Opportunities—*Team Exercise*	Barbara K.	Evaluate each opportunity to determine its impact on each of the five customer focus capabilities.
6. 3:00–3:15	15 min	Break		
7. 3:15–4:15	60 min	Next Steps	Brian L./ Barbara K.	Understand how to evaluate opportunities for revenue, cost, and risk.
8. 4:15–5:00	45 min	Workshop Debrief	Barbara K./ Brian L.	Capture and share the benefits of the workshop with colleagues.
9. 7:00–9:00	120 min	Group Dinner		

Lead Facilitator: Julia K.   Facilitators: Barbara K./Brian L.

1. SET THE STAGE— 45 MINUTES

The facilitator provides an overview of the workshop and its objectives, and has the participants introduce themselves. The objective of this workshop is for participants to understand and apply techniques that will help them evaluate potential business opportunities to ensure that they focus on enabling business success. Participants and facilitators need to read in advance materials that will be used for the warm-up exercise.

2. WARM-UP EXERCISE—60 MINUTES

The warm-up exercise is designed to identify potential business opportunities. Information from the toy company workshop will be used for illustration. A market survey designed around the company's strategies was undertaken to perceive customer and non-customer needs, wants, and desires. Copies of the thirty-page final report were provided to all the participants for advanced reading.

The facilitator starts the exercise by asking participants if they have read the materials provided. There are always a few people who didn't have the time and even those who have may be glad to refresh their thoughts. The facilitator reviews the instructions for the warm-up exercise by showing the group a slide. Figure 9–9 is the instruction slide used at the toy company workshop.

Reinventing Superior Customer Value

1. The facilitator will divide you into teams of three.

2. Review the reading material individually for *15 minutes*.

3. Spend the next *15 minutes* with your team identifying sources of potential opportunities.

4. Record your responses on the supplied template.

5. Signal to the facilitator when you have completed the exercise.

Figure 9–9. Sample Slide: Warm-Up Exercise Instructions

The facilitator informs participants that they can review the reading materials for fifteen minutes, after which they will work for another thirty minutes in groups of three to identify potential sources of opportunities based on the report findings. Teams will record their responses on the supplied worksheet.

The facilitator starts at the left of the room and assigns the first three people to team 1, the next group of three people to team 2, and so forth. He announces the current time and tells the group that he will inform them of the time at five-minute intervals.

At the end of the second fifteen-minute period the facilitator asks each team to identify potential opportunities. As each group presents its results, one of the facilitators records them on a template. The facilitator asks for additions or modifications, seeking group consensus before changing responses. Figure 9–10 is the completed consolidated template for the warm-up exercise at the toy company.

Competencies/Capabilities
1. We need to find out why it takes 12–18 months too long to develop new products.
2. We should include customers, child psychologists, pediatricians in our processes.
3. Our customers complain about our products being out of stock a lot of the time.
4. Our customers tell us we need to add electronics to our toys.
Competitors/Markets
1. We need to differentiate ourselves in the marketplace.
2. We need to find out why our market penetration is so weak in the West.
3. We need to identify how our competitors attract customers.
4. We need to identify new markets for our products.
Customers/Noncustomers
1. We should bring in customers/noncustomers and find out what they would do differently.
2. We need to identify how our competitors attract customers.
3. We need to better communicate with our customers.
4. We need to find better ways to capture our customer concerns.

Figure 9–10. Sources of Opportunities

The break is included as part of the warm-up exercise.

3. DETERMINING ALIGNMENT QUOTIENT FOR SELECTED OPPORTUNITIES—105 MINUTES

The facilitator starts off the exercise by telling the group that during the next 105 minutes they will be working in teams to identify the best opportunity from the sources of opportunities list developed in the warm-up exercise. At the toy company workshop the facilitator introduced the exercise this way:

> When my family plans a vacation we sit down at the dinner table and prepare a list of where each of us would like to go. Last year my wife wanted to go to the Jersey shore. My son wanted to go to California. My daughter wanted to go to Europe. Next we each prepared a list of our vacation objectives. We discussed them in great length and then agreed on three major objectives. First, we were all tired from a long year and we needed some rest but wanted to have some fun as well. Second, we all agreed that we wanted a warm weather climate. Third, we didn't want to travel far. Fourth, we wanted to go somewhere the family could do things together. We then reviewed the vacation that each of us had identified against the criteria we developed. We finally chose Disneyland.

When the facilitator finished he asked the group for conclusions they could draw from his family's vacation planning session. One participant said, "It's very organized. First you have everyone identify where they want to go and second you develop criteria by which to measure each vacation opportunity." The facilitator responded by telling the group that selecting business opportunities follows a similar process and then reviewed the alignment quotient dimensions during the next ten minutes.

The facilitator reviews the exercise instructions with the group (see Figure 9-11) and asks if there any questions. After answering the questions he tells the group that the team facilitators will help them through the process because the concepts for this exercise, although logical, are new to everyone in the group.

Developing Alignment Quotient for Selected Opportunities

1. Break into your teams and meet in your assigned break areas.
2. For the first *20 minutes* identify a specific opportunity using the list of opportunity sources developed in the warm-up exercise.
3. For the next *60 minutes* work with your team to develop the alignment quotient for the opportunity using the template provided.
4. Next to the alignment quotient record the reason for your score.
5. Be prepared to review your findings with the rest of the group in a *5–10-minute* presentation.
6. Return to the main meeting room when your team has completed the exercise.

Figure 9–11. Sample Slide: Team Exercise Instructions

The teams work with their team facilitators for the next 70 minutes, returning to the main meeting room to present their findings. The facilitator probes the teams for more insight into their rationale in scoring the opportunities. The facilitator asks a number of how questions: How would this opportunity improve the company's competitive position? How would this opportunity improve the company's core competency? and so forth. This technique helps to stimulate thought and requires a direct response. The group recommended some minor changes. (Tables 9–4, 9–5, and 9–6 are the completed worksheets from each of the teams at the toy company workshop.) The facilitator discusses the scores and asks the group what threshold score would indicate a favorable opportunity; he is looking for an answer of 3.0 or above. Because this is the first step in the opportunity selection process, a high score is not necessary. You do, however, desire a score that indicates alignment without much variability. Therefore, a score of 3.0 or above indicates a favorable opportunity to pursue to the next stage.

Table 9–4. Alignment Quotient Potential Opportunity #1

Description of Opportunity: Improve product development cycle.
Description of Benefit: Improve time to market (less development cost/improved revenues).

Alignment Dimensions		Response (Insert number that corresponds to your answer)
1=Not at all	**2=To a low degree** **3=To a moderate degree**	**4=To a high degree**
A. *COMPETITIVE POSITION*	To what degree would the potential opportunity improve your competitive position in the marketplace?	4 (Bring products to market faster/ahead of competitors.)
B. *CORE COMPETENCY*	To what degree would the potential opportunity improve or develop a core competency?	3 (Improve engineering design competency.)
C. *CORE CAPABILITY*	To what degree would the potential opportunity improve or develop a core capability?	4 (Improve new product development cycle.)
D. *VALUE CHAIN*	To what degree would the potential opportunity improve customer value in any one or more points of the value chain elements?	4 (We would be viewed as market leaders for innovative new products.)
E. *STRATEGY*	To what degree would the potential opportunity achieve your business strategy?	4 (Strategy is to develop new products quickly.)

Calculating Alignment Quotient
1. Total score for all questions (add responses).   19
2. Divide by 5. This is equal to the **OVERALL ALIGNMENT QUOTIENT.**   3.8

Table 9–5. Alignment Quotient Potential Opportunity #2

Description of Opportunity:	Integrate technology into our products.
Description of Benefit:	Respond to competitors/market needs (increased revenues, market share, customer satisfaction).

Alignment Dimensions		**Response** (Insert number that corresponds to your answer)
1=Not at all 2=To a low degree 3=To a moderate degree 4=To a high degree		
A. *COMPETITIVE POSITION*	To what degree would the potential opportunity improve your competitive position in the marketplace?	4 (Respond to customers and competitive market.
B. *CORE COMPETENCY*	To what degree would the potential opportunity improve or develop a core competency?	3 (Develop engineering competency.)
C. *CORE CAPABILITY*	To what degree would the potential opportunity improve or develop a core capability?	3 (Integrate technology into manufacturing process.)
D. *VALUE CHAIN*	To what degree would the potential opportunity improve customer value in any one or more points of the value chain elements?	4 (We would be viewed as market leaders for innovative new products.)
E. *STRATEGY*	To what degree would the potential opportunity achieve your business strategy?	4 (Incorporate technology into our products.)

Calculating Alignment Quotient
   1. Total score for all questions (add responses).   18
   2. Divide by 5. This is equal to the OVERALL ALIGNMENT QUOTIENT.   3.6

Table 9–6. Alignment Quotient Potential Opportunity #3

Description of Opportunity: Develop customer listening systems to capture customer needs, wants, and desires.

Description of Benefit: Improved customer satisfaction, retention, revenues, and profits.

Alignment Dimensions		Response (Insert number that corresponds to your answer)
1=Not at all **2=To a low degree** **3=To a moderate degree**		**4=To a high degree**
A. *COMPETITIVE POSITION*	To what degree would the potential opportunity improve your competitive position in the marketplace?	4 (Identify what customers want and how they buy.)
B. *CORE COMPETENCY*	To what degree would the potential opportunity improve or develop a core competency?	3 (Listening is a competency we don't have now.)
C. *CORE CAPABILITY*	To what degree would the potential opportunity improve or develop a core capability?	4 (Develop a series of effective processes that capture customer thoughts and ideas.)
D. *VALUE CHAIN*	To what degree would the potential opportunity improve customer value in any one or more points of the value chain elements?	4 (Customers want to be heard.)
E. *STRATEGY*	To what degree would the potential opportunity achieve your business strategy?	4 (We must become more customer-focused.)

Calculating Alignment Quotient
1. Total score for all questions (add responses).   19
2. Divide by 5. This is equal to the **OVERALL ALIGNMENT QUOTIENT.**   3.8

4. LUNCH—60 MINUTES

Lunch is an opportune time to reinforce learning as well as exchange ideas. At the toy company workshop the facilitators prepared questions for each of the tables to warm up the group for the afternoon team exercise. They handed out one alignment quotient worksheet to each table along with the following list of questions:

1. How will this opportunity help you improve the speed with which you respond to customers?

2. How will this opportunity affect the quality of the products and services you provide the customer?

3. Will this opportunity enable you to better perceive your customers' needs, wants, and desires?

4. To what degree will this opportunity improve your ability to respond to market changes?

5. Will this opportunity enable your enterprise to be more innovative?

The table facilitators were instructed to discuss these subjects in a relaxed manner. The idea is for the participants to start thinking about these questions, so they are better prepared for the afternoon team exercise.

5. DETERMINING CUSTOMER FOCUS CAPABILITY INDEX FOR OPPORTUNITIES—90 MINUTES

The facilitator starts off the workshop by asking the group about the discussion at lunch. One participant says, "It really made me think about the opportunity as it relates to our customers." Others agree. The facilitator then explains the next team exercise by showing the instruction slide to the group. Figure 9–12 is the slide used for the toy company workshop.

The facilitator asks, "Have any of you used these capabilities in any of the previous workshops?" A few participants raise their hands. He asks those who raised their hands to explain the concepts to the rest of the group. After a ten-minute discussion the facilitator asks the group to break into their teams and begin the exercise. He informs them of the current time and the time they are expected back in the meeting room for their presentations.

The team facilitator starts the exercise by asking if anyone in the team has used these concepts before. If so he or she can lead off the discussion. The facilitator needs to judge when to move on to the next part of the exercise, which is based on the team's comprehension of the concepts behind the customer focus capabilities.

The team facilitator takes a less active role as the team works to-gether to complete the exercise; his job is to ensure that team members can articulate their reasons for their scores.

Determining Customer Focus Capability Index

1. Break into teams and meet in your assigned areas.

2. For the first *15 minutes* the team facilitator will lead you in a discussion of the five customer focus capabilities.

3. During the next *30 minutes*, discuss with your team how each of these capabilities are affected by the opportunity.

4. In the next *30 minutes* determine the degree to which each capability will be affected by the opportunity, recording your responses on the supplied template.

5. Explain why your team arrived at the answer, recording your response next to the numerical score for each capability.

6. Be prepared to review your findings with the rest of the group in a *5–10-minute* presentation.

7. Return to the main meeting room when your team has completed the exercise.

Figure 9–12. Sample Slide: Team Exercise Instructions

When the teams return, each presents its results to the group. The facilitator asks *why* questions to determine the reasons for their answers and *how* questions to understand the process they used to arrive at their answers. He also asks if anyone has comments or questions about the team presentations. At the toy company workshop one participant asked, "Why did team 2, in evaluating the opportunity to integrate technology into our products, rate the degree it would affect speed as only moderate?" One of the participants from team 2 responded, "Integrating technology in and of itself won't improve the ability to create, develop, and deliver value. At a higher level it helps because we need to realize that speed is an integral part of our market strategy."

The facilitator should try to solicit two or three questions or comments from the group to stimulate a discussion. This adds to the learning process. Tables 9–7, 9–8, and 9–9 are the completed worksheets from the toy company workshop.

Table 9–7. Customer Focus Capability Index Potential Opportunity #1

Description of Opportunity: Improve product development cycle.

	Alignment Dimensions	**Response** (Insert number that corresponds to your answer)
1=Not at all	**2=To a low degree** **3=To a moderate degree**	**4=To a high degree**
A. *SPEED*	To what degree would the opportunity improve the speed at which you create, develop, and deliver customer value?	4 (Improve ability to get products to market more quickly.)
B. *CONSISTENCY*	To what degree would the opportunity improve the company's ability to provide a consistent product or service?	3 (We would have to make sure we did this consistently.)
C. *ACUITY*	To what degree would the potential opportunity improve the company's ability to perceive customer needs, wants, and desires?	2 (Perceive capability is independent of product development capability.)
D. *AGILITY*	To what degree would the potential opportunity enable the company to respond to changing market conditions?	4 (If we do this with speed and consistency we will be agile.)
E. *INNOVATION*	To what degree would the potential opportunity enable you to generate new ideas into revenue-producing products and services?	4 (It would force us to be more innovative.)

Calculating Alignment Quotient
  1. **Total score for all questions (add responses).**   17
  2. **Divide by 5. This is equal to the OVERALL ALIGNMENT QUOTIENT.**   3.4

Table 9–8. Customer Focus Capability Index Potential Opportunity #2

Description of Opportunity: Integrate technology into our products.

Alignment Dimensions		Response (Insert number that corresponds to your answer)
1=Not at all **2=To a low degree** **3=To a moderate degree**		**4=To a high degree**
A. *SPEED*	To what degree would the opportunity improve the speed at which you create, develop, and deliver customer value?	2 (Integrating technology wouldn't directly affect the speed.)
B. *CONSISTENCY*	To what degree would the opportunity improve the company's ability to provide a consistent product or service?	2 (Technology in the product will have minimal effect.)
C. *ACUITY*	To what degree would the potential opportunity improve the company's ability to perceive customer needs, wants, and desires?	4 (Provide what customers/non-customers are asking for.)
D. *AGILITY*	To what degree would the potential opportunity enable the company to respond to changing market conditions?	4 (If we do this with speed and consistency we will be agile.)
E. *INNOVATION*	To what degree would the potential opportunity enable you to generate new ideas into revenue-producing products and services?	4 (If we are creative we will be using our innovation skills.)

Calculating Alignment Quotient
  1. Total score for all questions (add responses).   16
  2. Divide by 5. This is equal to the OVERALL ALIGNMENT QUOTIENT.   3.2

Table 9–9. Customer Focus Capability Index Potential Opportunity #3

Description of Opportunity:	Develop customer listening systems to capture customers' needs, wants, and desires.

Alignment Dimensions	**Response** (Insert number that corresponds to your answer)
1=Not at all 2=To a low degree 3=To a moderate degree 4=To a high degree	
A. *SPEED* To what degree would the opportunity improve the speed at which you create, develop, and deliver customer value?	4 (We would be able to capture customer information early and respond to it.)
B. *CONSISTENCY* To what degree would the opportunity improve the company's ability to provide a consistent product or service?	4 (We would have to develop the quality of our listening systems.)
C. *ACUITY* To what degree would the potential opportunity improve the company's ability to perceive customer needs, wants, and desires?	4 (If we do this well we will perceive customer and market trends.)
D. *AGILITY* To what degree would the potential opportunity enable the company to respond to changing market conditions?	3 (We would have to deliver value to succeed.)
E. *INNOVATION* To what degree would the potential opportunity enable you to generate new ideas into revenue-producing products and services?	4 (We should be more innovative in providing values.)

Calculating Alignment Quotient
1. Total score for all questions (add responses).   19
2. Divide by 5. This is equal to the **OVERALL ALIGNMENT QUOTIENT.**   3.8

6. BREAK—15 MINUTES

The afternoon break is always the most difficult to control. Facilitators will probably be needed to ensure that the group reconvenes on time. The facilitator should announce the current time and the time the group is expected to return to the main meeting room.

7. NEXT STEPS—60 MINUTES

The facilitator explains to the group that reinventing superior customer value follows a four-step process and reviews the steps that were accomplished in this workshop. He explains that the exercises were designed to help the participants experience the process of identifying the opportunities, aligning them for business focus, and determining their impact against the five customer focus capabilities. This part of the workshop will be devoted to a brief overview of how to evaluate opportunities for revenue, cost, and risk.

The facilitator explains that it is easier to learn the four steps in this order because having some knowledge of the other steps contributes to an understanding of how to evaluate the opportunities for revenue, cost, and risk. The facilitator uses Table 9–2 as a brief overview of the process as well as other materials that he feels are appropriate. At the toy company workshop the facilitator used the section of this chapter on revenue, cost, risk, as a handout and reviewed it over a thirty-minute period.

8. WORKSHOP DEBRIEF—45 MINUTES

Sharing lessons learned using a short statement is an effective way to summarize the workshop. Below is the lessons learned slide from the toy company workshop.

Opportunities can come from different sources.	Opportunities have to be aligned for business focus.	Opportunities should impact the speed at which you respond.	The alignment quotient helps identify evaluate opportunities.	Opportunities should improve your level of innovation.
Evaluate each opportunity for revenue, cost, and risk.	The value chain is a good framework for identifying opportunities.	Risk is an area that is most times forgotten.	There is always downside and upside risk for every opportunity.	Probability theory helps to evaluate risk.
Opportunities should help you better respond to changing markets.	Opportunities help you reinvent superior customer value.	There is a downside, upside, and projected revenue for every opportunity.	Opportunities should help you improve your overall enterprise quality.	Opportunities should help you become more perceptive.

Figure 9–13. Lessons Learned

9. GROUP DINNER—120 MINUTES

The group dinner can be a venue where learning points are rein-forced. The facilitators can use this opportunity to seed a few ques-tions at each table to help the participants explore opportunities that have helped or hindered the company's growth. At the toy company workshop, senior management prepared a list of past opportunities that had succeeded or failed. This list was used by each table facilitator to discuss some of the reasons behind the suc-cesses and failures. Each facilitator used a briefing packet that was prepared by management and was instructed to ask probing ques-tions to solicit discussion among participants.

ENDNOTES

1. Erin Davies, "Selling Sex and Catfood—One Adman's Marketing Hall of Fame," *Fortune,* June 9, 1997, p. 36.

CHAPTER 10

HOW TO KEEP ON GETTING IT RIGHT

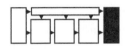

Our job is to sell more than just the box.

Jack Welch
Chairman of the Board
General Electric

Between 1990 and 1993 sales tripled to $3.8 billion at Microsoft while head count more than doubled from 5,600 to 13,400. Windows was the main strategy and Bill Gates didn't want to hear about the Internet or the World Wide Web. By the fall of 1995, 20 million people were surfing the Net and guess what! they weren't using a single Microsoft tool. In 1996 Bill Gates announced that Microsoft would indeed enter the Internet market. Since then the company has done a major about-face. It no longer thinks of the Internet as a toy some people will play with but calls it "the most important thing going on for us. It's driving everything. There is not one product we have where it's not at the center." In a short six months Gates took a thriving $8-billion company with 20,000 employees and made a 180-degree turn.[1]

Another company that has had the courage to radically transform itself in order to stay alive in one of its major markets is the Italian-based Olivetti Corporation. In 1992 Olivetti Office USA, located in Bridgewater, New Jersey, was vertically structured with 800 employees. It competed in the U.S. market primarily by selling European-made computers, printers, and other office products through approximately 3,000 distributors spread across the country. After a five-year period of increasing losses and dwindling revenues, in 1993 the company reported a loss of close to $12 million on sales of $60 million.

Senior management in Italy decided to take action. They asked Salomon Suwalsky, a long-time employee and management expert, to become President and CEO of Olivetti Office USA and turn the operation around. Suwalsky was not new to this kind of challenge. During his twenty-year career as executive manager with Olivetti he had helped to turn around other Olivetti divisions in many countries, including, Canada, Israel, Italy, and Norway. When he arrived at the New Jersey office it didn't take long for him to see what was wrong. Senior managers spent most of their time in their offices, dictating orders to the workforce, ignoring customers, and spending money on frivolous expenses. His first action was to eliminate the senior management team.

When he interviewed the second level of managers, he found they had many of the answers that would help the company. During an interview, with marketing director J. Todd Althoff, for instance, he asked what changes the director would make in marketing and product development to improve company operations. Althoff responded, "We lose money on every Olivetti product we sell. They are excellently made, but they are priced too high. Customers here don't care that the competition's products aren't as high quality, they like the low prices. So to sell, we mark our products down, and lose money on every item. We have the ideas for a new line of competitively priced products for the U.S. market, but we haven't been allowed to pursue them." Althoff was made vice president of marketing and product development on the spot. Similar interviews with similar outcomes also took place in the sales and operations areas.

Suwalsky stopped selling Olivetti products, and focused all efforts on the Royal office product line that the company had purchased a few years earlier. The line included calculators, organizers, and other office products, most of them made in the Far East, which were beginning to sell well in the U.S. His next step was more painful. Suwalsky realized that if the company could sell directly to nationwide organizations like Staples, OfficeMax, and Sam's Club, it wouldn't need hundreds of workers handling orders from thousands of dealers.

By the end of 1993 the workforce had shrunk to below 150, and was ready for action. His leadership style is to manage the boundaries and empower employees to do what they need to get the job done. He asked Althoff to come up with four new products for unveiling at the annual Consumer Electronics show six months away. Althoff met his first challenge ably, and the company has not looked back since.

Olivetti Office USA has improved its sales profile by almost $100 million and is now a profitable $150 million company that has taken some commanding leads in the U.S. office marketplace. Market share in cash registers is 75%; in calculators it is 24%; in electronic organizers under $50 it is 33%; for paper shredders under $70 it is 50%; and for laminators under $100 Olivetti market share is 42%.

Although Texas Instruments, Casio, and others are always a threat, Suwalsky's competitive strategy is simple: manufacture superior products, invest in packaging that attracts the consumer, and offer a good price. His biggest weapon is surprise. Every year the Royal product line changes. "This not only keeps our customers happy, it drives our competitors crazy. Olivetti Office USA constantly monitors the marketplace, their customers as well as the ultimate consumer. We know what our customers and their customers want and the changes we make each year are about satisfying our customers' needs. We do this through a constant and permanent dialogue with buyers, control groups, and customers."

Suwalsky is quick to point out that the heart of Olivetti's success lies with its workforce who, in his words, "have given its heart and soul to rebuild this company and deserves much of the credit for its success." Morale is high as you walk through the New Jersey headquarters. "We have an entrepreneurial spirit we never had before," says one manager. "Now we are left alone to do our jobs, and trusted to do them well, something the previous management team would never do." Todd Althoff is proud of the organization he is a part of. "Before everything was top down. The president rarely left his office. Today, ideas come from within the organization and we make it happen."

Olivetti prepared its workforce, perceived its markets, and is providing value to delighted customers. It was not afraid of change, even to the extent of scrapping virtually its entire product line, as well as an inefficient way of doing business. And if things are different tomorrow, you can be sure that Olivetti Office USA will not hesitate to change again.

In today's complex marketplace strategies have to be revisited constantly to ensure that market opportunities are not lost. The winners today are those companies, like Microsoft and Olivetti, that build organizations that can rapidly respond to changing market conditions and exploit new market opportunities. Microsoft's late entry into the Internet arena would not have been successful if it didn't have an organization that could respond rapidly. By having the capability to shift focus opportunities can be exploited for customer value.

NEW LEVELS OF SERVICE

In the post-World War II economy, manufacturing was the name of the game and company coffers were overflowing. Manufacturers couldn't produce fast enough, the marketplace gobbled up everything produced, and value was based on availability. Today the value proposition is completely different. Consumers are defining market needs. Products, therefore, are merely commodities, with the services that surround them becoming the new focus for value. Companies like GE, Xerox, Otis Elevator, and AT&T are redefining value for their customers in the commercial marketplace, while Hertz, Ritz Carlton, Walt Disney, and Home Depot are turning their products and services into memorable experiences for consumers. These market leaders have prepared their workforces to perceive the changing needs, wants, and desires of customers so they can provide superior value.

Jack Welch turned GE around beginning in 1982, when he took over the reins. His Work-Out program became the basis for many books on transformation and GE again became the global giant it had been. GE's stock rose 86 percent since early 1995 and the company has a total market capitalization of $157 billion as of October 1996. It expects profits of over $7 billion in 1997, making it the most valuable company on the globe.

But Jack Welch doesn't think the GE transformation is over. Today Welch tells his troops that GE can no longer prosper on manufactured goods alone; it has to provide the services that go along with them. In 1990 manufacturing generated 56 percent of GE's $58 billion in revenues. In 1995 it dropped to 43.5 percent and in the year 2000 it is expected to drop to 33 percent while sales will rise to $120 billion. The shift from manufacturing to service dominance is turning the global manufacturer into a giant consulting company with services playing an ever more important role in the corporate treasure chest.

Recently, GE entered into a multiyear deal with Columbia/HCA to service all its medical equipment, some of it made by GE's competitors. In the aircraft industry GE has signed a ten-year, $2.3 billion deal with British Airways to maintain and overhaul engines, including those built by its competitor Rolls Royce. It also is pursuing outsourcing deals in power generation, where its competency in building and operating power plants can save companies millions of dollars.[2] GE is not alone in moving into services. Other recognized names are also taking advantage of the new service economy.

Otis Elevator for many years sold elevators and provided support repair services. As elevator controls changed from electromechanical to electronic, more and more customers did not have the expertise to maintain them and signed service contracts with Otis. The company does its job so well that nearly two thirds of its $5 billion in revenue comes from service and maintenance.[3] The telephone companies have been in the service business for years, helping customers configure complicated communication systems. AT&T Solutions, headed by Victor Millar, the former head of consulting for Arthur Andersen, has built a billion-dollar system integration and services business based on competencies in networking and telecommunications.

Other companies that may not, at first glance, appear to be in the services business are breaking new ground. The Australia Post is reinventing itself as a distribution company and is offering its customers a range of services beyond mail delivery. In the automotive industry service was associated with car maintenance. New megadealers like CarMax and Auto-By-Tel are reinventing the retailing and distribution end of the business by offering buyers tremendous savings and quick individualized service through their sheer buying power.

Companies around the globe are focusing on delivering a level of service that no one ever imagined possible. These companies are the ones that will lead the market in the twenty-first century.

THE EXPERIENCE OF VALUE

Consumers are looking for value in a totally different way than ever before. People who purchase home improvement products go to Home Depot because of the experience they encounter. Well-prepared service representatives help customers by perceiving their problems. What may appear to be a request for a washer to fix a faucet may in fact be a requirement for a new faucet. If you don't know where to find something a service representative will personally guide you to it. Home Depot service representatives provide a level of value that customers enjoy being a part of. It's the experience that makes them come back.

Customers use Hertz because they like to see their name in lights when they walk up to get their car. Couples go to fancy restaurants not so much for the food but for the ambiance that makes the experience memorable. Planet Hollywood and Hard Rock Cafe have made millions because for the price of a hamburger their customers can briefly feel a part of the music or movie world. Revolutionaries like Starbucks are reinventing value by selling America not just on drinking coffee but experiencing cappuccino, latte, and frappuccino any way you like it. This notion of the market moving toward a new level of value is being explored by B. Joseph Pine II and James H. Gilmore, partners in Strategic Horizons LLP. Their new book talks about *staging experiences* or memorable events (like going to Disney World) that engage each individual in a personal way.[4]

More and more businesses today recognize that it's the experience that keeps customers coming back. Shopping malls, for example, are staging "events" to draw customers back into their stores. This trend toward staging experiences will change the way businesses interact with their customers and will develop into an entirely new business in its own right. Companies that focus on making the customer interaction an *experience* will improve their customer retention rate and overall profitability.

STAYING ON TOP

In the athletic shoe industry, Nike's CEO Phil Knight transformed his company into a giant that has increased shareholder return by 35 percent or more per year between 1986 and 1996 through a constant state of reinvention. "We're constantly reviewing how the world has changed and how we're reacting to it," says Knight. The Nike sneaker revolution made the company a household word, as its shoes—designed for serious athletes—swept the world. In 1993 and 1994, growth stalled. Knight realized that Nike was really limiting itself to one product line—shoes—and needed to reinvent itself. "We decided we're a sports company, not just a shoe company," says Knight. As a result, Nike began to refocus on apparel. "If you watch Arizona play basketball on television, you see their shoes about 10 percent of the time, but the uniform logo is visible about 75 percent of the time." With renewed growth Nike is ready for its next venture, producing Nike events from soccer matches to golf tournaments. "We promote our athletes and the brand while at the same time making money on the event," says Knight. You would think that a company that has posted a 47-percent average annual return would ride its success, but Nike is staying in motion, realizing this is the only strategy that will enable it to stay on top.[5]

IBM's surprise purchase of Lotus Notes in 1996 will help keep the company on top into the twenty-first century. As companies try to figure out how to maximize the productivity of today's knowledge worker, scientists and engineers at IBM are uncovering new ways for people to work together and share knowledge. Monsanto, a high-growth chemical company with 1996 revenue of $9.3 billion, is staying on top through its bio-agricultural business, which currently represents a quarter of its sales but generates almost half of its operating income. Monsanto is putting knowledge into seeds to improve crop yield, because the world population is forecasted to increase to more than 8.5 billion people by the year 2000. Between now and then, however, the amount of arable land is expected to decline. Farmers around the world, therefore, need help in boosting their yields. Monsanto has developed a seed that includes its own fertilizer, insect control mechanism, and other biological wizardry that enables farmers to improve crop yield by 200 to 300 percent. Even though this seed costs seven times the normal price, farmers are lining up to buy it.

The world of biotechnology will also change the way people communicate. British Telecom thinks future generations of portable phones will be implanted directly in your ear. Surgeons have performed about 17,000 cochlear implants on patients with hearing loss. "People are already walking around with chips in their heads," says Peter Cochrane, head of research at British Telecommunications PLC. This could enable an individual with a microcomputer chip implant to have a miniature telephone constantly ready to receive calls. "The pace of change is actually accelerating now," says Richard Howard, director of wireless research at Lucent Bell Laboratories. In the next two decades "we'll see explosive growth of communications, computing, memory, wireless, and broadband technology."

Sun Microsystems believes computer interfaces coupled with physiology will be a whole new frontier that will take it into the twenty-first century. Passengers in a car can feel the bumps in the road, or the pull of gravity in a turn, or the blast of wind, and the sound of an engine. Technology can enable you to have the same feeling while in your office monitoring information. Imagine datastreams appearing on the bottom part of your computer screen along with a soft sound. If your e-mail receives an important message the datastream will flash and the sound of waves hitting the beach will be transmitted over speakers. These sensations will help fuel an industry that will change the way we work in the future.

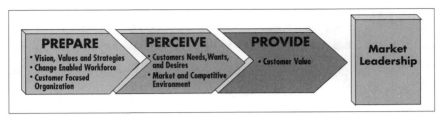

Figure 10–1. Prepare, Perceive, and Provide

Whether they succeed or fail, these companies have one thing in common: They don't accept the status quo. They realize products and services are no longer the key to success. It's the infrastructure and your ability to anticipate and respond to changing market conditions that will enable success. They challenge the future.

In the 1960s, '70s and '80s, executives sat atop their high-rise office buildings scanning the many reports (sales, margins, productivity, efficiency, downtime, and so on) that monitored and controlled the internal workings of their companies. They pretty much ignored what was happening in the business landscape. Today's market leaders have literally turned themselves inside out. Instead of looking within themselves as in the past, they focus externally on their customers, on their suppliers, and on strategic partnerships. As a result, the enterprise structure has grown more agile to accommodate new relationships and opportunities.

Leading companies understand their competition. They benchmark the best and can develop products and services ahead of market needs. They redesign their processes to optimize efficiency and to deliver a level of service and an experience of value that keeps customers coming back for more. Most importantly, these successful companies recognize that change is probably the only thing that is constant in today's marketplace and to stay ahead of the game they must prepare their workforce for change. Through their example, and with the help of the workshops and other practical tools in this book, you, too can get it right and transform your company into a market leader for the twenty-first century.

ENDNOTES

1. Kathy Rebello, "Inside Microsoft," *BusinessWeek,* July 15, 1996.

2. "Jack Welch's Encore," *BusinessWeek,* October 28, 1996, pp. 154-158.

3. Ibid.

4. B. Joseph Pine II and James H. Gilmore, *The Experience Economy,* Harvard Business School Press, to be published in 1998.

5. Julia Glynn and Otis Port, "Information Technology Report," *BusinessWeek,* June 23, 1997, p. 75.

BIBLIOGRAPHY

Amelio, Gil, and William Simon. *Profit from Experience*. New York: Van Nostrand Reinhold, 1996.

Ashkenas, Ron, Dave Ulrich, Todd Jick, and Steve Kerr. *The Boundaryless Organization*. San Francisco, CA: Jossey-Bass, 1995.

Berger, Lance A., and Martin J. Sikora. *The Change Management Handbook*. New York: Irwin, 1994.

Berry, Leonard L. *On Great Service*. New York: Free Press, 1995.

Blackburn, Joseph D. *Time-Based Competition*. Homewood, IL: Business One Irwin, 1991.

Boar, Bernard H. *The Art of Strategic Planning for Information Technology*. New York: John Wiley & Sons, 1993.

Camp, Robert C. *Benchmarking: The Search for Industry Best Practices That Lead to Superior Performance*. Milwaukee, WI: ASQC Quality Press, 1989.

Champy, James. *Reengineering Management*. New York: Harper Business, 1995.

Crego, Edwin T. Jr., and Peter D. Schiffin. *Customer-Centered Reengineering*. New York: Irwin 1995.

Cross, Kelvin F., John J. Feather, and Richard L. Lynch. *Corporate Renaissance*. Cambridge, MA: Blackwell, 1994.

Currid, Cheryl, et al. *Reengineering ToolKit*. Rocklin, CA: Prima Publishing, 1994.

D'Aveni, Richard A. *Hyper-Competition*. New York: Free Press, 1994.

Davenport, Thomas H. *Information Ecology*. New York: Oxford University Press, 1997.

Gale, Bradley, T. *Managing Customer Value*. New York: Free Press, 1994.

Goldratt, Eliyahu M. *The Goal*. New Haven, CT: North River Press, 1984.

Hall, Robert. *The Soul of the Enterprise*. New York: Harper Business, 1993.

Hamel, Gary, and C.K. Prahalad. *Competing for the Future*. Boston, MA: Harvard Business School Press, 1994.

Hammer, Michael and James Champy. *Reengineering the Corporation*. New York: Harper Business, 1993.

Harrington, James H. *Business Process Improvement*. New York: McGraw-Hill, 1991.

Harrington, James H. *Total Improvement Management*. New York: McGraw-Hill, 1995.

Katzenback, John R., and Douglas K. Smith. *The Wisdom of Teams*. Boston, MA: Harvard Business School Press, 1993.

Leonard-Barton, Dorothy. *Wellsprings of Knowledge*. Boston, MA: Harvard Business School Press, 1995.

Manganelli, Raymond L., and Mark M. Klein. *The Reengineering Handbook*. New York: AMACOM, 1994.

McGee, James, and Laurence Prusack. *Managing Information Strategically*. New York: John Wiley & Sons, 1993.

Mintzburg, Henry. *The Rise and Fall of Strategic Planning.* New York: Free Press, 1994.

Morris, Daniel, and Joel Brandon. *Re-Engineering Your Business.* New York: McGraw-Hill, 1993.

Morton, Michael S. Scott. *The Corporation of the 1990s.* New York: Oxford University Press, 1991.

Nonaka, Ikujiro, and Hirotaka Takeuchi. *The Knowledge Creating Company.* New York: Oxford University Press, 1995.

Oakley, Ed, and Doug Krug. *Enlightened Leadership.* New York: Fireside, 1994.

Pepper, Don, and Martha Rogers. *The One to One Future.* New York: Doubleday, 1993.

Peters, Tom. *Thriving on Chaos.* New York: Harper Collins, 1987.

Petrozzo, Daniel P., and John C. Stepper. *Successful Reengineering.* New York: Van Nostrand Reinhold, 1994.

Pine, Joseph B. II. *Mass Customization.* Boston, MA: Harvard Business School Press, 1993.

Porter, Michael E. *Competitive Advantage.* New York: Free Press, 1985.

Porter, Michael E. *The Competitive Advantage of Nations.* New York: Free Press, 1990.

Preiss, Kenneth, Steven L. Goldman, and Roger N. Nagel. *Agile Competitors and Virtual Organizations.* New York: Van Nostrand Reinhold, 1996.

Preiss, Kenneth, Steven L. Goldman and Roger N. Nagel. *Cooperate to Compete.* New York: Van Nostrand Reinhold, 1996.

Robert, Michael. *Strategy Pure and Simple.* New York: McGraw-Hill, 1993.

Schneider, Benjamin, and David E. Bowen. *Winning the Service Game.* Boston: Harvard University Business Press, 1995.

Senge, Peter M. *The Fifth Discipline.* New York: Doubleday, 1990.

Senge, Peter, and Arthur Kleiner, Charlotte Roberts, Richard Ross, and Bryan Smith. *The Fifth Discipline Fieldbook.* New York: Doubleday, 1994.

Slater, Robert. *Get Better or Get Beaten!* New York: Irwin, 1994.

Tapscott, Don, and Art Caston. *Paradigm Shift.* New York: McGraw-Hill, 1993.

Thurow, Lester. *Head to Head.* New York: William Morrow, 1992.

Treacy, Michael, and Fred Wiersema. *The Discipline of Market Leaders.* Reading, MA: Addison-Wesley, 1995.

Waitley, Denis. *Empires of the Mind.* New York: William Morrow, 1995.

Waldon,Gene, and Edmund O. Lawler. *Marketing Masters.* New York: Harper Business, 1993.

Walther, George R. *Upside-Down Marketing.* New York: McGraw-Hill, 1994.

Wellins, Richard S., William C. Byham, and George R. Dixon. *Inside Teams.* San Francisco, CA: Jossey–Bass, 1994.

Wheelwright, Steven C., and Kim B. Clark. *Revolutionary Product Development.* New York: Free Press, 1995.

Whiteley, Richard C. *The Customer Driven Company.* Reading, MA: Addison-Wesley, 1991.

Youngblood, Mark D. *Eating the Chocolate Elephant.* Richardson, TX: Micrografax Inc., 1994.

INDEX

333